The Theory and Interpretation of Narrative Series

Narrative as Rhetoric

Technique, Audiences, Ethics, Ideology

James Phelan

Ohio State University Press
Columbus

Publication of this book has been aided by a grant from the College of Humanities at The Ohio State University

Library of Congress Cataloging-in-Publication Data

Phelan, James, 1951–
Narrative as rhetoric : technique, audiences, ethics, ideology / James Phelan.
p. cm. — (The theory and interpretation of narrative series)
Includes bibliographical references and index.
ISBN 0-8142-0688-3 (cloth : alk. paper). —
ISBN 0-8142-0689-1 (pbk. : alk. paper)
1. Narration (Rhetoric) 2. Fiction—Technique. 3. Ideology and literature
I. Title II. Series
PN212.P485 1996
808—dc20 95-50365
CIP

Text design by Hunter Design Associates
Type set in Monotype Bembo
Printed by Bookcrafters, Inc., Chelsea , MI.

The paper used in this publication meets the minimum requirements of American National Standard for Information Sciences—Permanence of Paper for Printed Library Materials, ANSI Z39.48–1992.

9 8 7 6 5 4 3 2 1

For Betty, Katie, and Mike, with love
and gratitude for our vital rhetorical community

Contents

Preface

This book did me the great favor of sneaking up on me. I wrote it while procrastinating on a different, seemingly more daunting project. I'd get to that large body of work, I told myself many times over the last few years, right after scratching this itch, massaging that cramp, scrubbing away this dirt. After a while, I realized that I'd done so much scratching and scrubbing that I'd managed to create something with a discernible identity of its own. Whether the coherence and magnitude of this creature is sufficient—or sufficiently attractive—for anyone to want to spend much time in its company remains to be seen. But it is worth noticing here that the coherence derives from my consistent attempt to think through what it means to say that narrative is rhetoric, even as I've worked on the range of issues that give the book its first claim to magnitude: voice, progression, mimesis, the ethics of reading, kinds of textual recalcitrance, the paradoxes of first-person (or homodiegetic) narration, the role of ideology in telling and interpreting nonfictional narratives. At the same time, the thinking through occurs very much in connection with the practical work of interpreting particular narratives, and the range of these texts constitutes the other claim to magnitude: short stories by Joseph Conrad, Katherine Anne Porter, Ernest Hemingway, and Lorrie Moore; novels by William Makepeace Thackeray, Virginia Woolf, Hemingway, F. Scott Fitzgerald, Toni Morrison; nonfictional accounts of contemporary campus life by Dinesh D'Souza.

The progression of chapters here does show some shifts in my thinking about narrative as rhetoric: in particular, I start with but gradually move away from a model in which rhetoric consists of an author, through the narrative text, extending a multidimensional (aesthetic, emotive, ideational, ethical, political) invitation to a reader who, in turn, seeks to do justice to the complexity of the invitation and then responds. In the model I move to, the multidimensional quality of reading is retained, but the lines between author, reader, and text become blurred. In the revised model, rhetoric is the synergy occurring between authorial agency, textual phenomena, and reader response. Despite this shift, I don't regard the book as implicitly constructing a metanarrative, a Bildungsroman in which the initially flawed but sympathetic critic moves, with each succeeding chapter, nearer and nearer to the Great Enlightenment. If, as I maintain, author, text, and reader are in an endlessly recursive relationship, then any one essay will necessarily emphasize some features of that relationship more than others—and it will have been written at some particular moment in my ongoing relationship to the narrative. Consequently, the particular work of any essay here should remain both potentially useful and presumptively less than definitive regardless of when in the last few years I composed it. To help indicate some of the connections between the essays, I have written headnotes to each. To help the reader with the terminology of narrative theory I employ in the book, I have included a glossary of terms after the appendix.

While the book was sneaking up on me, I was getting help from many people. I owe thanks to Debra Moddelmog for introducing me to "Magic"; to Paul Smith, Scott Donaldson, and Mike Reynolds for encouraging me to think some more about Hemingway, and to Jackson Breyer and Jerry Kennedy for an inducement to do something with Fitzgerald; to Elizabeth Langland and Laura Claridge for the invitation to write about Thackeray and to Susan Griffin and Sandy Morey Norton for complicating my first conclusions; to Dan Schwarz for asking me to write about Conrad; to Monika Fludernik for prodding me to think about second-person narration; to Dinesh D'Souza for agreeing to participate in a dialogue about *Illiberal Education.* I am also indebted to a large group of students and colleagues who have over the years patiently listened to me go on about these texts and these issues (in one seminar, my worrying over "My Old Man," I later discovered, almost transformed the twelve vigorous participants into "My Prematurely Aged Grad Students"). I have named some of these people in notes to specific chapters, but here I want to acknowledge my deep and enduring appreciation for the help of four research assistants, Elizabeth Patnoe, Jane Greer, Susan Swinford, and Elizabeth

Preston. These people have each provided crucial material support and invaluable criticism and advice; without them, this book would be a lesser thing. To Peter J. Rabinowitz, I owe a special thanks: he read it all—much of it more than once—with a wonderful combination of generosity and rigor, and then took the time to walk me through his responses. In short, he exemplified what it means to enter into an authorial audience without losing oneself in the process. Finally, I am thankful for the rhetorical community in which I find most favor, that provided by my wife, Betty Menaghan, and our two children, Katie and Mike; this one is for all of you.

Different versions of the following chapters have appeared, in whole or in part, in the following publications. I thank all of them for permission to reprint.

Chapter 1 as "Character and Judgment in Narrative and in Lyric: Toward an Understanding of Audience Engagement in *The Waves*." In *Style* 24 (1990): 408–21.

Chapter 2 as "*Vanity Fair:* Listening as a Rhetorician—and a Feminist." In *Out of Bounds: Male Writers and Gender(ed) Criticism,* edited by Laura Claridge and Elizabeth Langland, 132–47. Amherst: University of Massachusetts Press, 1990.

Chapter 3 as "Distance, Voice, and Temporal Perspective in Frederic Henry's Narration: Powers, Problems, Paradox." In *New Essays on "A Farewell to Arms,"* edited by Scott Donaldson, 53–73. Cambridge: Cambridge University Press, 1990. Also as "The Concept of Voice, the Voices of Frederic Henry, and the Structure of *A Farewell to Arms*. In *Hemingway: Essays of Reassessment,* edited by Frank Scafella, 214–32. New York: Oxford University Press, 1990.

Chapter 4 as "What Hemingway and a Rhetorical Theory of Narrative Can Do for Each Other: The Example of 'My Old Man.'" In the *Hemingway Review* 12, no. 2 (1993): 1–14.

Chapter 6 as "Sharing Secrets." In *The Secret Sharer: A Casebook in Contemporary Criticism,* edited by Daniel R. Schwarz. Boston: Bedford Books, 1996.

Chapter 7 as "*Self-Help* for Narratee and Narrative Audience: How I—and You?—Read 'How.'" In *Style* 28 (1994): 350–65.

Chapter 8 as "Narrating the PC Controversies: Thoughts on

Dinesh D'Souza's *Illiberal Education.*" In *Narrative* 2, no. 3 (1994): 244–67. Reply to D'Souza's "Response" as "A Monologic Imagination." In *Narrative* 2, no. 3 (1994): 270–71.

Chapter 9 as "Toward a Rhetorical Reader Response Criticism: The Difficult, the Stubborn, and the Ending of *Beloved.*" In *Modern Fiction Studies* 39 (1993): 709–28.

Appendix as "Why Wayne Booth Can't Get with the Program; or, The Nintentional Fallacy." In *Rhetoric Society Quarterly* 22, no. 3 (1992): 54–58.

Introduction

Narrative as Rhetoric: Reading the Spells of Porter's "Magic"

Reading a Narrative of Rhetoric

What does it mean to treat narrative as rhetoric? Although this question, a natural way to begin a book entitled *Narrative as Rhetoric,* tempts me to deliver a long, theoretical disquisition on authors, readers, narrative techniques, structures, conventions, and the concept of rhetoric, I will spare you that and opt for illustration by offering a rhetorical reading of a particular narrative. The narrative I choose is a narrative *of* rhetoric, that is, a narrative whose central event is the telling of a story, Katherine Anne Porter's "Magic."

Magic

And, Madame Blanchard, believe that I am happy to be here with you and your family because it is so serene, everything, and before this I worked for a long time in a fancy house—maybe you don't know what is a fancy house? Naturally . . . everyone must have heard sometime or other. Well, Madame, I work always where there is work to be had, and so in this place I worked very hard all hours, and saw too many things, things you wouldn't believe, and I wouldn't think of telling you, only maybe it will rest you while I brush your hair. You'll excuse me too but I could not help hearing you say to the laundress maybe someone had bewitched your linens, they fall away so fast in the wash. Well, there was a girl there in that house, poor thing, thin, but well-liked by all the men who called, and you understand she could not get along with the woman who ran the house. They quarreled, the madam cheated her on her checks: you know, the girl got a check, a brass one, every time, and at the week's end she gave those back to the madam, yes, that was the way, and got her percentage, a very small little of her earnings: it is a business, you see, like any other—and the madam used to pretend the girl had given back only so many checks, you see, and really she had given many more, but after they were out of her hands, what could she do? So she would say, I will get out of this place, and curse and cry. Then the madam would hit her over the head. She always hit people over the head with bottles, it was the way she fought. My good heavens, Madame Blanchard, what confusion there would be sometimes with a girl running raving downstairs, and the madam pulling her back by the hair and smashing a bottle on her forehead.

It was nearly always about the money, the girls got in debt so, and if they wished to go they could not without paying every sou marqué. The madam had full understanding with the police; the girls must come back with them or go to the jails. Well, they always came back with the policemen or with another kind of man friend of the madam: she could make men work for her too, but she paid them very well for all, let me tell you: and so the girls stayed on unless they were sick; if so, if they got too sick she sent them away again.

Madame Blanchard said, "You are pulling a little here," and eased a strand of hair: "and then what?"

Pardon—but this girl, there was a true hatred between her and the madam. She would say many times, I make more money than anybody else in the house, and every week were scenes. So at last she said one morning, Now I will leave this place, and she took out forty dollars from under her pillow and said, Here's your money! The madam began to shout, Where did you get all that, you——? and accused her of robbing the men who came to visit her. The girl said, Keep your hands off or I'll brain you: and at that the madam took hold of her shoulders, and began to lift her knee and kick this girl most terribly in the stomach, and even in her most secret place, Madame Blanchard, and then she beat her in the face with a bottle, and the girl fell back again into her room where I was making clean. I helped her to the bed, and she sat there holding her sides with her head hanging down, and when she got up again there was blood everywhere she had sat. So then the madam came in once more and screamed, Now you can get out, you are no good for me any more: I don't repeat all, you understand it is too much. But she took all the money she could find, and at the door she gave the girl a great push in the back with her knee, so that she fell again in the street, and then got up and went away with the dress barely on her.

After this the men who knew this girl kept saying, Where is Ninette? And they kept asking this in the next days, so that the madam could not say any longer, I put her out because she is a thief. No, she began to see she was wrong to send this Ninette away, and then she said, She will be back in a few days, don't trouble yourself.

And now, Madame Blanchard, if you wish to hear, I come to the strange part, the thing recalled to me when you said your linens were bewitched. For the cook in that place was a woman, colored like myself, like myself with much French blood just the same, like myself living always among people who worked spells. But she had a very hard heart, she helped the madam in everything, she liked to watch all that happened, and she gave away tales on the girls. The madam trusted her above everything, and she said, Well, where can I find that slut? because she had gone altogether out of Basin Street before the madam began to ask the police to bring her again. Well, the cook said, I know a charm that works here in New Orleans, colored women do it to bring back their men: in seven days they come again very happy to stay and they cannot say why: even your enemy will come back to you believing you are his friend. It is a New Orleans charm for sure, for certain, they say it does not work even across the river. . . . And then they did it just as the cook said. They took the chamber pot of this girl from under her bed, and in it they mixed with water and milk all the relics of her they found there: the hair from her brush, and the face powder from the puff, and even little bits of her nails they found about the edges of the carpet where she sat by habit to cut her finger- and toenails; and they dipped the sheets with her blood into the water, and all the time the cook said something over it in a low voice; I could not hear all, but

> at last she said to the madam, Now spit in it: and the madam spat, and the cook said, When she comes back she will be dirt under your feet.
>
> Madame Blanchard closed her perfume bottle with a thin click: "Yes, and then?"
>
> Then in seven nights the girl came back and she looked very sick, the same clothes and all, but happy to be there. One of the men said, Welcome home, Ninette! and when she started to speak to the madam, the madam said, Shut up and get upstairs and dress yourself. So Ninette, this girl, she said, I'll be down in just a minute. And after that she lived there quietly.

In saying that "Magic" is a narrative of rhetoric, I want to call attention, first, to the rhetorical dimensions of the maid's action: she is *telling a particular story to a particular audience in a particular situation for, presumably, a particular purpose.* I want to call attention, second, to the parallel between the maid's action and Porter's: the particular story that Porter is telling is the maid's telling of Ninette's story. In analyzing these parallel acts of telling, I want to focus on teller, technique, story, situation, audience, and purpose: all the elements that help determine the shape and effect of the story.

By approaching both the maid's telling and Porter's telling as parallel rhetorical acts, we can recognize a crucial element of its construction that may not initially jump out during a first reading: "Magic" is a narrative with three interrelated levels. These are (1) the inner level, narrated by the maid: the story of Ninette, the madam, and the cook; I shall refer to this level as Ninette's story; (2) the middle level, narrated by the heterodiegetic narrator, who appears only twice: the report of the maid's telling Ninette's story to Madame Blanchard; I shall refer to this level as the maid's story; and (3) the outer level, constructed and designed by Porter as implied author: the largely covert communication from Porter to her audiences, implied and real, of the narrator telling the maid's story of Ninette's story; I shall refer to this level as Porter's story.

In looking first at the technique of "Magic," notice that, rather than calling attention to the three different levels, Porter's presentation blurs the borders between them, especially the border between Ninette's story and the maid's story. Porter starts in the midst of things and does not even use quotation marks for the maid's story (*And* Madame Blanchard, I am happy to be here [emphasis mine]); furthermore, she has the heterodiegetic narrator speak only after Ninette's story is well under way and, as noted above, only twice in the whole story—and each time very briefly. As a result, Porter elides the difference between Ninette's story and the maid's story—or perhaps, better, she foregrounds Ninette's story and backgrounds the maid's. Given this technique, it is not surprising that, as Helen Leath has noted, many critics focus on Ninette to the exclusion of the maid. Surely, one effect of the technique is to engage us strongly in the horrors of Ninette's story.

Indeed, as we attend to those horrors, we also recognize the major disparity between the maid's version of Ninette's story and Porter's: in Porter's version Ninette is not defeated by the cook's magic spell but rather by the social forces lined up against her. Ninette returns to the fancy house looking sick and wearing the same clothes because she has had no money to live on and has not been able to find another way to support herself. Ninette's story in Porter's version is not about magic but rather about failed rebellion and victory for the oppressive madam and her support system of police and well-off men.

This first act of seeing beneath the surface of Ninette's story quickly moves us into the next, richer area of the rhetorical exchange, that involving the ways that Ninette's story, the maid's story, and Porter's story intersect. As soon as we infer that Porter does not expect us to believe in magic, we are inclined to ask whether the maid does—and whether the maid expects Madame Blanchard to. The answers are not immediately obvious, but merely posing these questions highlights the fact that the maid seizes upon the pretext of Madame Blanchard's remark about her laundry being bewitched to tell Ninette's story. This recognition in turn prompts the questions that form the interpretive crux of "Magic": what are the maid's motivations for telling Ninette's story, what does she hope to achieve by telling it, and does she achieve any of her goals? In short, what rhetorical purposes does the maid want her narration to serve, and does it achieve those purposes?

Porter's technique of eliding the first two levels of the narrative suggests that the answer can be found in parallels and contrasts between them. Porter provides many. First, there are the two madams.

Though they move in different social spheres, both are powerful women—they have money, authority, employees. At the same time, their power itself depends on a larger patriarchal structure: the madam provides a service to the men of New Orleans, and when they complain about Ninette's absence, the madam responds; Madame Blanchard's wealth and comfort depend, to some extent at least, on her marriage to M. Blanchard. Second, there are the maid and Ninette: they are both subservient employees of a madam. Third, and most strongly, there are the maid and the cook: both have "mixed racial blood"; both have lived always among people who work spells; both like to watch all that happens; both apparently like to tell tales.

All these parallels help us answer the questions about the maid's rhetorical purposes, though we have a multitude of possibilities rather than any single answer. The maid may be giving Madame Blanchard a warning: If you do not treat me well, I will, like Ninette, oppose you—and because I am like the cook, I will be more successful in my opposition than she. The maid may be trying to ingratiate herself, saying in effect, "Like the cook, I am willing to help my Madame in all things." Or the maid may be signifying on Madame Blanchard's remark that the sheets are bewitched in order to scare Madame Blanchard: Like the cook, I can do powerful magic; if you think those sheets are bewitched, you ain't seen nothin' yet.

Because the end of the maid's story coincides with the end of Ninette's, we cannot know which is her primary purpose and we do not know whether she has achieved it. But the two appearances of the heterodiegetic narrator and the two interjections by Madame Blanchard do direct our attention in specific ways. The power struggle between employer and employee that defines Ninette's story seems to be very much the subtext of the maid's story. It is when the maid is telling about the madam's general ill-treatment of her employees that the maid pulls Madame Blanchard's hair: a quiet assertion of the maid's power even as she is serving her mistress. Madame Blanchard reasserts control by gently stopping the hair pulling, but she also reveals that she has been caught by the power of the maid's storytelling: she asks the rapt audience's perpetual question, "And then what?" In the second appearance, just after the maid recounts the cook's spell, the heterodiegetic narrator calls attention to Madame Blanchard's closing her perfume bottle "with a thin click." Since Ninette's madam asserted her power over her employees by beating them with bottles, Madame Blanchard's clicking her own perfume bottle shut at this moment suggests that she feels some need to remind herself—and the maid—of her power. But, like the first interruption of the maid's telling, this one also ends with Madame Blanchard asking the engaged audience's question: "Yes, and then?"[1]

More generally, the more we look at the interaction of Ninette's story, the maid's story, and Porter's story, the more it seems that Porter wants us to view the maid's telling of Ninette's story as the prime example of the maid's magic. Like the cook, the maid casts a spell. By calling her story "Magic," Porter makes the same claim for herself: just as the maid seeks to catch Madame Blanchard in the spell of Ninette's story, so too does Porter want to catch us up in her telling of the maid's story.

In this way, the rhetorical exchanges in which we participate as we read and interpret Ninette's story, the maid's story, and Porter's story eventually lead us to reflect on the power of narrative. We do not know exactly what the effect of the maid's telling on Madame Blanchard will be, but the clues about the subtext of power relations and the evidence of Madame Blanchard's being caught by the maid's spell strongly suggest that it will have some effect. And the effect of this conclusion on us is to reinforce our sense of the magic of narrative and to take pleasure in our consenting to Porter's spell. In this respect, the open-endedness of the story is all to the good. The more interpretations we find of the maid, her motive, her story, and its likely effect, the more we are both drawn into her world and made cognizant of the magical power of narrative.

Concepts of Rhetoric: Deconstruction, Pragmatism, Communication

There is more to say about the concrete particularities of "Magic," and I will return to them shortly, but I turn now to consider the theoretical principles I have been using to discuss the story so far. First, the phrase "narrative as rhetoric" means something more than that narrative uses rhetoric or has a rhetorical dimension. It means instead that narrative is not just story but also action, *the telling of a story by someone to someone on some occasion for some purpose.*[2] Furthermore, as the analysis of "Magic" indicates, this basic configuration of teller-story-situation-audience-purpose is at least doubled in most narrative: there is the narrator's telling the story to his or her audience and then the author's telling of the narrator's telling to the author's audience. Consequently, the narrator's telling is part of the author's construction of the whole narrative, and in that sense, what is a matter of the telling at one level becomes a matter of the told at the next. Before exploring the details of this rhetorical configuration, I would like to highlight some of its key assumptions and emphases by comparing the general approach with the ones that follow from two other widely circulating conceptions of rhetoric: deconstruction and pragmatism.[3]

I call deconstruction's conception of rhetoric "widely circulating" with full knowledge that deconstruction's heyday has passed and that most critics and theorists are currently more concerned with reinventing historical criticism and merging literary with cultural studies in ways that foreground the politics and ideology of both cultural and critical texts. I engage deconstruction here because its *legacy* is so influential: it is to deconstruction that we owe the wide acceptance of the principles that language is inherently unstable, that there is no transcendental anchor to textual meanings, and that textual meanings are more likely to be at odds with one another than not. Like most other contemporary theorists, I acknowledge the value of these deconstructionist principles for complicating our understandings of language, textuality, and interpretation. At the same time, however, I find these views less compelling than many other critics do, and although I am not interested in trying to repudiate deconstruction, I do want, first, to show how the principles of my approach to narrative as rhetoric differ from deconstruction's and, second, to suggest that, despite appearances, deconstruction does not invalidate or otherwise supplant those principles.[4]

I call pragmatism's conception of rhetoric a widely circulating one because, through the efforts of Stanley Fish and Richard Rorty, this conception has come to be seen as part and parcel of poststructuralist antifoundationalism. Again, my efforts here are less to argue either for or against pragmatism as a philosophical position than to locate my approach to narrative as rhetoric in relation to it—and, more specifically, to make a space for that approach in the contemporary critical landscape.

Paul de Man's famous essay "Rhetoric and Semiology" illustrates the fundamental emphasis of deconstruction's approach to rhetoric: a rigorous reading of language as a system of tropes and a rigorous analysis of the logic implied by the tropes of any text. De Man argues that the grammar and rhetoric of texts frequently diverge, but efforts to decide whether one should be privileged over the other are doomed to failure precisely because there is no decisive evidence in the text. He brilliantly illustrates this logic of deconstruction in his tour de force reading of an interchange from the 1970s television show *All in the Family*. When Edith Bunker asks her husband, Archie, whether he wants the laces on his bowling shoes tied over or under, he impatiently replies, "What's the difference?" Under de Man's gaze, Archie's question is fully explicable, first, as what its rhetoric suggests—a rhetorical question revealing Archie's belief that there is no difference—and, second, as what its grammar suggests, that is, a genuine question, asking for an explanation of difference. As a genuine question, it is a kind of challenge to Edith—if you're going to ask me such a question, I want you to explain the difference to me. It is worth noting that de Man's analysis includes the rhetorical situation but that he does not believe that an appeal to the situation can decide the case. Since the fault line between grammar and rhetoric is so wide, since the text finally does not contain sufficient evidence for its own interpretation, appealing to author, audience, occasion, or purpose for a resolution to the undecidability is not a valid move but instead an imposition of the interpreter's will on the text.

What deconstruction's attention to textual rhetoric means for narrative analysis is very nicely encapsulated in J. Hillis Miller's entry "Narrative" in *Critical Terms for Literary Study*. The "basic elements" of narrative, Miller declares, are three: plot, personification, and trope. Not surprisingly, he gives special emphasis to trope, arguing, in effect, that narrative inevitably tropes over itself. That is, narrative develops some pattern or repetition of trope, and this patterning invariably generates "fundamentally incongruous meanings" or "narrative disjunctions that can never be brought back to unity" (77).

Turning back to "Magic," then, we can see that a deconstructionist would be willing to accept much of the analysis I have presented so far but would go on to say that it stops too soon, that it does not do a sufficiently rigorous reading of the logic of Porter's narrative. The conclusion that the story demonstrates the magical power of narrative does not attend sufficiently to the first move of my analysis: the inference that Porter's story tells us that Ninette comes back not because of the cook's spell but because of the madam's power. Once we reexamine that inference, we can see that the powers of all the spells found through the analogies made in my analysis—between the cook's spell, the maid's story, and Porter's story—are built on an illusion. Consequently, Porter's story simultaneously demonstrates the power of narrative and exposes narrative as powerless. Everyone may be caught in the spell of narrative, but the spell is, finally, based on an illusion.

Furthermore, we can push the logic of Porter's technique of elision to its logical conclusion. The spell in Ninette's story that brings her back is cast by the cook, whereas the spell in the maid's story is cast by the maid's own telling. But it is just as much the spell cast by the maid's story that brings Ninette back, because there is no evidence other than the maid's word that Ninette came back in seven days. Indeed, there is no evidence that any of the events of the tale actually occurred or that Ninette is anything other than the maid's invention. Again, the effect is to demonstrate narrative's power and simultaneously to expose its powerlessness. The maid's narrative makes things happen—and makes them happen so vividly as to catch Madame Blanchard in its spell—but the things it makes happen may have happened only through the act of the maid's telling. If saying makes things so, then our sayings are powerful indeed; but if saying makes things so, then, to anyone's saying, we can say, "So what?" And of course, this same logic applies a fortiori to Porter's story.

Before discussing the relation of this deconstructive reading to the one I have offered, I would like to consider the pragmatist conception of rhetoric and its resultant claims for both readings. This conception, represented in the work of Richard Rorty, Stanley Fish, Steven Knapp and Walter Benn Michaels, and others, is well summarized in Fish's chapter entitled "Rhetoric" in *Doing What Comes Naturally.* This view sees the world—especially that part of the world concerned with knowledge—as constituted by rhetoric. Our discourse about the world makes the world what we find it to be. In his essay, Fish points to two attitudes toward rhetoric that have been present in different forms throughout the history of Western thought: (1) the attitude that rhetoric is a means by which a truth independent of our discourse is folded, spindled, mutilated, or otherwise manipulated; and (2) the attitude that rhetoric is inescapable because truth is not independent of but rather constituted by our discourse about it. Fish emphasizes the point that the ancient quarrel can never be resolved, but upon reflection we can see that this emphasis itself indicates his preference for the second view. Someone committed to the position that truth is independent of our discourse would think that this truth could be demonstrated sufficiently for the quarrel to be resolved, whereas someone committed to the position that truth is constituted by our discourse about it can see both positions as consistent with the general principle—and therefore as engaged in a quarrel in which neither can win.

A pragmatist view of narrative as rhetoric would view narrative as inescapably bound up with its interpretation and its interpretation as endlessly malleable—according to the needs, interests, and values of the interpreter on any given occasion. Consequently, the pragmatist would regard both my analysis of "Magic" and that of the deconstructor as different instances of the same phenomenon: each is construing Porter's narrative in a particular way for its particular purposes. What neither view realizes, however, is how partial and particular it is, how much the questions it asks and the assumptions it makes—about language, the nature of narrative, readers, and many other things—participate in the construction not just of the interpretation but also of the text. And what each view needs to recognize is that no final resolution of disagreements is possible. There is no fixed ground, no foundation—either in the narrative text, in authorial agency, in reader response, or, indeed, in any general theory of interpretation—that would allow for any satisfactory adjudication. However, the pragmatist would also say that the difference between my analysis and the deconstructive one is the difference between a foundationalist and an antifoundationalist view of truth. From the pragmatist perspective, my analysis seems to assume Porter's narrative has some essential character that the interpretation seeks to describe, whereas the deconstructive analysis sees the textual rhetoric as frustrating any access to such an essential character. Although the pragmatist would want to qualify the deconstructor's claim for the necessity of the deconstructive reading, the pragmatist would also favor it over the one I have proposed.

Let me now reconsider my analysis in light of these critiques. As always, I find that the deconstructive analysis seems simultaneously counterintuitive and virtually irresistible: once the premises of deconstruction are granted, its logic is very persuasive. However, thinking about this logic from the pragmatist's antifoundational perspective clarifies the strength and weakness of deconstruction's appeal. From the pragmatist perspective, the logic is intriguing because it is an instance of what it describes, an enactment of the power and powerlessness of narrative. That is, the logic leads to a strong account of Porter's narrative, one capable of disrupting the analysis I proposed, but the logic also leaves us powerless to move beyond its contradictory assertions about power and powerlessness. To describe the logic this way is to make clear how deconstruction's claim to be reading the text more closely than anyone else can be legitimately questioned: the logic depends on two interpretive leaps. The first leap is to key terms—in this case, *magic* and *narrative,* as opposed, say, to *race* and *class;* the second is to a narrative about those terms in the text—in this case, the narrative about the power/powerlessness of narrative. In other words, the antifoundational perspective helps point out that although no narrative and no interpretation is deconstruction-proof, deconstruction's logic about textual logic is not as inevitable and necessary as its attention to textual rhetoric makes it appear. Laying bare the leaps that form the basis of the deconstructor's operation shows that deconstruction cannot really claim to be closer to the literal text than other approaches.

With this understanding in mind, we can return to the most important question that the deconstructive reading presents to the one I offered: what is the relation between the cook's magic spell and the maid's magic of narration? Does our awareness that the cook's magic is illusory make us suspect that the magic of narrative is similarly illusory? A closer look reveals that Porter's story, in effect, recognizes the deconstructive hypothesis but then sets out its affirmation of the power of narrative. That is, Porter's story indicates that the maid's narrative is more powerful than the cook's spell because the maid's narrative catches the powerful Madame Blanchard, whereas the cook's spell is not really responsible for Ninette's return and both that spell and the return may be a product of the maid's magic. Furthermore, the parallel between the maid and Ninette also works to point to the story's ultimate affirmation of narrative. Ninette, though sufficiently wily and resourceful to save enough money to leave the brothel, is not sufficiently wily and resourceful to construct a narrative for her madam that will allow her to keep the money and successfully escape. Regardless of whether the maid wants to ingratiate herself with Madame Blanchard, to scare her, or to warn her, the maid uses narrative in an effort to establish a different relationship with her employer than the one Ninette has with the madam. To be sure, Porter leaves open the question of whether the magic of the narrative will have any real effect. But in these situations "where it was almost always about the money"—situations faced by Ninette, the cook, and the maid—where the powerful have money and the powerless minorities and women have none, Porter's story suggests that the best weapon or best defense of the powerless is narrative. Porter's story, of course, does not offer any guarantee of the maid's success, but it certainly suggests that her odds are better than Ninette's.

Before turning from the deconstructionist to the pragmatist challenge, I would like to call attention to some other dimensions of the spell Porter casts in "Magic." To read the story is not only to inquire into the maid's motives but also to situate ourselves emotively and ethically in relationship to Ninette, the French cook, the two madams, the maid, and Porter herself. In Ninette's story, the emotive and ethical lines are clearly drawn: our sympathies are with Ninette in her nervy effort to escape the domineering, abusive madam (and her willing helper, the cook); we experience the madam's victory as a dispiriting defeat. In the maid's story, however, the emotive and ethical lines are blurry. Because we have no strong evidence of Madame Blanchard's ethical character, the maid's storytelling, in contrast to Ninette's efforts at escape, has the quality of a preemptive strike. Our inferences about Ninette's story and what it suggests about the plight of the powerless woman certainly make the maid's action understandable, and these inferences may incline us to sympathize with and even admire her ingenuity and resourcefulness. However, once we recall that the maid may have simply fabricated Ninette's story, the maid's character—and the ethical balance of her story—shift. If the maid has invented Ninette's story, then she is someone who aggressively manipulates her environment, someone who, above all, looks out for number one. Of course, with either construction of the maid's character, Madame Blanchard does not change. We never see her as a victim of the maid, and, indeed, she may remain ultimately unaffected by the maid's storytelling. Nevertheless, our reflections on the maid enable us to recognize more fully how charged this domestic scene of one woman brushing another's hair may be. It is certainly a subtle power struggle; it may also be one with an underlying threat of violence. If Ninette's story is dispiriting, the maid's is chilling: although its outcome is unknown, the story itself is full of ominous notes.

Moving to Porter's story, we can recognize that her technique of plunging us into this situation works not just to involve us cognitively but also to affect us emotionally and to challenge us ethically. Each inference we make about the maid's storytelling situation also leads us, first, to a tacit judgment of the maid's action, motives, and character, and second, to our sense of how powerfully the scene is charged. But virtually each new inference (the maid is telling a story from her past; the maid is making up this story) leads us to a reexamination of these same things, a reexamination that involves us in such ethical questions as how much we take the maid's side, regardless of her motives, how much we care about whether she is making up Ninette's story, how much we judge Madame Blanchard simply on the basis of her name and her class. In short, Porter's story so successfully casts its spell because it so efficiently arouses and so tightly interweaves the audience's cognitive, emotive, and ethical responses.

If, on the one hand, my effort to make space for my approach to narrative as rhetoric alongside the deconstructive one has been successful, it may, on the other, nevertheless serve to sharpen the pragmatist objection: the approach is based on a fundamental epistemological error, the notion that there are facts and truths outside of our discourse. Now note that the pragmatist, especially the pragmatist called Stanley Fish, works with a strict either/or logic: either language describes the world or language constructs the world; either there is transcendent Truth or there is no truth; either there are facts outside of discourse or discourse creates facts and truths. My response to the pragmatist objection is that this either/or logic inadequately captures the complexity of the relationship between facts, hypotheses, and theories, or in the realm of literary criticism, texts, interpretations, and approaches. I can better substantiate this claim after you read the following narrative, which I have entitled "Institutional Magic."

During a session at a conference I recently attended called "The Politics of Interpretation after Poststructuralism," I witnessed a disturbing event. A white middle-aged man was reading a paper arguing that the political consequences of much mainstream poststructuralist thought are inimical to the politics of multiculturalism and that this antithesis highlights some serious theoretical limitations of poststructuralism. His delivery indicated both that he felt very strongly about the political dimension of his argument and that he was very nervous about making this case at a conference where the reigning assumption seemed to be that the theoretical (non)foundations of poststructuralism were beyond question. After he had been talking for about ten minutes, a man in the audience began to hiss. At first the sound was barely audible, but the hisser gradually grew bolder and louder. Then the woman sitting next to him joined in. And then another person and another, until everyone in the room, including the speaker, could hear it. The speaker became increasingly flustered until, unable to stand it anymore, he looked up from his text and berated the audience: "You see, this is exactly the kind of negative political consequence I am talking about." But this chiding only incited the hissers to increase their volume. The speaker tried to return to his text but was now so distraught that he could not find his place. The hissing continued unabated, and the speaker's distress turned to panic: shouting, "The hell with it!" he threw his paper into the air and ran from the podium and out of the room. As he left, the hissing turned to applause.

Horrified by this event, I wrote two letters: one to the speaker to express some sympathy and support, and one to the conference organizer to complain about the behavior of the audience and to inquire whether any formal action was going to be taken. Within a few weeks I had two replies: a very brief thank-you from the speaker, and a longer letter from the conference organizer with a very surprising enclosure. Since an unsolicited apology had just arrived, he was not going to pursue any formal action; I would understand, he said, when I read the enclosed copy of the letter of apology. This letter, you see, was from the speaker. In addition to apologizing, the speaker detailed his conversion to a position much more sympathetic to poststructuralism, and he expressed gratitude for the audience's "creative resistance" to his earlier, erroneous argument. Finally, the speaker hoped that the organizer would be willing to consider the paper he wrote about his conversion experience for publication in the conference volume, adding as an aside that the acceptance of one more essay would clinch his pending tenure case.

Let us now consider the pragmatist question about the existence and force of the "facts" of this story and my use of it. There are, I maintain, numerous kinds of facts involved here: (1) Facts that will not be disputed—for example, that I asked you to read "Institutional Magic." (2) Facts that depend on the employment of our interpretive faculties—for example, that there are recognizable parallels between this story and Porter's "Magic," especially between Ninette's defeat and the conference speaker's change of heart. (3) Facts that depend on an even deeper excursion into the realm of interpretation so that the line between fact and interpretation is extremely blurry—for example, that the speaker's capitulation in "Institutional Magic" is different from Ninette's because he is more complicit in the oppressive system. Beyond this point, we get so deep into the territory of interpretation that rather than facts we have questions whose answers most will agree deserve the name "interpretations": How much is the "I" of "Institutional Magic" like the maid in "Magic"? How much is the "I" constructing you as a reader in a role like the one Madame Blanchard has in "Magic"? What is the relation between the "I" of "Institutional Magic" and the "I" of *Narrative as Rhetoric*? What is the veiled communication I want to make? Is "Institutional Magic" less open-ended than Porter's story? Given the context in which I have used it, how much is "Institutional Magic" thematizing narrative?

According to the pragmatist view, even this delineation of kinds of facts and this consideration of the interrelations between facts, interpretations, and questions needs to be seen as the product of a kind of discourse: everything I've said about "Magic" and "Institutional Magic" can be seen as arising from a set of beliefs and assumptions that in turn influence my way of talking about narrative, literary critical arguments, academic audiences, and other issues. Without those beliefs and assumptions and without that discursive framework, both "Institutional Magic" and the things I have said about it—indeed, perhaps most of the things you have thought about it—are not recognizable and therefore cannot be considered as facts of any kind. If we stepped out of the discursive framework provided by my beliefs and assumptions and moved into one that attended, say, only to the reproduction of the black marks on the white page, then even the data and the givens of my case apparently disappear.

With the point that there are no facts outside of some framework for describing them I am in complete agreement. It is the next step of the pragmatist logic, the conclusion that truth is constituted by our discourse about it, that gives me pause. That our facts change as our discursive frameworks change does not prove that there are no facts; it proves rather that there are multiple facts and multiple ways of construing facts. Thus the same phenomenon, for example, the phrase "happy to be here," may be, in one discursive frame, an ironic comment that reveals something about a character, while in another frame something that tells us about the importance of the letter *h*. In making this claim, I am not asserting that my rhetorical approach to "Magic" or "Institutional Magic" is the standard or foundation against which all other ways must be compared. But I am asserting that the approach makes a legitimate claim to propose one kind of truth about both stories: the way each functions as a communication from author to reader.

To put the point another way, to accept the pragmatist position would be to accept that your experience in reading "Institutional Magic"—its arousal of horror, pleasure, disgust, indifference, or anything else—is not primarily a function of textual phenomena and their shaping by me (under Porter's influence) but rather is rooted in something else—a set of beliefs about the academy, about stories, and about stories about the academy. My alternative view is quite simple: we should reject the institutional magic of pragmatism that makes the story and its techniques disappear, because those techniques and that shaped story do influence the experience. Indeed, I have told this story about the academy rather than a whole range of others precisely because I believe in its power to evoke a strong response from my expected audience. You will be willing to accept my alternative to the extent that you find yourself convinced that the shaped story is important to (though not necessarily determinative of) whatever response it evokes in you.

In countering the either/or logic of the pragmatist by arguing that there are multiple facts and multiple ways of construing them, I am proposing a different kind of antifoundationalism. The position is antifoundationalist because it insists on the incompatibility of the multiple facts, the impossibility of finding the one true account of them and their connection to each other. At the same time, my antifoundationalist position departs from Fish's version by insisting that although facts are always mediated, always seen from within the confines of a given perspective, the perspective does not create the facts. In doing interpretation, then, we will encounter narratives capable of providing recalcitrance to the rhetorical critic; furthermore, the perspectives of other approaches have the potential to complicate, revise, or even overturn the initial results of a rhetorical interpretation.

Rhetoric in Relation to Other Interests

As many readers will have already recognized, my approach is indebted to rhetorical theorists such as Kenneth Burke and Wayne C. Booth who also emphasize narrative as a distinctive and powerful means for an author to communicate knowledge, feelings, values, and beliefs to an audience: indeed, viewing narrative as having the purpose of communicating knowledge, feelings, values, and beliefs is viewing narrative as rhetoric. There are various metaphors, all somewhat inadequate, that might be applied to this relationship between author, text, and audience: *interaction, exchange, transaction, intercourse. Interaction* is unexceptionable because unexceptional and bland. Both *exchange* and *transaction* carry connotations of buying and selling, and while these connotations are not entirely inappropriate, they are also reductive.

Gift exchange is better (see Sharp), but it does not quite capture the effort frequently involved in the reader's half of the exchange. *Intercourse* is, well, sexy. Its calling attention to the play of desire and the erotic component in the writing and reading of narrative (see Barthes) are genuine advantages, but again, it strikes me as too narrow. What I want is a shorthand term that might include all these things—interaction, transaction, (gift) exchange, intercourse. Rather than search for another metaphor, I propose to let *rhetoric* function as this shorthand. That is, in this book, when I talk about narrative as rhetoric or about a rhetorical relationship between author, text, and reader, I want to refer to the complex, multilayered processes of writing and reading, processes that call upon our cognition, emotions, desires, hopes, values, and beliefs.

Given this larger interest, I am more specifically interested in the elements of narrative (e.g., character, event, setting, narrative discourse) and in techniques, forms, structures, genres, and conventions of narrative for the ways in which they enable, enrich, interfere with, or otherwise complicate narrative as rhetoric. I am interested in the author in a way that parts company with Booth's highly influential rhetorical approach. Booth emphasizes the author as Constructor of the text, whose choices about the elements of narrative largely control the responses of the audience. As a result of this emphasis, Booth's work moves in the direction of defending the Author and the importance of authorial intention for determining the meaning of a text.[5] I do not see authorial intention as fully recoverable and as controlling response, even as I want to insist that when we read rhetorically we encounter something other than ourselves. The approach I am advocating shifts emphasis from author as controller to the recursive relationships among authorial agency, textual phenomena, and reader response, to the way in which our attention to each of these elements both influences and can be influenced by the other two. Shifting the emphasis this way also helps to open the rhetorical approach to the insights of many other approaches—from feminism to psychoanalysis, from Bakhtinian linguistics to cultural studies—about agency, response, and text. These insights, when integrated into the general approach, can complicate interpretations, even as the main concern with the rhetorical transaction of reading remains.[6]

In the case of "Magic," the rhetorical analysis I have presented so far benefits especially from being complicated by the insights of a feminist analysis. Attending more closely to issues of gender and especially to issues of gender and power in "Magic," several important points emerge or at least take on greater importance. First, although all the main actors and tellers in the story are women and, indeed, the maid's story occurs in a distinctly female space, there is a larger system of patriarchy controlling the events. The madam of the "fancy house" is, in one sense, not entirely successful in her battle with Ninette because she has to give in to the demands of the male customers and take steps to bring her back. Furthermore, this development helps bring to the fore the way in which the brothel's existence depends upon the indulgence of the police and the larger patriarchal society. And why is Ninette unable to support herself except as a prostitute? This question is easily answered in light of the way the class-gender system worked in New Orleans of the 1920s (and still works in many places today) to prevent a poor woman from having any serious economic opportunity outside marriage. Ninette's parallel with the maid and the madam's with Madame Blanchard are also important in this connection. The maid's opportunities are severely limited by her gender, class, and race, and her effort to overcome these limitations through narrative becomes more important the more we attend to these limitations. If the madam of the brothel is dependent on a bargain she has made with patriarchal society, so, too, is Madame Blanchard. The difference, of course, is that her bargain seems to have left her better off. But Madame Blanchard's particular interest in Ninette's story may now appear as some kind of recognition, however unconscious, of some fundamental similarity among women that cuts across differences of class and race. Attending to these issues also suggests that we should not be too quick to move from the horror of Ninette's story to Porter's thematizing of the power of narrative: to do so is to blunt the narrative's genuine social critique. Indeed, it is the rhetorical power of the first-level story upon which all the effects of the narrative are built.

What is true of such a feminist approach is also true of other approaches: each of them is a potential source of complication for the rhetorical precisely because the rhetorical is interested in the multilayered relationships between authorial agency, textual phenomena, and reader response and because it believes that reading is endlessly recursive. Consequently, I could continue the analysis of "Magic" by bringing the conclusions reached so far into dialogue with some things I've barely touched on, such as the story's location in New Orleans in the 1920s. But rhetorical criticism must reach a (provisional) end, even if rhetorical reading, like relationships between people, stops nowhere.

Prelude

The rest of this book offers essays based on the underlying conception of narrative as rhetoric that I have sketched in this introduction, but each essay takes its particular shape from the particular problem or issue it seeks to address. Where this introduction has been concerned with illustrating, situating, and articulating the fundamental principles of my approach, the succeeding chapters are concerned with deploying it in the service of specific interpretive and theoretical problems. In this respect, my strategy of advancing the case for my approach will shift from direct comparison with other approaches to demonstration of the kinds of analysis this approach makes possible—or, more generally, to the way in which it can be an effective means of both identifying and resolving a wide range of theoretical and interpretive problems. No chapter is designed to produce a comprehensive analysis of any narrative, but each one is designed to explore some relation between particular features of a specific narrative and general issues in narrative theory. Because the essays were originally composed on different occasions for different purposes and different audiences, I have found it helpful to write headnotes for the occasion and audience of this book. Therefore, I will not describe the essays in detail here, but just offer the following brief remarks about their arrangement and their concerns.

I have organized the essays into three groups, but there is considerable overlap among the groups. In the first group are essays concerned primarily with progression and narrative discourse. In my previous book of narrative theory, *Reading People, Reading Plots,* I sketched an approach to character and narrative progression that seeks to describe the way in which the internal dynamics of narrative directed our attention to different dimensions of characters—to what I called their mimetic, thematic, and synthetic components. The essays in this first group, in effect, expand upon the model I developed in *Reading People* by first considering Virginia Woolf's *The Waves,* whose progression is more lyric than narrative, and second by attempting to theorize the role of "voice" in narrative with particular attention to Thackeray's *Vanity Fair* and Hemingway's *A Farewell to Arms.* The essay on Hemingway also begins to move into the territory of the second group of essays, on mimetic conventions, ethics, and homodiegetic narration, because it moves beyond voice to consider some of the powers and limits associated with Frederic Henry's narration.

The first two essays in part 2, on Hemingway's "My Old Man" and Fitzgerald's *The Great Gatsby,* consider two problems in homodiegetic narration that both relate to the larger question of what constitutes mimesis in homodiegetic narration. In Hemingway's story, the issue is unselfconscious narration and paralipsis, the narrator telling less than he or she knows. My effort there is not only to address some interpretive problems in "My Old Man" but also to show why the paralipsis is a paradox but not a problem. In *The Great Gatsby,* the issue is paralepsis, the narrator telling more than he knows, and its relationship to narrative reliability and unreliability. I attempt to show that understanding the rhetorical reasons for the paralepsis helps understand the ways in which the relationship between the narratorial and the character functions of homodiegetic narrators such as Nick Carraway can fluctuate considerably in the course of a novel. In both essays, questions of ethical judgment figure prominently, but in the third essay in this group, on Conrad's story "The Secret Sharer," I make ethics the primary focus as I examine the way in which the technique and the progression complicate the ethical positioning of the authorial audience.

This interest in the ethics and ideology of reading continues in the third group of essays. Here I combine issues of form and technique with questions of ideology and audience. The first essay in this section considers the question of audience in relation to second-person narration, particularly that in Lorrie Moore's short story "How." Bringing structuralist theory's concept of "narratee" and rhetorical theory's concept of "narrative audience" together, I attempt to show that the complexity of effects generated by Moore's story can best be explained by recognizing the complementarity of the two concepts. In the next essay, I consider the form of Dinesh D'Souza's storytelling in *Illiberal Education* and how his ideology shapes that storytelling and my ideology shapes my critique. Although *Illiberal Education* is no longer receiving the attention it once did, I offer this essay as an illustration of how approaching narrative as rhetoric can perform effective work in the public arena. In the final essay of the book, I consider the problem of interpreting Toni Morrison's character Beloved as an instance of a textual recalcitrance that is designed not to yield to our efforts at interpretation. This "stubbornness," I suggest, has implications for my efforts as a white male reader to come to terms with Morrison's narrative. This essay also experiments with a possible new direction in rhetorical reading by trying to mirror in some of the critical prose the complexity of the reading experience itself. Finally, I have included an appendix written in a different voice, which assesses the work of Wayne C. Booth, the theorist who has most advanced the profession's thinking about rhetoric and narrative.

In sum, this book represents a series of inquiries into a range of texts and problems with a corresponding range of emphases on textual form, authorial agency, and reader response, especially those components of response involving judgment, ethics, and ideology. Taken together, these essays are an attempt to offer a rounded, albeit not exhaustive, view of what it means to claim that narrative is rhetoric; as rhetorical acts themselves, they are an attempt to show the power of the antifoundationalist, ethical, ideological, and audience-oriented rhetorical approach applied here to the spells of Porter's "Magic."

Part One

Narrative Progression and Narrative Discourse: Lyric, Voice, and Readerly Judgments

1

Character and Judgment in Narrative and in Lyric: Toward an Understanding of Audience Engagement in *The Waves*

In this essay, I focus on the relation between textual phenomena and audience response, proposing a distinction between lyric and narrative that has less to do with particular formal features of texts than with particular ways in which audiences respond to those features. Developing a point I learned from Sheldon Sacks many years ago, I propose that the key difference between the genres is in the role of judgments by readers: narrative requires audiences to judge its characters; lyric requires audiences not to judge its speakers. I relate this insight to the theory of character and progression I proposed in Reading People, Reading Plots *(the summary in this essay is also relevant to later chapters) and then sketch how these ideas begin to explain the complicated invitation for engagement offered by* The Waves, *the way it both draws us in and pushes us away from Bernard, Susan, Rhoda, Jinny, Neville, and Louis. I want to stress the word* begin *in the previous sentence: I realize that there's much more work to do with the complexities of Woolf's narrative experiment.*

It [the novel of the future] will resemble poetry in this that it will give not only or mainly people's relations to each other and their

> activities together, as the novel has hitherto done, but it will give the relation of the mind to general ideas and its soliloquy in solitude. For under the dominion of the novel we have scrutinized one part of the mind closely and left another unexplored. We have come to forget that a large and important part of life consists in our emotions toward such things as roses and nightingales, the dawn, the sunset, life, death, and fate; we forget that we spend much time sleeping, dreaming, thinking, reading, alone; we are not entirely occupied in personal relations; all our energies are not absorbed in making our livings. The psychological novelist has been too prone to limit psychology to the psychology of personal intercourse. . . . We long for some more impersonal relationship. We long for ideas, for dreams, for imaginations, for poetry.
>
> —Virginia Woolf, *Granite and Rainbow*

> I am not trying to tell a story.
>
> —Virginia Woolf, *Writer's Diary,* 28 May 1929

An Approach to Character and Narrative Progression

Although it is a critical commonplace to think of *The Waves* as a lyrical novel, and although Woolf's experiment has received much insightful commentary about both her themes and her techniques (especially by Freedman, Graham, Richter, Fleishman, Caws, and Dick), we do not yet have an adequate account of the reading experience the novel offers. Central to any account of that experience will be an understanding of how we respond to Woolf's six speakers. Just what kind of emotional and intellectual engagement does Woolf ask her implied audience to have with Bernard, Susan, Louis, Jinny, Neville, and Rhoda as she presents their voices against the backdrop of the interludes?[1] Is J. W. Graham overstating the case or getting at something important about our response when he claims that, since *The Waves* is an antinovelistic work, "such critical terms as 'plot,' 'character,' and 'setting' are the wrong instruments for exploring its nature as fiction" (193)?

I think that these questions about character in Woolf's novel are best approached after addressing some broader theoretical issues. To decide whether it is appropriate to call Woolf's speakers "characters," we need some working conception of that term, so I will begin by reviewing a model for understanding character in narrative that I have developed elsewhere. To decide whether our designation of *The Waves* as a lyrical novel captures something important about our response to the characters, I will first extend the model to include an account of character in the lyric and then apply those findings, with the necessary modifications, to Woolf's experimental work. Although I will be sketching an interpretation of *The Waves* here, my purpose is less to offer a new reading of the work than to develop a new understanding of the conditions of our response to it, especially the principles upon which Woolf has constructed her characters.

The model for analyzing character I develop in *Reading People, Reading Plots* has three main parts: (1) Character consists of three components—the mimetic (character as person), the thematic (character as idea), and the synthetic (character as artificial construct). (2) The relationship between these components varies from narrative to narrative. The mimetic may be undermined by the foregrounding of the synthetic, usually for some thematic purpose (as in some metafiction); the mimetic may be highly developed and the synthetic kept covert (as in most realistic fiction), but then either the mimetic or the thematic may be finally given greater emphasis. To account for the variety of characters and relationships, I distinguish between *dimensions* and *functions*, between the potential to signify in a certain way and the realization of that potential. On the mimetic level, a character may have dimensions without functions when s/he has traits that do not coalesce into the portrait of a possible person (e.g., Jonathan Swift's Gulliver, whose traits change in each of his journeys as Swift adapts new targets for his satire). On the thematic level, a character may have dimensions without functions when traits are not thematized, not made part of the work's ideational content. On the synthetic level, dimensions are always also functions, but they may be more or less foregrounded. Thus, within the terms of this model, Graham is overstating the case when he claims that "character" is an inappropriate term to apply to *The Waves*. Woolf's speakers have mimetic, thematic, and synthetic components; on the mimetic level, it may be debatable whether they have functions or only dimensions, but they are still characters. (3) The relations between the components are determined by narrative progression, the way in which the narrative initially establishes certain issues or relationships to be the center of its implied audience's interest, and the way in which the narrative complicates and resolves (or fails to resolve) those interests. Progressions are generated in two ways: through instabilities, that is, some unstable relationships between or within characters and their circumstances, and through tensions, that is, some disparity of knowledge, value, judgment, opinion, or belief between narrators and readers or authors and readers. Let me leaven this dense description of the model with the discussion of a concrete case.

In Jane Austen's *Pride and Prejudice* the synthetic component of character remains in the background, and the mimetic is foregrounded as the progression introduces and complicates the instabilities created by the entrance of Bingley and Darcy into the Bennets' neighborhood. (Further instabilities are introduced by the arrival of Collins and Wickham, but these are eventually tied to the main line of the progression.) As the progression develops, the implied audience is asked to see Lizzy's various traits as forming the portrait of a possible person and to respond to her accordingly, that is, to become actively involved in her dilemmas and choices, and eventually to feel emotional satisfaction in her engagement to Darcy. At the same time, Austen sets the action in a context that focuses our attention not just on general thematic issues of pride and prejudice but more particularly on what it means for a woman to get married—or not—in this society. Thus, after we read the famous first sentence ("It is a truth universally acknowledged that a single man in possession of a good fortune must be in want of a wife"), and after we see such actions as Charlotte Lucas's decision to marry Collins and Lady Catherine's attempt to tell Lizzy that she is not worthy of marrying Darcy, we respond to Lizzy's final happiness not only for its mimetic power but also for its thematic significance, for the way in which it signals Austen's belief in both the necessity and the possibility of marrying for the right reasons in the face of all the pressures that operate on a woman to marry for the wrong reasons.

Within this general construction of the narrative, Austen builds many nuances that I cannot go into here, but my main point is that the model for analyzing character and progression improves our understanding of how we relate to Austen's characters and how we generally participate in the narrative as we read from beginning to end.

Reading People, Reading Plots seeks to develop and substantiate the model's power by analyzing a broad range of characters, progressions, and audience involvements. But the book does not address the issue of character in the lyric, something that needs to be done for an adequate understanding of character in *The Waves*.

Distinguishing Lyric from Narrative

In her essay "Lyric Subversions of Narrative in Women's Writing: Virginia Woolf and the Tyranny of Plot," Susan Stanford Friedman invokes a generally held conception of the difference between lyric and narrative. "Narrative," she says, "is understood to be a mode that foregrounds a *sequence* of events that move dynamically in space and time. Lyric is understood to be a mode that foregrounds a *simultaneity*, a cluster of feelings or ideas that projects a gestalt in stasis. Where narrative centers on *story*, lyric focuses on *state of mind*, although each mode contains elements of the other" (164).[2] As the final clause indicates, this account of the difference between the modes indicates *tendencies* in each, but does not adequately capture their essential difference. It is an easy matter to think of lyrics that "move dynamically in space and time" ("Because I Could Not Stop for Death") and of narratives that focus on states of mind (*Ulysses* and its progeny). Furthermore, if we think of progression not just as something internal to the text (a question of whether a character or a speaker "goes" anywhere between beginning and end) but also as something linked to its audience's understanding of the text, then the opposition between story and gestalt in stasis also becomes less than adequate: the very temporality of reading means that the effects of both narrative and lyric depend in part upon sequence. If the opposition between sequence and stasis does not adequately pinpoint the difference between lyric and narrative, if the difference cannot be fully located in the content or the arrangement of that content, then we must shift our attention elsewhere. Since the material of lyric and narrative can so easily overlap, I suggest that we look to discriminate between them according to the attitudes we are asked to take to that material. I want therefore to examine the interaction between character and judgment in the two modes.[3] I will anchor the discussion in two well-known poems by Frost: "Nothing Gold Can Stay," in which the speaker is not individualized and is not placed in any specific situation, and "Stopping by Woods on a Snowy Evening," in which the speaker is somewhat individualized and speaking in a clearly specified situation.

Suppose, first, that a character in a traditional narrative were to make an argument for the evanescence of beauty that began with the description of particular things in nature ("Nature's first green is gold / Her hardest hue to hold / Her early leaf's a flower / But only so an hour"), invoked some notion that this is the Order of Things ("So Eden sank to grief"), and ended with a generalization about that evanescence ("Nothing gold can stay"); suppose, that is, that the character uttered the text of Frost's poem. Our response to that utterance would follow the same logic as our response to any other speech by that character: the response would be mediated powerfully by our previously established sense of the character. If this character has frequently been exposed as lacking in understanding, then we would either suspect that the author did not stand behind the argument contained in this new utterance or, depending on other cues in context, that the author wants to suggest some alteration in the character's understanding. In either case, the poem would be important for its contribution to the characterization of the speaker and to the sequence of judgments we are making about her. Furthermore, that characterization and those judgments would be *required* for anyone who wanted to participate in the experience offered by the narrative's design. In that sense, the judgments would be internal to the narrative itself, part of the logic of its construction. We might later evaluate whether being asked to judge the character as we do for the reasons that we do enhances or detracts from the value of the text, but such an evaluation obviously depends on our having understood the characterization and made the judgment. In that sense, such an evaluation would be an external judgment.

Read in its usual context, as a lyric by Frost, "Nothing Gold Can Stay" obviously has a very different effect. The speaker's character is not a functional part of the poem; instead, it fades back into the image of the implied author. In other words, the distinction between speaker and author does not exist here. If we describe the speaker as having the mimetic dimension of possessing the belief in the evanescence of beauty, we are also describing the implied author. If we describe the implied author as having certain powers of expression as exhibited in the poem's diction, rhythm, and rhyme, we are also describing the speaker.[4] With the conflation of the nondramatized speaker and the implied author, our attention is directed away from any mimetic representation of that speaker and toward the poem's thematic point about beauty. We are not asked to judge the speaker and use that judgment as part of our overall understanding of the poem, but instead are asked to take in, understand, and contemplate the speaker's argument for its own sake. To be sure, Frost presents the argument as something of value, and our response to the poem is not complete until we make some judgment of that value. This judgment will necessarily include some judgment of the speaker. But this judgment is not internal to the poem but external to it: it is part of evaluating what we are asked to take in and, in effect, it is an evaluation of the implied author and the poem itself. In short, a crucial difference between narrative and lyric is that in narrative internal judgments of characters (and narrators) are required, while in lyric such judgments are suspended until we take the step of evaluation.

Now what of lyrics where we have dramatized speakers and thus situations that more closely resemble narratives? A poem such as Frost's "Stopping by Woods on a Snowy Evening" is at first glance strikingly different from "Nothing Gold Can Stay" because it presents a speaker in a specified situation that calls for—and receives—some response from him. Indeed, the poem has the ingredients of narrative: a character, an unstable situation, a resolution of the instability. Furthermore, it is helpful to think about the design of the poem in terms of the speaker's character and the progression of his emotions and thoughts. The first three stanzas, with their descriptions of the woods, the snow, the wind, and the darkness, gradually reveal the instability: the speaker's desire to stop traveling, to give himself up to the woods, the snow, and the darkness, a desire that finds its veiled expression in the first line of the last stanza—"The woods are lovely, dark and deep." The last three lines then resolve the instability as the speaker voices his decision not to yield to the desire. The poem is complete once the choice is made: the repetition of "And miles to go before I sleep" in the last two lines signals both the power of the desire—the decision needs to be restated—and the finality of the resolution.

The poem nevertheless remains lyric because of the way characterization and judgment work.[5] Speaker and author are not identical here, as we can see by reflecting that we intuitively assign the rhymes of the poem to Frost rather than to the speaker. Our covert awareness of Frost's presence through the rhymes is also a sign that the synthetic component of the speaker's character remains in the background. Yet the mimetic component of the speaker's character is highly restricted—his main trait is his desire for surcease. This restricted characterization allows readers to project themselves into the poem, to experience vicariously the speaker's desire and choice. As Rader says about the dramatic lyric in general, "The figure in the poem is imagined from within, so that we participate in his mental activity as if his eyes and experience had become the poet's and our own" (142).

This effect is also possible because once again we are not asked to make an internal judgment of the speaker. Neither his desire nor his decision are held up for evaluation by Frost, though of course we may come to think of that desire and that decision—and thus, the whole poem—as trivial, profound, sentimental, inspiring, or something else. What Elder Olson says about "Sailing to Byzantium" applies as well to "Stopping by Woods"—the speaker performs an act of choice "actualizing and instancing his moral character" (286)—but that choice and that character are presented not for us to judge but to project ourselves into. Consequently, experiencing the progression here is closer to experiencing the progression of "Nothing Gold" than to experiencing that of a narrative such as "Magic": we do not develop hypotheses about the motivation for the telling nor expectations or hopes or desires about the resolution of the instability. Furthermore, the thematic dimensions of the speaker do not become functions. We do not thematize the desire of the speaker in "Stopping by Woods" the way we thematize the maid's motivations in "Magic," and we do not consider whether Frost is sympathetic or unsympathetic toward him the way in which we must consider whether Porter is sympathetic or unsympathetic toward the maid. (It is, of course, possible for the speaker of a lyric to describe his or her situation in thematic terms as, for example, Matthew Arnold's speaker does in "Dover Beach," but this thematizing is a variable rather than an essential of the lyric situation.)[6]

Although I have been focusing on the text of "Stopping by Woods," I have also been articulating the set of conventions we bring to the reading of lyric. It would be misleading to argue that the "text itself" is the sole basis upon which we will experience the poem as lyric rather than as narrative. Part of the difference in experience is also a consequence of our choice to employ the conventions of lyric rather than those of narrative in our reading of the poem. At the same time, the fit between the conventions of lyric and the text is tighter than the fit between the conventions of narrative and the text: as in "Nothing Gold Can Stay" and in contrast to "Magic," there is no textual material that moves us toward internal judgments of the speaker.

Speech and Lyric in *The Waves*

Consider now the episode of "the primal kiss" (Fleishman, 156) in section 1 of *The Waves*. The episode contains material with the potential to establish instabilities that could be the source of much of the later narration—instabilities between Jinny and Louis (when she kisses him, he says, "all is shattered"), between the two of them and Susan, who witnesses the kiss and is pierced with anguish, between Susan and Bernard, who goes to comfort her, and between Bernard and Neville, who resents Bernard's leaving him to comfort Susan. Although the episode is referred to several times later, its potential to set in motion a chain of events is never actualized. That potential is never actualized because of what Woolf has done before this incident, because of how she treats the incident itself, and because of what she does later.

The influence of the first "stream" of narration, the impersonal narrator's description of the sun rising over the ocean waves and gradually illuminating a garden and a house, is subtle but powerful even in the first section. The impersonality of the voice, especially its distant psychological stance, provides a context of distance within which we read the voices of the characters in the second "stream" of narration. This distance combines with the juxtaposition of the scene in nature with the characters' speeches to move us away from a full involvement with any developing story involving the characters and toward the thematic connections we can make between the juxtaposed scenes. More important, the initial group of speeches establishes the separateness of the speakers:

> "I see a ring," said Bernard, "hanging above me. It quivers and hangs in a loop of light."
>
> "I see a slab of pale yellow," said Susan, "spreading away until it meets a purple stripe."
>
> "I hear a sound," said Rhoda, "cheep, chirp; cheep, chirp; going up and down."
>
> "I see a globe," said Neville, "hanging down in a drop against the enormous flanks of some hill."
>
> "I see a crimson tassel," said Jinny, "twisted with old threads."
>
> "I hear something stamping," said Louis. "A great beast's foot is chained. It stamps, and stamps, and stamps." (9)

We do not have different perceptions of a common phenomenon or different participations in a common action, but rather different consciousnesses with different perceptions (some hear, some see, but no perceptions overlap) following one another in sequence. This separateness of the speakers is reinforced by the stylized language and by Woolf's technique of simply shifting our attention from one speech to the next without providing any narrative presence that might comment on the speeches or relate them to each other. The pattern of separate consciousnesses reporting by turns is solidified in the next few rounds of speech, where even imperatives spoken by one character are not responded to by the others: When Bernard says, "Look at the spider's web," or when Jinny says, "Look at the house," the next voices do not comment on the web or the house. This feature of the discourse prompts one to label even these opening speeches soliloquies (although that label does not apply to all the speeches of the text, for sometimes characters clearly address and respond to each other).

Since we are not reading the speeches as responses to each other, we are invited to adopt the perspective of each one much as we are invited to adopt the speaker's perspective in the lyric. That is, we are asked to see the world through the speaker's eyes without making a judgment on that vision. Woolf maintains the same effect throughout the incident of the primal kiss, as we can see by looking at Neville's speech, which closes the incident.

> "Where is Bernard?" said Neville. "He has my knife. We were in the tool-shed making boats, and Susan came past the door. And Bernard dropped his boat and went after her taking my knife, the sharp one that cuts the keel. He is like a dangling wire, a broken bell-pull, always twangling. He is like the seaweed hung outside the window, damp now, now dry. He leaves me in the lurch; he follows Susan; and if Susan cries he will take my knife and tell her stories. The big blade is an emperor; the broken blade a Negro. I hate dangling things; I hate dampish things. I hate wandering and mixing things together. Now the bell rings and we shall be late. Now we must drop our toys. Now we must go together. The copy-books are laid out side by side on the green baize table." (19)

In a traditional narrative, we would be asked to evaluate Neville and Bernard in light of this speech: is Bernard insensitive for leaving Neville "in the lurch," or is Neville selfish for resenting Bernard's following Susan? In this narrative, the issue does not arise, both because of the pattern already established and because of the way Woolf handles the link between Neville's expression of resentment and his confession of hate. Woolf uses Neville's resentment of Bernard primarily as a way to reveal something about Neville—"I hate dangling things. . . I hate mixing things together"—rather than as a way to build some future conflict between the two that the narrative will focus on and develop. As flesh-and-blood readers we may of course judge Neville for his resentment, but Woolf never makes that judgment functional within the progression of the narrative. In this passage, after revealing Neville's feeling, Woolf takes things in a new direction—back to narration—and so we are left contemplating Neville rather than anticipating any consequences of his feelings for the later action. This effect is reinforced by the beginning of the next speech in which Louis, who has last said, "all is shattered," makes no reference to anything that Jinny, Susan, or Bernard have done, but begins this speech with the clause, "I will not conjugate the verb" (19). Through this jump in Louis's consciousness, Woolf signals that we have now moved into a new lyric moment.

Progression and Audience Engagement in *The Waves*

To say that the speeches often function as lyric utterances is only to take a first step toward understanding our engagement with Woolf's narrative. There are several ways in which this view needs to be complicated or supplemented. First, the utterances often follow the pattern of Neville's and move from narration to lyric revelation and back again. The narration always functions to give us information about some situation or action in which the characters are placed; sometimes it also functions to advance our sense of the character's particular way of perceiving things. When the characters' speeches are giving us information about their situation rather than their particular perceptions, the speeches work to invite thematic connections between the situations they describe and the scene in nature described in the previous interlude. Take, for example, Louis's description of the boys' last day at school. Although it becomes lyric by the end ("I see wild birds, and impulses wilder than the wildest birds strike from my heart"), initially the speech is not important for what it reveals about Louis's perspective; instead, it focuses our attention on a particular stage of the boys' lives as an analogue to the stage in the sun's progress toward the horizon we have read about before section 2:

> "Now we have received," said Louis, "for this is the last day of the term—Neville's and Bernard's and my last day—whatever our masters have had to give us. The introduction has been made; the world presented. They stay, we depart. The great Doctor, whom of all men I most revere, swaying a little from side to side among the tables, the bound volumes, has dealt out Horace, Tennyson, the complete works of Keats and Matthew Arnold suitably inscribed." (57–58)

A second important supplement in our understanding of lyric in *The Waves* is that Woolf varies the kinds of lyric utterance she gives to the speakers. Sometimes, she orchestrates a revelation of feeling such as we have seen in Neville's speech, a revelation triggered by some action or situation—often described in the first few sentences of the speech—external to the character. At other times, Woolf orchestrates a lyric of perception and sensation, exemplified in miniature by the opening speeches and exemplified more fully by Bernard's description of being bathed: "Water pours down the runnel of my spine. Bright arrows of sensation shoot on either side. I am covered with warm flesh. My dry crannies are wetted; my cold body is warmed; it is sluiced and gleaming. Water descends and sheets me like an eel" (26). The consequence of this variation is that Woolf is able to incorporate an enormous range of experiences into the text. Thus, for example, Susan's utterances range from the revelation of her intense reaction to Jinny's kissing Louis to the report of her baking bread in her country kitchen, and Bernard's range from his cool assessment of Dr. Crane to the revelation of his deeply mixed emotions at the combined news of Percival's death and the birth of his son.

A third complication is that the same material will sometimes be revisited and rendered differently. This movement helps Woolf adapt the lyric utterances to her larger narrative purpose because it shows the speakers in a changed relation to the original material as they move through life. Nevertheless, the sense of lyric remains strong because the new relation is not presented as more valid than the old; it is different in a way that reflects the different stage of the speaker's life. When Bernard, for example, remembers his bath, he is less concerned with the sensations he captured so vividly the first time than he is with their consequences: "Mrs. Constable raised the sponge above her head, squeezed it, and out shot, right, left, all down the spine, arrows of sensation. And so, as long as we draw breath, for the rest of time, if we knock against a chair, a table, or a woman, we are pierced with arrows of sensation—if we walk in a garden, if we drink this wine" (239).

A fourth complication is that the speakers' utterances function not just to reveal themselves and their perspectives but also to reveal the other characters more fully. Because of what Neville says in section 1, for example, we see not only Neville but also Bernard in a new way. More generally, Woolf uses each character's view of the others to help us form our understanding of each, and thus we can have a greater participation in their lyric utterances as the work progresses. We develop this understanding through a fusion of the perspectives offered by the other characters and the perspectives we gain from our inside views of each. In this way, we develop a sense of these characters as individuals that is far greater than anything that occurs in any dramatic lyric such as "Stopping by Woods." The question about the mimetic component of Woolf's speakers can now be resolved: Each of the six has a fully developed mimetic function, one that, though easily recognized in the reading, is not easily summarized.[7]

Mimetic, Synthetic, and Thematic Components of *The Waves*

We can move from this account of the characters' speeches to a fuller account of our response to them. The lyric mode of their utterances invites a very strong mimetic involvement with them and their visions of the world. Yet this mimetic involvement is itself complicated by the way in which Woolf's technique makes us aware of the synthetic component of the characters and by the way the progression makes us respond to them thematically. In the first section, the gap between the speakers' ages and their powers of expression calls attention to the artifice of the text. That their voices remain largely the same from childhood to middle age further reinforces that artifice. That the language of one speaker sometimes overlaps with the language of another or with the language of the interlude narrator is a third strong sign of their artifice. Because the artifice of Woolf's technique shows through in these ways, our mimetic involvement is juxtaposed with—and somewhat diminished by—our awareness of Woolf's experimenting with narrative form here.

I said above that the first stream of narration distances us from the second. The distance derives in part from the impersonality of the voice and in part from what the voice describes. As we follow the descriptions of the sun, the waves, the birds, the garden, and the house as the day proceeds from sunrise to sunset and the seasons proceed from spring to winter, we read the second stream with an awareness that the characters lack: we see them as like the sun, waves, and birds, i.e, as unwittingly following some natural laws that are governing their movement from childhood to death.[8] Furthermore, because we always read the characters' speeches against the situation in nature described in the interludes, we come to view the individual lyric utterances as part of this overall progression of the six characters from childhood to death. Consequently, the characters become representative figures as well as mimetically differentiated individuals, figures of Childhood, Young Adulthood, Middle Age, and figures of Responses to Life Events such as marriage, birth of children, the death of a friend. This heightening of the thematic component also contributes to our overt awareness of the synthetic component of the characters and thus works against a full mimetic involvement of the kind that we have in either a dramatic lyric such as "Stopping by Woods" or in a narrative such as "Magic" or *Pride and Prejudice.*

Why should Woolf want to involve us in her characters in this way, to ask us to participate in the mimetic sphere while also giving us signals that work against that participation? The reason, I think, can be found in her larger thematic intention. As noted earlier, Woolf uses the characters' utterances to express many different kinds of experience at many different stages of life. In doing that, she is also able to explore many thematic issues: the nature of identity, the difficulty of connecting with others, the intensity of life, its chaos, its beauty, its pain, its ordinariness, its strangeness, its value. But the juxtaposition of these explorations with the impersonality of the interludes leads to a larger emphasis on a double vision: the lyric utterances collectively insist on the intensity and value of life, while the distance between them and the interlude descriptions implicitly questions the significance of those lyric moments. This point is made perhaps with its greatest impact at the very end of the narrative, when Bernard's ringing defiance of Death, "Against you I will fling myself, unvanquished and unyielding, O Death!" is juxtaposed with the impersonal description of inexorable nature, "The waves broke upon the shore."[9]

The point is also made for us in the experience of reading the text as we move from a strong engagement with the characters, their visions, and emotions to a more detached assessment of them as constructs serving Woolf's thematic and synthetic purposes. They matter intensely to us as individuals, and then again they don't. They live intensely and diversely, but their lives do not make a dent in the universe. To experience the narrative fully we need to experience both sides of Woolf's vision.

If the previous analysis is at all accurate, then Woolf has offered us a most unusual kind of engagement with her characters. We are asked not only to be simultaneously and overtly aware of their mimetic, thematic, and synthetic components but also to refrain from making judgments of them or to develop attachments to them of the kind we develop toward Elizabeth Bennet that makes us expect and desire certain outcomes for them. It is, I think, the very peculiarity of our response that leads critics such as Graham to say that the term *character* is the wrong instrument for discussing Woolf's creation. But I hope that this essay has shown that we do better justice both to *The Waves* and to our reading experience if, rather than turning away from the term, we deepen our understanding of what character is and of the complicated relations that readers can have to it.

2

Gender Politics in the Showman's Discourse; or, Listening to *Vanity Fair*

As the title suggests, this essay is an effort to think about the relationship between reading narrative and listening to it. More particularly, it is concerned with developing an understanding of "voice" and illustrating how voice functions as part of narrative discourse. Influenced by Mikhail Bakhtin, I emphasize the connection between voice and ideology: to listen to narrative is, in part, to listen to values associated with a given way of talking. Thackeray's Vanity Fair *provides a rich site for exploring voice because the Showman's virtuoso performance is fascinating in itself and revealing of Thackeray's attitudes toward Victorian patriarchy. As in the essay on* The Waves, *my emphasis here is more on the textual phenomena and their shaping by an implied author than on readerly subjectivity, though once I move to evaluate the Showman's voices, my ideological commitments as a flesh-and-blood reader become significant.*

The first version of this essay was written for a collection concerned with complicating our views of male writers' relations to patriarchy, Out of Bounds: Male Voices and Gender(ed) Criticism, *edited by Laura Claridge and Elizabeth Langland (Amherst: University of Massachusetts Press, 1990). In that version I distinguished between my rhetorical approach to Thackeray's discourse and what I called "one kind of feminist perspective." In this revision, I have eliminated that differentiation because, for reasons I discuss in the introduction, it now seems to me misleading. In looking at voice rhetorically, I am looking at ideology, and my evaluations of that ideology are very much influenced by my interactions with feminist theory (and many flesh and blood feminists). For these reasons, my rhetorical analysis and evaluation is consistently informed by "one kind of feminist" ideology.*

Thackeray's decision to survey the booths of Vanity Fair by charting the progress of Becky Sharp and Amelia Sedley, two very different women, leads him into numerous representations of and reflections on women in patriarchy, while his own virtuoso performance as the Showman of Vanity Fair leads him to adopt many poses and to speak in many voices. Consequently, *Vanity Fair* provides fertile ground for investigating voice and its relation to ideology as well as for exploring the role of voice in relation to other elements of narrative. I will undertake such an investigation and exploration here by first setting forth a rhetorical understanding of voice and then employing that understanding in the analysis of two passages whose gender politics seem to be significantly different from one another.[1] I will extend the analysis by evaluating Thackeray's deployment of voice and by considering how my rhetorical and ideological commitments shape that evaluation.

The Concept of Voice: Some Rhetorical Principles

Voice is one of those critical terms (*genre, theme, style, irony, pluralism* are others) that are frequently used but rarely defined with any precision. The result is that we now have no commonly accepted meaning for the term, no clear understanding of what constitutes voice, let alone what makes one kind of voice more effective than another.[2] The understanding I propose here is dictated in large part by my purpose in defining it: I want to talk about voice as a distinct element of narrative, something that interacts with other elements like character and action but that makes its own contribution to the communication offered by the narrative.

My understanding of voice comprises four interrelated principles about language in use. (1) *Voice is as much a social phenomenon as it is an individual one.* This principle follows from the observation that wherever there is discourse there is voice. Just as there can be no utterance without style, there can be no utterance without voice—although, of course, just as some styles are more distinctive than others so too are some voices. In the case of, say, a letter from the university registrar to the faculty stipulating that grades must be submitted by a certain date, one might be tempted to say that there is no voice in the discourse, that what speaks is some bureaucratic machine. In one sense, this might be true: the discourse may not be at all expressive of the registrar himself or herself. But that is just the point: the letter does not signal the absence of voice but rather the presence of one voice rather than another. We recognize that voice not because we recognize the author of the letter but because as social beings we have heard that voice speak to us on other occasions.[3] The example also indicates that, in adopting this principle, I am postulating that although voice is a term that seems to privilege speech over writing, it is a concept for identifying a feature of both oral and written language.

(2) Though mediated through style, voice, as Bakhtin suggests, is more than style and in a sense is finally transstylistic. *Voice is the fusion of style, tone, and values.* There are markers of voice in diction and syntax, but the perception of voice also depends on inferences that we make about a speaker's attitude toward subject matter and audience (i.e., tone) and about the speaker's values. Style will reveal the register of a voice and sometimes its location in space and in time relative to the things it describes and to its audience. But for inferences about personality and ideological values, style is a necessary but not a sufficient condition: by itself style will not allow us to distinguish among possibilities. The same sentence structure and diction may carry different tones and ideologies—and therefore different personalities—while the same personality and ideology may be revealed through diverse syntactic and semantic structures. For example, in the first chapter of *Pride and Prejudice,* Mrs. Bennet echoes the diction of the narrator's famous opening remark that a "single man in possession of a good fortune must be in want of a wife" by referring to Mr. Bingley as "a single man of large fortune." The similar style is spoken with different tones—the narrator's voice is playfully ironic, Mrs. Bennet's is serious and admiring—and communicates different values: the narrator mocks the acquisitiveness behind Mrs. Bennet's speech. Austen uses the similar style to emphasize their different voices, their different

values and personality. Later, in describing Mrs. Bennet at the end of the chapter, Austen changes the tone of the narrator's voice. "The business of her life was to get her daughters married; its solace was visiting and news." Although the change in tone indicates a difference in the voice, the consistency of the values expressed enables us to regard the difference as a modulation in the voice rather than the adoption of a whole new one.

A corollary of the principle that voice is more than style is that voice is also more than speech act or, to put it another way, the relation between style and voice is similar to the relation between voice and speech acts. If a speaker typically gives commands rather than making requests or extending invitations, this speech behavior will influence our perception of her voice. Nevertheless, a request and a command can be spoken in the same voice. Imagine an even-tempered benevolent middle manager who would say first to his supervisor and then to his secretary, "Could you please give me the documentation on that?" The illocutionary force of the sentence, when directed to the supervisor, is that of a request, and, when directed to the secretary, the illocutionary force is that of a command. Provided that the middle manager conveys the same respect to each and the same understanding of the power hierarchy in the organization, the voice of each utterance will still be the same. Two commands can be spoken in two different voices, as Shakespeare shows us through Lady Macbeth: "Come, spirits, unsex me here!" and "Out! Out! Damned spot!" In sum, locutionary and illocutionary acts both contribute to but do not determine our sense of voice.

(3) As Wayne C. Booth and Mikhail Bakhtin (among numerous others) have amply demonstrated, the voice of a narrator can be contained within the voice of an author, creating what Bakhtin calls the situation of "double-voiced" discourse. Significantly, *the presence of the author's voice need not be signaled by any direct statements on his or her part but through some device in the narrator's language—or indeed through such nonlinguistic clues as the structure of the action—for conveying a discrepancy in values or judgments between author and narrator.* (In fact, one of the defining features of homodiegetic narration is that all such discrepancies must be communicated indirectly.) In the first sentence of *Pride and Prejudice,* Austen's style and tone allow her to communicate the way

she is undermining a literal reading. In homodiegetic narration, our perception of the authorial voice may have less to do with style and tone than with the social values at work in the discrepancy between the voices. When Huck Finn makes his famous declaration, "All right, then, I'll go to hell," there is nothing in Huck's sincerely resolute voice to signal that Twain is double-voicing his utterance. We hear Twain's voice behind Huck's because we have heard and seen Twain's values earlier in the narrative; we thus place Huck's sincere resolution within a wider system of values that allows us to see his decision to accept damnation as a decision confirming his ethical superiority.

Double-voicing can, of course, also occur within the explicit syntax or semantics of an utterance. When Voltaire has a speaker say, "As luck would have it, providence was on our side," he is using the style to bring two different social voices into conflict. In cases such as this one, the author's voice functions as a crucial third member of the chorus by establishing a hierarchy between these voices.

(4) *Voice exists in the space between style and character.* As we attribute social values and a personality to voice, we are moving voice away from the realm of style toward the realm of character. But voice, especially a narrating voice or a "silent" author's voice, can exist apart from character-as-actor. Voice has a mimetic dimension, but it need not have a mimetic function. That is, voice exists as a trait of a speaker, but it need not be the basis for some full portrait of that speaker. In many narratives, especially ones with heterodiegetic narrators, the voice of the narrator will be his or her only trait, though modulations within a voice will reveal more traits. In homodiegetic narratives, the narrator's voice is more likely to be one trait among many. The same holds true for the voices of characters in dialogue.

Two main consequences follow from these four principles. (1) Voice is an element of narrative that is subject to frequent change as a speaker alters tones or expresses different values, or as an author double-voices a narrator's or character's speech. The corollary of this point is that even as voice moves toward character, it maintains an important difference in its function. Whereas many narratives require consistency of character for their effectiveness, *consistency of voice is not necessary for its effective use.* (2) Voice is typically a part of narrative manner, part of the how of narrative rather than the what. That is, like style, it is typically a mechanism (sometimes a crucial one) for influencing its audience's responses to and understanding of the characters and events that are the main focus of narrative.[4] Like any other element, voice could itself become the focus of a specific narrative (arguably this situation obtains in *Tristram Shandy*), but more commonly it will be a means for achieving particular effects. Thus, *we cannot expect an analysis of voice to yield a comprehensive reading of most narratives,* though we should expect that such an analysis will enrich significantly an understanding of the way any narrative achieves its effects.

Just as the first three principles in my account of voice move the concept away from style and toward character, these two consequences of the principles move the concept back toward style. The point again is that voice exists in the space between style and character.

Some Functions of the Showman's Multiple Voices

To understand the functions of the Showman's voices, we need a fuller explanation of the context in which they are heard. Broadly defined, Thackeray's purpose in the narrative is to expose the condition of universal vanity he describes in the final paragraph: "Ah! *Vanitas Vanitatem!* Which of us is happy in this world? Which of us has his desire? or, having it, is satisfied?"[5] To achieve this purpose, Thackeray invents his dramatized male narrator and has him tell the story of the progress of two very different women through a society that consistently reflects and reveals the ineradicable but multifarious vanity of its inhabitants. This story is frequently (even ubiquitously) linked with gender issues: not only does the male narrator comment on the careers of the women but those careers themselves expose the patriarchal structures as well as the vanity of society. Again speaking schematically, we can see that Thackeray takes his two female characters, places them in the same setting but in different circumstances in the opening chapters, then sends them off in different directions so that he might conduct a relatively comprehensive survey of nineteenth-century society. He then reunites them at the end of the narrative as a way to achieve closure.

He uses Amelia to explore the workings of vanity in the private sphere—the realm of the home and the heart—and he uses Becky to explore those workings in the public sphere—the realm of social climbing and social status. In keeping with his overriding thematic purpose, Thackeray uses Amelia and Becky to expose the vanity of others and to exemplify certain vain behaviors. In the case of Becky, the procedure is effective and straightforward: he gives her a temporary license to succeed in her vain pursuits by playing on the greater vanity of others, and then once she has exposed that vanity in creatures ranging from Miss Pinkerton to Lord Steyne, he takes the license away and emphasizes what has never been far from the foreground of the narrative: Becky's own vanity-driven life. In the case of Amelia, however, the situation (though not her character) is more complicated: he uses her constancy, love, and dependence on George first as a way to expose the vanity of George and those like him; later Thackeray tries to expose the negative side of these very same qualities as he shows how they ultimately undermine Dobbin's estimation of her worth—and the chance for their happiness together when he finally succeeds in marrying her.

Although the stories of Becky and Amelia have clear beginnings, middles, and ends, although the characters move from an initial situation to a final one, the principle controlling the linking of episodes is, for the most part, additive rather than integrative. That is, unlike a novel by Jane Austen in which the significance of each episode derives from its consequences for and interaction with later episodes, *Vanity Fair* is built upon episodes that typically derive their significance from their contribution to the overriding theme of ubiquitous vanity.[6] One consequence of this broad design is that it allows Thackeray to vary the way in which he treats his characters. Sometimes they appear to be autonomous beings for whom he wants us to feel deeply, sometimes they are obvious artificial devices for making his thematic points, and sometimes they are largely incidental to the Showman's disquisitions about the workings of society. In other words, Thackeray's narrative fluctuates the audience's attention between the mimetic, thematic, and synthetic components of the narrative.

One consequence of this narrative design is that it allows the Showman great freedom in his use and selection of voice: he can move from intimacy to distance, from formality to informality, from treating the characters as puppets to treating them as people provided that the movement remains in the service of the thematic end. Indeed, because of the additive structure and the length of the whole narrative, it is almost incumbent upon Thackeray to take full advantage of that freedom and make the narrator's performance one source of our sustained interest in the narrative.[7] The performances I will focus on here, while not fully representative, illustrate many other transactions that go on between Thackeray and his audience.

As this way of talking about the narrative performances indicates, I see the Showman as Thackeray's mouthpiece: the only distance between author and narrator is created by the audience's knowledge that the narrator is created. On this reading, the Showman is the knowing source of the numerous ironies of the narrative discourse. Thackeray, in other words, does not communicate to his audience behind the Showman's back, but rather uses the protean Showman as the orchestrator of virtually all the narrative's effects.[8]

In chapter 3, the Showman comments on Becky's interest in Jos Sedley:

> If Miss Rebecca Sharp had determined in her heart upon making the conquest of this big beau, I don't think, ladies, we have any right to blame her; for though the task of husband-hunting is generally, and with becoming modesty, entrusted by young persons to their mammas, recollect that Miss Sharp had no kind parent to arrange these delicate matters for her, and that if she did not get a husband for herself, there was no one else in the wide world who would take the trouble off her hands. What causes young people to "come *out,*" but the noble ambition of matrimony? What sends them trooping to watering-places? What keeps them dancing till five o'clock in the morning through a whole mortal season? What causes them to labor at piano-forte sonatas, and to learn four songs from a fashionable master at a guinea a lesson, and to play the harp if they have handsome arms and neat elbows, and to wear Lincoln Green toxophilite hats and feathers, but that they may bring down some "desirable" young man with those killing bows and arrows of theirs? What causes respectable parents to take up their carpets, set their houses topsy-turvy, and spend a fifth of their year's income in ball suppers

> and iced champagne? Is it sheer love of their species, and an unadulterated wish to see young people happy and dancing? Psha! they want to marry their daughters; and, as honest Mrs. Sedley has, in the depths of her kind heart, already arranged a score of little schemes for the settlement of her Amelia, so also had our beloved but unprotected Rebecca determined to do her very best to secure the husband, who was even more necessary for her than for her friend. (28)

For the most part, the Showman speaks here in the sociolect of the genteel upper middle class. He is someone who knows and feels comfortable in the social circuit of that class: the well-informed gentleman speaking politely but firmly—and with a certain air of superiority—to a group of women from the class. His diction is generally formal, but he will occasionally drop the register to something more familiar: "mammas" or "take the trouble off her hands." Furthermore, the genteel and formal qualities of the voice are reinforced by the parallel structure of the rhetorical questions and their well-chosen concreteness, as, for example, in "four songs from a fashionable master at a guinea a lesson." In adopting his air of knowing gentility, the Showman also positions himself at a considerable distance from Becky: he calls her "Miss Rebecca Sharp" at the outset, and even later when he speaks of her as "our beloved but unprotected Rebecca," his sympathy does not overpower the distance. As a result of the genteel stance and the cool distance from Becky, the voice appears to be considering her as a "case," one that he is finally sympathetic to, but one that he is interested in as much for what it generally illustrates.

Within this general sociolect, there are significant modulations—so significant, in fact, that even as we read we come to see the dominant voice as a pretense, one that the Showman puts on to expose the limitations of the values associated with it. The Showman's strategy is twofold: he occasionally lets a certain aggressive element enter the genteel voice and, more dramatically, he temporarily shifts to a voice that is critical of the dominant one and then lets this voice invade and subvert the dominant. One major consequence of this strategy is that while making his apologia for Becky, the Showman offers a powerful indictment of courtship behavior in this male-controlled society.

The Showman adopts the genteel voice right away, but in the second half of the first sentence the voice momentarily drops into a different, franker register as the Showman mentions "the task of husband-hunting." The phrase not only calls to mind the image of the social circuit as a jungle where women are the predators, men the prey, but also insists on the hunt as work rather than sport. Although the Showman quickly regains his genteel voice, everything he says in the rest of the sentence is now double-voiced, undermined by the candid, antigenteel voice of the earlier phrase.

When the genteel voice calls the business of the hunt "delicate matters," we register the discrepancy between this description and "the task of husband-hunting" and the corresponding conflict between the values associated with each; in addition, the use of "delicate matters" privileges the antigenteel voice: his reference to "the task of husband-hunting" makes the phrase "delicate matters" an ironic euphemism.

When the Showman modulates his voice from genteel to informal and affectionate with his reference to "mammas," the earlier presence of the frank, antigenteel voice strongly ironizes the new modulation—and indeed, the whole clause in which it appears. When he tells us that the task of husband-hunting is "generally, and with becoming modesty, entrusted by young persons to their mammas," we recognize the disparity between the image of the hunt and the alleged modesty of those in the hunting party. Moreover, we infer that the "young persons" have no choice about "entrusting" the hunt to their "mammas": the mammas manage, whether the daughters wish them to or not, as we learn later when we are told that "Mrs. Sedley . . . has arranged a score of little schemes for the settlement of her Amelia." We see, in short, that the real predators are those we usually call "mammas." This realization in turn adds another layer of irony to the phrase "kind parent to arrange these delicate matters."

The initial reference to husband-hunting as a "task" is echoed in the aggressive note that repeatedly creeps into the Showman's use of the genteel voice: "what sends them trooping to watering-places?" "What keeps them dancing?" "What causes them to labour?" (It is worth noting here, if only in passing, that the grammar of the passage suggests that "them" refers to "young people" but "young people" actually means "young women.") "What causes respectable parents to take up their carpets, set their houses topsy-turvy, and spend a fifth of their year's income?" The aggressive note is given more emphasis toward the end of this series of questions, when the Showman slides smoothly from the genteel voice to the franker, antigenteel one of the first sentence. His reference to the young people wearing "Lincoln Green toxophilite hats and feathers" is parallel to the previous phrases about their learning musical instruments. But once the topic of archery is introduced through this description of their clothes, the Showman quickly appropriates the earlier hunting metaphor: what keeps them doing all these things "but that they may bring down some 'desirable' young man with those killing bows and arrows of theirs?" The result is that the Showman strongly reinforces the subversion of the social values implied in the dominant voice: These genteel "young persons" and their "mammas" are no better than prisoners of their patriarchally imposed task, the purpose of which no one has even mentioned yet—nor has anyone apparently given any thought to what happens once the hunter has bagged her game.

The critique of "courtship" in the Fair reaches its high point in the final sentences of this passage as the Showman turns to answer his own questions about the motives for the behavior he describes. His interjection, "Psha!" followed by the direct assertion, "they want to marry their daughters," marks the entrance into the passage of a third voice—a more honest, more direct voice than the genteel one that has been speaking so far. With this third voice, the Showman is overtly setting himself above his genteel audience to reject their pretense and speak a truth that they also know but don't usually admit. This shift then sets up the final statement as an apologia for Becky's behavior, one that is convincing according to the values associated both with the genteel language he once again adopts—"so also had our beloved but unprotected Rebecca determined to do her very best to secure the husband"—and, significantly, with the new superior voice: "who was even more necessary for her than for her friend."

Because the new voice is clearly superior to the dominant one and because it is not ironized the way that the genteel one is (note all the undercutting in the description of "honest Mrs. Sedley" and her "schemes"), the apologia has real force. Yes, what Becky is doing is no different from what every other woman in this jungle does; yes, precisely because she has "no kind parents," a husband is more necessary for her than for Amelia. Yet the presence of the earlier subversion of the dominant voice and its values complicates this apologia. The case for Becky works only in terms of the values that we have been made to question by the earlier interaction between the voices; the case does not recognize how the very role that Becky "justifiably" adopts (i.e., mamma's role) has been exposed as itself constrained by patriarchy. Consequently, by the light of the values associated with the frankest voice of the passage, the apologia is unconvincing. In this sense, then, the superior voice of the last few sentences of the passage is itself undercut; though it drops the pretenses of the genteel voice, it does not question the basic assumptions and values of the upper-middle-class social circuit.

Evaluating the Showman's Voices

The interaction between this superior voice and the earlier, antigenteel one highlights an important effect of the passage that is characteristic of Thackeray's position throughout the novel. By insisting on both the limitations of and the constraints on Becky's behavior, the Showman offers a critique without offering an alternative. The power of the Fair is such that virtually no one can get outside it. The corollary of this point has been well illustrated by the analysis of the passage: the power of the patriarchy is also often such that no one can get outside it. It seems fair to conclude—at least tentatively—that Thackeray's analysis of Vanity Fair is in part a critique of the patriarchy by one of its own, the Showman. Let me now probe that conclusion, first by looking at some other elements of the chosen passage, at the novel more generally, and at one more passage (albeit not with the same degree of attention to detail).

The very positioning of the male voice in relation to the "ladies" addressed in the passage raises a question about the thoroughness of the critique, about whether the rhetorical setup of the passage works against the message conveyed through the modulation of the voices. Note, first, that the address to "ladies" is made in the Showman's genteel voice, the one that is most undercut in the whole passage. As that voice takes on and reflects the values of the genteel society, it takes on the assumption that the man can tell the "ladies" the truth about their behavior. When we see that this voice doesn't have the truth, this assumption is itself called into question. In that respect, the narrator-audience relationship reinforces rather than undercuts the message conveyed through the voices.

The passage, to be sure, does not suggest that the "ladies" see the full critique; instead, it presupposes that they will agree with the superior voice of the final sentences. But that presupposition does not mean that the Showman is talking down to them as much as it suggests that these "ladies" of genteel society, like Becky, the mammas, and the superior male voice, are caught in the trap of patriarchy.

Nevertheless, even as the analysis indicates Thackeray's considerable virtuosity in the manipulation of voice, it also suggests a potentially negative—or at least rhetorically risky—side to that virtuosity. The complex interplay of voices and their effects leads us back to their source, to what we might call the metavoice of the Showman. In addition to the qualities of wit, intelligence, learning, and a willingness to criticize, the Showman's virtuosity here involves a fondness for ironic one-upmanship: his communication to us comes at the expense of his addressed audience of "ladies." We—male and female readers alike—are invited to stand with him, to compliment him and ourselves on our superior knowledge as we look down on the Fair and those caught in it. Although there are places in the narrative when the Showman indicates that he too can't escape the traps of vanity, his frequently displayed penchant for one-upmanship at the expense of his characters and his addressed audiences creates a problem for many flesh-and-blood readers who seek to join the authorial audience. The invitation to stand with the Showman looking down on Amelia, Dobbin, George, Becky, Jos, Jones at his Club, genteel ladies, or whoever else the Showman names makes such readers uncomfortable: we feel that we're asked to participate in the metavoice's smugness or snideness or superciliousness.[9] This feature of the metavoice obviously has consequences for any evaluation of it, but it has an especially noteworthy role in our efforts to assess Thackeray's attitude toward Victorian patriarchy.

When we look at the novel more broadly than we have so far, we soon see that the Showman is hardly Jane Eyre's brother under the skin. His most obvious limitations are that he does not follow through on his insights into the patriarchy's shaping of women's behavior and that he sometimes reveals his own complicity with the patriarchy. Many instances could be cited to make these points, especially his ambivalent treatment of Amelia, but perhaps the clearest evidence is in the famous passage in chapter 64 describing Becky as "syren."

> I defy any one to say that our Becky, who has certainly some vices, has not been presented to the public in a perfectly genteel and inoffensive manner. In describing this syren, singing and smiling, coaxing and cajoling, the author, with modest pride, asks his readers all round, has he once forgotten the laws of politeness, and showed the monster's hideous tail above water? No! Those who like may peep down under waves that are pretty transparent, and see it writhing and twirling, diabolically hideous and slimy, flapping amongst bones, or curling round corpses; but above the water line, I ask, has not everything been proper, agreeable, and decorous, and has any the most squeamish immoralist in Vanity Fair a right to cry fie? When, however, the syren disappears and dives below, down among the dead men, the water of course grows turbid over her, and it is labor lost to look into it ever so curiously. They look pretty enough when they sit upon a rock, twanging their harps and combing their hair, and sing, and beckon to you to come and hold the looking-glass; but when they sink into their native element, depend on it those mermaids are about no good, and we had best not examine the fiendish marine cannibals, revelling and feasting on their wretched pickled victims. And so, when Becky is out of the way, be sure that she is not particularly well employed, and that the less that is said about her doings is in fact the better. (617)

The interplay among voices is characteristically complex here, as the Showman gives the very picture he is praising himself for having suppressed. He uses a refined, almost prissy voice to compliment himself for his decorum, and then, when talking about what he has not done, he adopts a melodramatic voice that likes to dwell on the seamier side of things. The alternation between these voices is clear and striking throughout but perhaps nowhere more so than when it occurs within the same sentence: "has he once forgotten the laws of politeness, and showed the monster's hideous tail above the water?" The hierarchy established between the voices brings the snideness of the Showman's metavoice into play. The melodramatic voice is privileged here: the chief effect of the passage is to convey the Showman's clear condemnation of Becky as a hideous female creature.[10] The refined voice acts as a cover under which the Showman asserts that Becky is ugly, fiendish, and murderous. Thackeray's early understanding of how Becky's behavior can be seen as shaped and constrained by the patriarchy seems to have vanished. Instead, the Showman enjoys himself at Becky's expense and asks us to do the same as he links her with a whole group of creatures whose evil derives in part from their femaleness and especially from their female sexuality.

In linking Becky this way, the Showman is performing an all-too-familiar misogynist maneuver, one that ought to be kept in mind as a severe limit on any unqualified claim that Thackeray's critique of Vanity Fair is also a critique of patriarchy. Furthermore, the snideness with which the whole maneuver is carried out makes the Showman's voice not simply one that is complicit with the values of patriarchy but one that is actively perpetuating them.

At the same time, Thackeray's sliding away from the critique of patriarchy in his representation of his female characters is worthy of further thought. Why should his representation be inconsistent in this way? Or, to put the question another way, are there good—or at least plausible—reasons, within the working of the narrative itself, why his attitude toward the patriarchy would seem to shift from one point in the narrative to another?

Thackeray is a moralist as well as a social analyst, and he insists on locating some instances of vanity and its related sins—as well as its opposite virtues—in individuals themselves: consider his treatment of Jos Sedley on the one side and of Dobbin (for most of the narrative) on the other. Since his aim is to show the multifarious and ubiquitous operations of vanity, sometimes he uses Becky and Amelia as instruments for exposing vanity in others or in the structures governing the society, and at other times as exemplars of certain manifestations of the problem. If Thackeray used his female protagonists only as instruments of exposure, then his critique of patriarchy would be stronger and more consistent, but his demonstration of the omnipresent workings of vanity would be weakened. At the same time, of course, there is no *necessary* link between his location of vanity within individual women and the kind of misogyny that emerges in the passage we have just examined. Furthermore, on this last point, I think that a defense based on an appeal to historical and cultural difference is only partially successful. It is sensible and important to remember that we cannot expect Thackeray or any other author to escape entirely the ideology of his or her time and place and that, therefore, we ought not to evaluate voices and ideologies solely according to their conformity with our own. At the same time, an act of evaluation is, to some extent at least, an assessment of a text's value to us now, so our own values do matter. If condemning the entire book for the misogyny of the Becky-as-syren passage (and some others) would be a rash judgment, then overlooking or dismissing that ideology would be an evasion of the evaluative task. At the same time, we need to be clear about the nature of our evaluative claims. It is one thing to object to Thackeray's larger narrative project as we might do if we concluded that he should have written a consistent critique of patriarchy. It is quite another thing to say, as I have done here, that in the execution of his critique of the operations of vanity in Victorian society, he himself sometimes critiques patriarchy, sometimes trades in misogynistic stereotypes. More generally, the analysis suggests that listening to the Showman's voices deepens our engagement with Thackeray's narrative to the point that we must talk back to it—and that talking should in turn provoke more listening.

3

Voice, Distance, Temporal Perspective, and the Dynamics of *A Farewell to Arms*

This chapter builds on the model of voice outlined in the essay on Vanity Fair *by deploying it to reexamine Hemingway's famous style in* A Farewell to Arms *and to offer an account of how voice contributes to the novel's progression. Although I want to claim some originality for my specific analyses, the overarching goal of the first part of the chapter is quite traditional: to show how the technique is working in the service of the narrative's larger effects. Later, however, I expand my focus from voice to the autodiegetic narration more generally and investigate not just positive contributions of the technique but also some instructive problems and an interesting paradox in Hemingway's use of it. In looking at the problems, I am exploring the space where authorial agency and textual phenomena are in some tension, where intentionality seems to pull in one direction and the textual signs pull in another. In looking at the paradox, which concerns how the knowledge Frederic Henry arrives at through his experience does and does not inform his narration of that experience, I am trying to show how attending to narrative progression helps readers to understand a peculiarity of many autodiegetic narratives.*

Voice and Style in *A Farewell to Arms*

Taken collectively, critical discussions of *A Farewell to Arms* are striking in at least two respects: there is considerable consensus about the nature and effect of Hemingway's style, and there is considerable disagreement about the nature and effect of the narrative as a whole. Here I shall try to develop new grounds for consensus about its larger design by disrupting—or better, complicating—the consensus about the style. My contention is that *A Farewell to Arms,* though marred by Hemingway's characterization of Catherine, traces a coherent process of growth and change in Frederic Henry that culminates, tragically and ironically, in the moment of his greatest loss. Furthermore, I believe that Hemingway's representation of this process cannot be fully appreciated until we combine our attention to style, character, and structure with careful attention to voice. Thus, I will focus on Frederic's voice, with an occasional glance at the voices of other characters, in order to assess how Hemingway's modulation of voices helps to reveal—and contribute to—the novel's gradually unfolding design.

Larzer Ziff offers an apt and characteristic, albeit incomplete, description of Hemingway's style: a predominance of simple sentences; the frequent use of "blank" modifiers such as *nice;* the restricted use of figures of speech; the frequent use of proper nouns; the frequent use of indirect constructions (e.g., "took a look" rather than "looked"). In an essay subtitled "The Novel as Pure Poetry," Daniel Schneider adds imagery as an element of style, notes the recurrence of images of rain, desolation, impurity, and corruption in *A Farewell to Arms,* and offers the strongest statement of its effect: the style creates "the perfect correlative . . . of the emotions of despair and bitterness. . . . Virtually every sentence says, 'Death, despair, failure, emptiness.' . . . The novel begins with this state of mind, and it is established so firmly, through the repetition of the central symbols, that any emotions other than despair and bitterness may thereafter intrude only with difficulty" (273–75). In general, discussions of the style assume not only that it is consistent within the narrative but also that it has consistent and predictable effects. One burden of my argument will be to show that similar stylistic features of Frederic's discourse actually create widely divergent effects because they are spoken by recognizably different voices.

The disagreement about the effect of the whole no doubt has multiple causes, but one of them surely is the problem of establishing with any confidence the relation between Hemingway as implied author and Frederic. Some of the different relations posited can be seen in even a brief sampling of critical commentary: Schneider argues that the novel is a lyric expression of despair, failure, and emptiness; just as the speaker in a lyric poem may be distinguishable from the author even as that speaker expresses the author's attitudes, so too Frederic is distinguishable from but a surrogate for Hemingway. Earl Rovit views the novel as an epistemological tale "though not a tragedy"; Frederic learns something as he goes along—in a sense, narrator moves closer to author—but he does not attain tragic stature. Scott Donaldson maintains that the narrative is Frederic's failed apologia; he has taken advantage of Catherine and is now unsuccessfully trying to avoid taking responsibility for his behavior; in Donaldson's reading, author and narrator are consistently distant from each other. Gerry Brenner contends that the narrative is Frederic's unsuccessful attempt to make sense of his experience before he takes his life; on his account, Hemingway and Frederic are miles apart. Given these divergent readings, I want to investigate what happens to our understanding of the author-narrator relationship when we try not only to see it but to hear it.

There is just one feature of the long discussion of voice in chapter 2 that I want to repeat here because it bears directly on the author-narrator relationship. When we detect a discrepancy between an author's values and those expressed in a narrator's voice, we have the situation of a double-voiced discourse: the narrator's voice is contained within—and its communication thereby complicated by—the author's. In such situations, I will employ the term *distance* to refer to the relationship between the authorial voice and the narrative voice.[1]

The Voices of Book 1

Let us listen to Frederic Henry at the beginning of the narrative.

> In the late summer of that year we lived in a house in a village that looked across the river and the plain to the mountains. In the bed of the river there were pebbles and boulders, dry and white in the sun, and the water was clear and swiftly moving and blue in the channels. Troops went by the house and down the road and the dust they raised powdered the leaves of the trees. The trunks of the trees

too were dusty and the leaves fell early that year and we saw the troops marching along the road and the dust rising and leaves, stirred by the breeze, falling and the soldiers marching and afterward the road bare and white except for the leaves. (3)

This paragraph is often cited (and parodied) as a quintessential example of Hemingway's style, and in fact at least two critics have been moved to recast Frederic's prose into verse.[2] Critical disagreements about Frederic himself, however, begin right here. Commenting on this passage and the descriptions of it as emanating from the voice of a "tough guy" (Walker Gibson) or the voice of a "spiritually maimed" individual (John Edward Hardy), Gerry Brenner writes, "Both the 'tough' and the 'maimed' labels judge Frederic's style upon the basis of the perennial illusion that Hemingway, a crippled tough, a sentimentalist masquerading behind he-man brusqueness, wants his reader to endorse Frederic's values, to emulate his conduct, and to imitate his style" (34). Brenner wants to accept the label "maimed" but to see its consequences differently: Frederic is not maimed and tough, but maimed and "disoriented." I will try to adjudicate these different conclusions by attending to both the stylistic and transstylistic features of the voice.

As has often been noted, the use of the definite article ("the late summer") and the demonstrative adjective ("that year") indicate that there are to be no preliminaries here: we are asked to recognize that the narratee already knows the narrator and the year referred to—or we are asked to conclude that the speaker is disoriented.[3] The style of the rest of the passage does not give other evidence of disorientation. Instead, it locates the voice in space (at the window of the house in the village) and gives an orderly description of what can be seen from that window, a description that continues beyond this paragraph as the narrator's gaze moves from the river and the road to the plain and then the mountains. We can conclude, at least tentatively, that the voice addresses an audience that already has some knowledge of the context of the utterance.

Strikingly, however, this shared knowledge between voice and audience does not form the basis for emotional intimacy. As many others have already noted, the voice does not share feelings or evaluations but focuses on the sensual surface of things. The voice, in effect, becomes a camcorder: this is where I was; these are some things I could see; this is what happened as I kept my eye on the passing scene. The clear, controlled style and the evenness that comes with the paratactic syntax—we saw this and this and this—give Frederic's apparent objectivity and neutrality a self-assured, authoritative quality. Nevertheless, the lack of evaluation is conspicuous. This voice could be "tough" or "maimed" or many other things we might project onto it.

Once, however, we consider the trans-stylistic features of the voice and the way that its discourse is actually double-voiced, we can better assess its quality. Behind the paratactic sentence structures we sense another consciousness and thus another voice—Hemingway's—conveying information that the narrator's voice is not aware of. As we move in the authorial audience from the description of the river ("In the bed of the river there were pebbles and boulders, dry and white in the sun, and the water was clear and swiftly moving and blue in the channels") to the description of the troops, whose marching disrupts the natural order of things ("and the leaves fell early that year"), we make inferences about the war's negative effect on nature, even in its apparently nonviolent activities such as the marching of troops. These inferences, as I will argue at some length below, are controlled by the authorial voice but not the narrating voice.

Furthermore, what is true about the distance between Frederic and Hemingway in this opening passage remains true for most of the narration in book 1 of the novel. In making this statement, I am parting company with most other critics of the novel, who see Frederic's later experiences coloring his retrospective account of his life.[4] In terms of Gérard Genette's distinction between who sees and who speaks, between, that is, vision and voice, I find that Hemingway typically restricts us to Frederic's vision and voice at the time of the action, even though he is narrating after the fact. This technique highlights the limits of Frederic's understanding early in the narrative—and nowhere more so than in the passage at the end of the first chapter: "At the start of the winter came the permanent rain and with the rain came the cholera. But it was checked and in the end only seven thousand died of it in the army"(4).

The air of authority and the paratactic structure are again joined here. But the discrepancy between Frederic and Hemingway arises not through any particular linguistic signal but rather through our awareness of the difference in values between them. Frederic is voicing an official party line here, mouthing the military's position on the damage done by the cholera; his personal voice is inhabited by the social voice of the military command. Hemingway asks his audience to recognize the severe limits of the values expressed in that voice: seven thousand lives can be dismissed with the adverb "only" and the lives of those outside of uniform simply do not count. For all the authority of his voice at the beginning of the narrative, Frederic Henry is strikingly ignorant; the implied presence of Hemingway's voice, which gives the sentence its pointed irony, makes Frederic's voice naive. This gap between Frederic and Hemingway is arguably the most important revelation of the first chapter. It establishes a tension between author and narrator that is one major source of our continued interest in the narrative, and it helps define the major initial instability of the narrative: Frederic's situation in a war whose effects and potential consequences he is ignorant of.

Since, as I noted above, this way of hearing the voice is not the one adopted by previous critics and since it has significant consequences for my claims about the larger dynamics of the narrative, I would like to consider the basis of my case more fully. Since Frederic is telling the tale after the fact, we should consider the hypothesis that he, not Hemingway, is the source of the irony in that last sentence of the first chapter: the knowledge he has gained from his experience would inform his discourse, and we would be asked to know that he knows. The problem with this hypothesis is that we have no evidence that his knowledge is informing his narration. The past tense in fictive narration may function as narrative present[5]—and in the absence of clear signs to the contrary, that is the way it typically functions. Since there is nothing in the chapter—no switch to the present tense, no clue of self-conscious narration—signaling that his *vision* is that of the man who has lived through these events and now sees them differently, it makes sense to conclude that both Frederic's vision and his voice are those of the time of the action. Indeed, the definite articles of the chapter's first sentence seem designed in part to indicate right from the outset that Frederic is offering his vision at the time of the action: we are back there with him in "*the* house in the village that looked across *the* river and trees to *the* mountains."

Consider his later statement, also in the past tense, where the relationship between narrator's and author's voices, though perhaps more readily apprehended, works the same way: the war, Frederic says, "seemed no more dangerous to me myself than war in the movies" (37). Again we have the vision and the voice of Frederic at the time of the action, and again the discourse is double-voiced by Hemingway, who has already shown us that the war is dangerous to everybody. An even more extreme statement along these lines that Hemingway at one point placed just after Catherine's arrival in Milan was deleted from the final version of the novel:

> The world had always been a fine place for me. I saw the things there were to see and felt the things that happened and did not worry about the rest. There were always plenty of things to see and something always happened. You needed a certain amount of money and you did not need the gonorrhea but if you had no money and had the gonorrhea life was still quite passable. I liked to drink and liked to eat and liked nearly everything. The war was bad but not bad for me because it was not my war but I could see how bad it could become. (Ms. pp. 206-7)

Hemingway does not need this passage because he has already presented its content in more dramatic fashion, but its unironic presentation of Frederic's clearly limited view is consistent with the effect of the narrative discourse as I have been analyzing it: Frederic's voice conveys his beliefs at the time of the action, while our awareness of Hemingway's voice conveys the distance between narrator and implied author.

The more general issue raised by the question of whether Frederic or Hemingway is responsible for the ironic effects of the discourse is one about Frederic's degree of self-consciousness. To read Frederic's voice in book 1 as if it is infused with the vision he has at the time of the narration is to entail the conclusion that Frederic is a self-conscious narrator, aware that he is presenting double-voiced discourse, aware of the ironic effects he is creating by portraying himself in this way. On this reading, Frederic becomes a kind of Humbert Humbert of the AWOL set, that is, a narrator much like Vladimir Nabokov's self-conscious artist in *Lolita,* one who carefully constructs his narrative as a work of art. To argue that Hemingway rather than Frederic is responsible for the double-voicing is to entail the conclusion that Frederic is not self-consciously creating the narrative's effects. The control of the effects, in other words, belongs not to Frederic but to Hemingway. The manuscript shows that at one stage of composition, Hemingway thought to have Frederic talk about his difficulty with the narration:

> This is not a picture of war, or really about war. It is only a story. That is why sometimes it may seem there are not many people in it, nor enough noises, nor enough smells. There were always people and noises unless it was quiet and always smells but in trying to tell the story I cannot get all in always but have a hard time keeping to the story alone and sometimes it seems as though it were all quiet. But it wasn't quiet. If you try and put in everything you would never get a single day done. (Ms. p. 174)

Although the passage emphasizes Frederic's lack of control, Hemingway's decision to delete it supports my point. By showing that Frederic was self-conscious about the task of telling his story, the passage interferes with the effects of the narrative discourse Hemingway left. As I have been suggesting, the discourse indicates that Frederic describes the way things looked and the way he felt in a manner that comes naturally to him; Hemingway arranges those descriptions so that we can understand more than Frederic is aware he is communicating.[6]

There are other places in the early part of the narrative where Frederic's apparently distinctive voice mouths conventional positions that he has not closely examined and that Hemingway clearly disapproves of. I will look at two especially important instances, the first involving his argument with Passini about the justification for the war, the second involving his interaction with Catherine. Just before he is wounded, Frederic debates Passini on the need for the war. Their positions are very clear and very opposed. Passini argues, "There is nothing worse than war," while Frederic counters, "Defeat is worse" (50). Again Frederic is clear, authoritative—and, in a significant sense, naive. His authoritative tone again depends in part on the paratactic structure and in part on his own confidence in conventional justifications: "They come after you. They take your home. They take your sisters." "I think you do not know anything about being conquered and so you think it is not bad." "I know it is bad but we must finish it"

(50). Passini's voice of respectful authority, by contrast, is established through its reference to concrete possibilities and its firm but carefully argued rejection of the conventional wisdom:

> "War is not won by victory. What if we take San Gabriele? What if we take Carso and Monfalcone and Trieste? Where are we then? Did you see all the far mountains to-day? Do you think we could take all them too? Only if the Austrians stop fighting. One side must stop fighting. Why don't we stop fighting? If they come down into Italy they will get tired and go away. They have their own country. But no, instead there is a war." (50–51)

Hemingway shows that Passini has the greater share of wisdom not only by letting him "win" the debate but also by following it with the landing of the shell that kills Passini and wounds Frederic.

The difference in Frederic's voice when he describes the landing of the shell and Passini's death clinches the point: the voice is urgent, anxious, and focused on the concrete; it also makes way for the more urgent and anguished voice of physical pain that springs from the dying Passini. We recognize, though Frederic does not, that his voice of conventional wisdom loses its force when juxtaposed with the voices involved in the concrete rendering of the scene:

> and then I heard close to me some one saying "Mama mia! Oh, mama Mia!" I pulled and twisted and got my legs loose finally and turned around and touched him. It was Passini and when I touched him he screamed. His legs were toward me and I saw in the dark and the light that they were both smashed above the knee. One leg was gone and the other was held by tendons and part of the trouser and the stump twitched and jerked as though it were not connected. He bit his arm and moaned, "Oh mama mia, mama Mia," then, "Dio te salve, Maria. Dio te salve, Maria. Oh jesus shoot me Christ shoot me mama mia mama Mia oh purest lovely Mary shoot me. Stop it. Stop it. Stop it. Oh Jesus lovely Mary stop it. Oh oh oh oh," then choking, "Mama mama mia." Then he was quiet biting his arm, the stump of his leg twitching. (55)

Besides Frederic's relation to the war, the other major instability of the early part of the narrative is his relation to Catherine. Again, one way that Hemingway establishes the instability is through the discrepancy between Frederic's voice and his own. Frederic remains the objective recorder speaking from the time of the action, but one of the things he records is Catherine's dialogue. By skillfully juxtaposing their conversations with Frederic's commentary, Hemingway plays Frederic's voice against Catherine's and double-voices Frederic's narration. Here is Frederic's rendering of part of his third meeting with Catherine:

> "You did say you loved me, didn't you?"
> "Yes," I lied. "I love you." I had not said it before.
> "And you call me Catherine?"
> "Catherine." We walked on a way and were stopped under a tree.
> "Say 'I've come back to Catherine in the night.'"
> "I've come back to Catherine in the night."
> "Oh, darling, you have come back, haven't you?"
> "Yes."
> "I love you so and it's been awful. You won't go away?" . . .
> I kissed both her shut eyes. I thought she was probably a little crazy. It was all right if she was. I did not care what I was getting into. This was better than going every evening to the house for officers where the girls climbed all over you and put your cap on backward as a sign of affection between their trips upstairs with brother officers. I knew I did not love Catherine Barkley nor had any idea of loving her. This was a game, like bridge, in which you said things instead of playing cards. Like bridge you had to pretend you were playing for money or playing for some stakes. Nobody had mentioned what the stakes were. It was all right with me. . . .
> [Catherine:] "This is a rotten game we play isn't it?"
> "What game?"
> "Don't be dull."
> "I'm not, on purpose."
> "You're a nice boy," she said. "And you play it as well as you know how. But it's a rotten game."
> "Do you always know what people think?"
> "Not always. But I do with you. You don't have to pretend you love me. That's over for the evening." (30–31)

Clearly, Frederic's commentary is self-indicting in its selfishness, its calculation that playing this game with Catherine is better than going to the house for officers, its indifference to the consequences of his actions. But Hemingway's orchestration of the voices does more than that with the scene. Hemingway shows Catherine insisting that Frederic adopt a particular voice and speak the language of romantic love so that she too can adopt that voice. Yet to speak the language of love on command is to speak without sincerity, to mouth the words but be detached from the feelings they're intended to express. By thus commanding Frederic to speak a language that can never be sincerely spoken on command, Catherine puts herself in a position where her response to Frederic's words must also be at some remove from her feelings. To act as she does is indeed to act "a little crazy." Then after Hemingway inserts Frederic's voice of selfishness in his address to the reader, the voice of the male on the make, Hemingway returns to Catherine and shows her speaking sincerely and frankly. The movement from her earlier voice to this one is so great that Frederic cannot keep up with it, and he tries to maintain the pretense of sincerity by feigning ignorance. With this move in the play among the voices, Hemingway shows us that Frederic's statement about what he is doing with Catherine is not just extremely selfish but is also woefully inadequate in its understanding of Catherine and what she knows about the way each of them is behaving. Frederic is out of his depth with her just as he is out of his depth in the war.

More generally, by establishing considerable distance from Frederic's commentary and some from Catherine's behavior in the earlier part of the scene, Hemingway is implicitly revealing his beliefs about love. It is unselfish, other-directed, based on honesty; Hemingway expresses some of what is implicit here in the priest's later words, "When you love you wish to do things for. You wish to sacrifice for. You wish to serve" (72). Another significant measure of Frederic's distance from Hemingway will be where he stands in relation to this authorial norm.

Closing the Distance

One of the striking features of *A Farewell to Arms* is how skillfully Hemingway gradually closes the distance between himself and

Frederic and how he uses the narration to signal Frederic's changes. In Frederic's conversation with the priest after he returns from Milan to the front, Frederic articulates one of his traits, which in turn sheds light on Hemingway's general strategy in the novel: "I never think and yet when I begin to talk I say the things I have found out in my mind without thinking" (179). Frederic typically recounts his experiences without commenting on his feelings and thoughts about them. The devices that Hemingway uses to have us assess Frederic's progress are, for the most part, the ones we have seen in the passages already discussed: asking us to see behind what Frederic explicitly says to what he unwittingly reveals; using the dialogue of another character to give us a perspective different from—and sometimes superior to—Frederic's. In addition, by making Frederic more of a recorder than a reflector, Hemingway is able to emphasize those places where Frederic does explicitly reveal his feelings. For example, when Frederic, after engaging in the drinking contest at the mess and then rushing to the hospital only to find out that Catherine could not see him, tells us, "I had treated seeing Catherine very lightly, I had gotten somewhat drunk and had nearly forgotten to come but when I could not see her there I was feeling lonely and hollow" (41), we see the passage as a very powerful signal of his movement past the attitudes expressed in the "I didn't care if she was crazy" passage. The importance of Frederic's feelings here is further emphasized by Hemingway's use of "there." The adverb indicates that Frederic's vision is shifting in this passage from the time of the action (when he says "to come" he is locating himself at the hospital) to the time of the narration (he steps back and looks at himself "there") and thereby indicates the importance of the event in his memory.

This passage, however, also illustrates Hemingway's habit of asking us to see more than Frederic tells us. Even as Frederic is moving past his "I don't care if she is crazy" attitude, he remains self-centered. He does not think about Catherine and how she might be feeling, though Ferguson has told him that Catherine is "not awfully well." He thinks only about himself and his feelings: "I was lonely and hollow."

In the second half of the novel, after his long convalescence in Milan with Catherine, Frederic does change—and so does his voice. When Frederic returns to the front after his summer in Milan, he discusses the war with the priest.

> [Priest:] "I had hoped for something."
> [Frederic:] "Defeat?"
> [Priest:] "No. Something more."
> [Frederic:] "There isn't anything more. Except victory. It may be worse." (179)

Frederic's voice here now echoes Passini's; the conventional wisdom has been replaced by the values of the Italian peasant. Furthermore, as Frederic voices values more in line with Hemingway's, the authoritative quality of the voice is softened to some extent: victory "*may* be worse." As I have argued at some length in *Reading People, Reading Plots,* the main reason for Frederic's change is Catherine. His time with her in Milan has exposed him to a world based on values of commitment, tenderness, and service, values that had been absent from his life before he met her. When he returns to the front, the contrast is sharp enough to shock him into articulate knowledge in this conversation with the priest.

Perhaps the best evidence of the change in his attitude toward Catherine occurs in a scene during the retreat from Caporetto in which her voice inhabits his. Early in the narrative—just before Frederic makes his comment about playing a game with Catherine—Catherine pretends that Frederic is her dead boyfriend, and she asks him to say, "I've come back to Catherine in the night." She then says, "Oh, darling, you have come back, haven't you." When Frederic says yes, she continues, "I love you so and it's been awful. You won't go away?" (30). Her voice here is romantic and committed at the same time that its dominant note is wistfulness: she knows she is only pretending, reaching back beyond Frederic for her lost love. During the retreat, Frederic dreams that he is with Catherine again. Still in the dream, he is surprised that they are together:

> "Are you really there?"
> "Of course I'm here. I wouldn't go away. This doesn't make any difference between us."
> "You're so lovely and sweet. You wouldn't go away in the night, would you?"
> "Of course I wouldn't go away. I'm always here. I come whenever you want me." (197–98)

This time it is Frederic who says, "You wouldn't go away." Intermingled with Catherine's voice this way, the utterance here conveys his attachment and dependence, his wistful desire to reach beyond the retreat and be reunited with Catherine.

Just before this part of the dream, we hear Frederic adopt not Catherine's specific words but her voice and its values:

> "Good-night, Catherine," I said out loud. "I hope you sleep well. If it's too uncomfortable, darling, lie on the other side," I said. "I'll get you some cold water. In a little while it will be morning and then it won't be so bad. I'm sorry he makes you so uncomfortable. Try and go to sleep, sweet." (197)

This is Catherine's voice of solicitude and service, a voice that we hear Frederic using for the first time in connection with Catherine's pregnancy. Away from Catherine but slowly moving back to her ("You could not go back. If you did not go forward what happened? You never got back to Milan" [216]), Frederic shows more concern for Catherine's pregnancy than he did at any time in Milan. Living in the gap between his life with her and his life at the front, Frederic is learning what Catherine already knows: what it means to be in love. Again, as he learns, his voice moves closer to Hemingway's.

Both Frederic's changed understanding of the war and his commitment to Catherine undergird his decision not just to save his own life by diving into the Tagliamento but also to defect from the Italian army. This development resolves the instabilities surrounding Frederic's relation to the war, but those instabilities now give way to those surrounding Frederic and Catherine's attempt to construct their own haven from the malevolent world. In effect, they seek to establish a world based on the values of her voice. As they set about this task, there are further changes in Frederic's voice, but I will restrict my focus for now to those involving Frederic's relationship to and understanding of that larger world because in that way I will be best able to assess Frederic's voice at the very end of the narrative.

Soon after he and Catherine are reunited, Frederic speaks from the time of narration; his voice merges temporarily with Hemingway's and he articulates what his experience has taught him about the world:

> If people bring so much courage to this world the world has to kill them to break them, so of course it kills them. The world breaks every one and afterward many are strong at the broken places. But those that will not break it kills. It kills the very good and the very gentle and the very brave impartially. If you are none of these things you can be sure it will kill you too but there will be no special hurry. (249)

The effectiveness of this famous passage is partially hindered because Hemingway's voice overrides Frederic's to some extent. The passage gives us a voice that is too great a departure from any of the voices that we have heard Frederic use to this point. Although the syntax is characteristic of Frederic, the sententiousness of the language is not. The passage sounds a little too much like a set piece of Hemingway's.[7]

Frederic's voice is more authentically his own as he tells us his thoughts in the hospital after he learns of the baby's death: "That was what you did. You died. You did not know what it was about. They threw you in and didn't tell you the rules and the first time they caught you off base they killed you. Or they killed you gratuitously like Aymo. Or gave you the syphilis like Rinaldi. But they killed you in the end" (327). Given everything that the narrative has shown us to this point, from the rain and the cholera to the disastrous retreat, from Passini's death to Aymo's, Frederic's response here seems appropriate: he is articulating a vision of the world that Hemingway has presented as true. Nevertheless, through the repetition of the phrase "they killed you" and especially through its first disruptive appearance in the baseball metaphor ("the first time they caught you off base they killed you"), Frederic's voice also carries a heavy tone of frustration and complaint. It has not yet fully merged with Hemingway's; indeed, a distinctive element of the "If people bring so much courage to this world" passage is that, instead of a complaining tone, it incorporates a kind of ironic acceptance: "if you are none of these, it will kill you too but there will be no special hurry."

Now consider the final sentence, the ending that Hemingway produced so many alternatives to. "After a while I went out and left the hospital and walked back to the hotel in the rain" (332). The emphasis on sequence and the use of coordination with *and* recalls a significant feature of the style of the opening paragraph: this happened and this and this. But the relation of Frederic's voice to Hemingway's is substantially different here. Just before this sentence, Frederic has told us about his attempt to say a melodramatically romantic good-bye to Catherine:

> "You can't come in now," one of the nurses said.
> "Yes I can," I said.
> "You can't come in yet."
> "You get out," I said. "The other one too."

He is imperious here because of the strength of his romantic fantasy. But the reality of Catherine's death destroys the fantasy: "But after I got them out and shut the door and turned off the light it wasn't any good. It was like saying good-by to a statue" (332). The shift to honest, matter-of-fact assertion beneath which lies very deep feeling sets up the last sentence.

If the voice of the first passage was naive in its lack of evaluation, the voice of the last sentence is wise in that lack. If the author of the first passage spoke behind the style to reveal that naïveté, he speaks here to reveal a strength in the face of knowledge. Frederic now knows the destructiveness not only of the war but also of the world; indeed, he has experienced that destruction firsthand in the most excruciating way imaginable. The world has destroyed his life by destroying Catherine. He has no illusions about the finality of the destruction. But as the voice speaks and as we hear Hemingway's voice behind the sentence, we see that Frederic is not really destroyed. Despite what he knows he acts. Despite what he knows he speaks without frustration and without complaint. Both the voice and the action are slow and deliberate, controlled and dignified (compare Hemingway's version to "Then I headed back to the hotel in the rain"). He has no reason to live, no hope for the future: "That was what you did. You died." But the control in the voice and the deliberateness of the action signal a refusal to be crushed by that world. Furthermore, in sending that signal, the control and the deliberateness also signify that Frederic has taken the final step in his remarkable growth from authoritative spouter of conventional wisdom to understated but informed source of Heming-way's own values. The final sentence is one of the times Hemingway got it just right.

Problems with the Technique

I have argued that by making Frederic a character who is not much given to reflection on his experience and a narrator who is an unselfconscious but faithful recorder of those experiences, Hemingway has communicated more to us than Frederic realizes in two main ways. Hemingway double-voices Frederic's narration and he uses the dialogue of other characters to offer perspectives whose significance Frederic does not fathom. I turn now to consider the limits of what Hemingway can accomplish with this technique by focusing on two problematic segments of the narrative: Frederic's shooting the Italian sergeant and Frederic and Catherine's interlude in Switzerland.

As I briefly indicated above, one of Hemingway's tasks in his representation of the retreat from Caporetto is to trace Frederic's gradual evolution from a committed, competent leader of the ambulance corps to a justified fugitive who makes his separate peace. Early in the retreat, we see Frederic at his most decisive and most active: leading Aymo, Bonello, and Piani, he decides that Aymo can bring the virgins, that they can give a ride to the sergeants, that they should ride in a certain order, when they should ride, when they should eat, when they should rest, when they should get off the main road. In short, he is dedicated to carrying out their orders to get to Pordenone. He is also dedicated to certain group values: they share the food they find, they help each other out, they do not harm the young women, they help the sergeants, they do not plunder the farmhouse where they stop for food. The sergeants, on the other hand, violate many of these values: they take the ride, but they want to save their own skins; they enter the farmhouse to see what they can steal from it; having eaten, they don't care whether the others eat. Their greatest violation occurs when the ambulance gets stuck and they take off. All this comes through

Frederic's narration very clearly. The problems arise when Frederic reacts to their greatest offense by shooting at them and wounding one, who is then killed, with Frederic's approval, by Bonello.

How much distance is there between Hemingway and Frederic at this point? Does Hemingway want us to see Frederic's response as justified in some way? Or is the shooting a sign that the violence of the war is infecting Frederic as well? What is the significance of the placement of the incident so soon after Frederic's dream about being together with Catherine again? How does the incident fit in with the two other shootings during the retreat—Aymo's by the Germans, and those by the carbinieri at the Tagliamento? Developing satisfactory answers to these questions is an extremely murky business, and the murkiness is inextricably wound up with Hemingway's particular deployment of the autodiegetic narration.

Just as we can be confident that Hemingway does not endorse the values behind the assertion at the end of the first chapter, we can be confident that he does not fully endorse Frederic's reaction here. Given Hemingway's attitudes about the war's destruction, we can infer that shooting to kill under these circumstances is overdoing it. One sign of Hemingway's disapproval is that he slightly distances Frederic from the killing by having Bonello fire the fatal shot. If Hemingway wholeheartedly endorsed the shooting, it would make sense to have one of Frederic's shots kill the man. Bonello's dialogue also provides a clue to Hemingway's values here. Bonello is proud of what he has done, but his boasting reveals the problems with his viewpoint: "all my life I've wanted to kill a sergeant" (207). His joke about what he will say in confession, "Bless me, father, I killed a sergeant," also underscores this reading of Frederic's action. When we recall the standard way of beginning a confession, "Bless me, father, for I have sinned," we can see how Hemingway is double-voicing Bonello's utterance here. Bonello is not just melding the language of war onto the language of religion. He is also transforming the confession of guilt into a source of pride—bless me, I did something good in killing the sergeant. By asking us to read the religious formula underneath Bonello's line, Hemingway reminds us that Bonello has in one sense "sinned." Significantly, Bonello's joke does not succeed with Frederic; he reports not that "We all laughed" but that "They all laughed" (208). Frederic's inability—or unwillingness—to laugh is a further sign that he has overreacted. Although Frederic never reflects on the incident, we see that one source of his uneasiness is that he has been operating by the same code of war that sanctions Bonello's actions and Bonello's comments. The code says that a commanding officer has the right to command obedience; violations of that command are punishable by death. Despite other moves Frederic has been making away from the war, he is still bound by the military mentality.

But Hemingway apparently wants to communicate other things with the scene as well. His representation of the sergeants as consistently violating the values of sharing and respect being honored by Frederic and the others suggests that the scene is also showing Frederic taking some kind of stand about those values. This issue is important because Frederic has earlier been someone who simply did what was easiest. By showing Frederic reacting so strongly to the sergeants' violations of the group's values, Hemingway seems to be showing—or trying to show—some significant change in Frederic as well. Again, Hemingway's technique for conveying this aspect of the incident is the use of another character's dialogue. Immediately after the shooting, Piani delivers a judgment about the sergeants whose accuracy we must recognize: "the dirty scum" (204). Later he returns the group's conversation to Frederic's action, saying with approval, "You certainly shot that sergeant, Tenente" (207).

Viewed in this way, the incident becomes an important checkpoint by which to measure the alterations Frederic undergoes during the retreat. When he shoots the sergeant he is simultaneously entrapped in the code of the military and committed to values that will eventually move him to make his separate peace. The subsequent events of the retreat, especially the shooting of Aymo and the executions at the Tagliamento, push him finally and completely away from the military code.

The trouble with this view of the incident is that I am not sure it is fully substantiated by the narration. The reading hangs heavily on the few lines of dialogue given to Bonello and Piani—and even more on my sense of how what Hemingway is doing with Frederic in the rest of the novel has implications for what he needs to do with his character here. The dialogue of the minor characters, especially Piani's, seems susceptible to alternative interpretations: Piani can be seen as closer to Bonello than my reading suggests; Piani does, after all, laugh at Bonello's joke. The more positive side of Frederic's action may not really be built into the incident. But then Hemingway's previous choices in representing the sergeants and in showing Frederic's commitment to certain values seem problematic. This second-guessing of my reading is not meant to dislodge it, only to indicate that I do not believe it can be as well substantiated as the earlier interpretations I have offered. The larger point is that if Hemingway had given Frederic different traits as a narrator and a character, if Frederic not only recorded but explicitly interpreted the incident through reflecting on it, Hemingway would be able to communicate its complexities far more firmly than he can through Frederic's tight-lipped, recording, time-of-the-action perspective. But to alter Frederic that way would be to lose much of the power of the rest of the book.

The situation with the events in Switzerland is both similar and different. Hemingway again wants to accomplish something complex: to show that Frederic and Catherine have reached a place that is both idyllic and impossible to maintain; to show also that Frederic and Catherine sense that their life has no future; to show further that if the world were different, Catherine and Frederic would always be very happy, and that the reason they are only sometimes so lies not with them but with that world and their knowledge of it. All these effects will serve the larger purposes of his narrative. By showing that their union is very attractive, he will increase the sense of loss we feel in Catherine's death. By showing that they have no real future, he will reinforce his thematic point about the malevolence of the world. By showing that they sense their own plight, he will add another dimension to their situation and will be able to make a further thematic point about how best to respond to a knowledge of the world.[8]

Part of Hemingway's strategy in chapters 38 to 40 is to use Frederic's narration to achieve these different effects at different times, but there are places where the effects interact. Consider the end of chapter 38. Frederic reports that he and Catherine awaken in the night. She had been thinking, she says, about the time when they first met and she was a "little crazy"; she insists that she is no longer crazy, just "very, very, very happy" (300), and she proposes that they both go back to sleep at exactly the same moment. The disturbance underneath her waking and her proclamation of happiness prevents Frederic from going back to sleep when she does. "I was awake for a long time thinking about things and watching Catherine sleeping, the moonlight on her face" (301).

Why should Catherine wake? Because she, who has known about the world all along, knows that their idyll can't last and she is disturbed by that knowledge. Why should Frederic not be able to fall back asleep? Because he senses what she knows. He makes a similar point at the end of chapter 40: "We knew the baby was very close now and it gave us both a feeling as though something were hurrying us and we could not lose any time together" (311). But earlier in chapter 38, Hemingway has also used Frederic's record of a long conversation with Catherine to show that she is worried about his feelings for her, a worry that also comes from her recognition that they have no real future. In the conversation, Catherine asks Frederic whether he is bored or restless, asks him about his having gonorrhea and says that she wished she'd had it, says that she wants to be exactly like him. Hemingway's sexism comes through clearly here, but so does a rather different consequence of Catherine's worry about their future. Her fear of what's coming also makes her somewhat desperate about the present: there seems to be some lack in the here and now that she wants to fill. Thus, when she wakes at night and proclaims that she is very, very, very happy, we can't help inferring that she protests too much.

But how do I know that it is her fear of the future that makes her desperate about the present? One could plausibly argue that her desperation is a sign of Frederic's present inadequacy and her own endless insecurity. Again, I think that what has happened is that Hemingway has run up against the limitations of his narrative perspective, only here those limitations become even stronger because of the sexism. Just as Hemingway turns in the shooting incident from Frederic's recording to the dialogue of Piani and Bonello to create his effects, he turns here to Catherine's dialogue. In addition to the limits Hemingway faces as a consequence of Frederic's tight-lipped recording, he faces the problem of the way the narrative perspective constrains our view of Catherine. Because the perspective allows us to see

Catherine only from outside—and because Hemingway has conceived her character in a sexist way—her conversation can give rise to interpretations that the trouble with their life in Switzerland is not the world but the two of them. Such interpretations alter our view of Catherine's death: it becomes not the culmination of the tragedy but a convenient way for Frederic to escape from this sterile, constricted relationship. Although I think that the larger progression of the narrative finally calls such interpretations into question, I would also suggest that the limits of the autodiegetic narration make them appear more plausible.

The Paradox of Frederic's Narration

I turn finally to the way in which much of what I have been saying about Frederic's narration implies that it is built on a paradox. Strikingly, this paradox has the potential to undermine the novel's illusion of realism, yet that potential is never realized. The paradox arises from three features of the narration, two of which I have already discussed explicitly. (1) With few exceptions, Frederic speaks from his perspective at the time of the action. (2) The growth or change in Frederic's character occurs at the time of the action, not during the time of the narration or through the act of narration. Thus, when I read the last sentence of the novel ("After a while I went out and left the hospital and walked back to the hotel in the rain") as a sign of Frederic's growth, I am also understanding that the growth occurred then. The understated style is capturing Frederic's control during his walk, not a control that he has acquired through the act of writing. (3) Frederic is a recorder, not a self-conscious narrator. He is intent on telling his story, but he is no artist, no Humbert Humbert trying to render the most artistically effective narrative that he can muster for some rhetorical purpose that serves as his motivation for telling the story.

Since it is always possible—even easy—to find confirmation for the hypothesis that Frederic is self-consciously crafting the narrative (it's clearly his story, and his story clearly shows evidence of careful crafting), I want to pick up once again the issue of how we determine whether a homodiegetic or autodiegetic narrator is self-conscious.

One of the conventions of homodiegetic narration is that unselfconscious narration is the unmarked case: that is, we take the homodiegetic narrator as unselfconscious unless we are given reason to do otherwise. Thus, we assume that the homodiegetic narrator is not the source of such things as foreshadowing, patterns of imagery, parallelism of incidents, the lyricism of a particular style—unless we have some signal that calls our attention to the narrator's self-consciousness. For example, when Huck Finn describes the sunrise over the Mississippi in sentences with impressive poetic power, we don't marvel at Huck's artistic prowess and his selective display of it; instead, we see Huck as the window through which Twain's artistry is being revealed. On the other hand, when Nabokov wants to create Humbert Humbert as a self-conscious narrator, he has Humbert frequently comment on his own narration: in chapter 1, he says, "You can always count on a murderer for a fancy prose style" (11); later, he says, "Oh my Lolita, I have only words to play with!" (34); and finally, of course, Humbert talks about his narrative—and its artistry—as an attempt to compensate for the crimes he has committed against Lolita: "I see nothing for the treatment of my misery but the melancholy and very local palliative of articulate art" (285). "One had to choose between [Clare Quilty] and H. H., and one wanted H. H. to exist at least a couple of months longer so as to have him make you live in the minds of later generations. I am thinking of aurochs and angels, the secret of durable pigments, prophetic sonnets, the refuge of art" (311). Frederic is clearly more like Huck than like Humbert.

The second reason that I want to argue for Frederic as recorder is the internal evidence of the narration. In addition to the evidence I have discussed earlier, I would like to add a final example, one in which Frederic does fluctuate between his perspective at the time of the action and his perspective at the time of the narration. In chapter 7 just before Frederic proclaims that the war "was no more dangerous to me myself than war in the movies" (37), he mentions that he had met two British gunners when he was on his leave in Milan. "They were big and shy and embarrassed and very appreciative together of anything that happened. I *wish* that I was with the British. It would have been much simpler. Still I would probably have been killed. Not in this ambulance business. Yes, even in the ambulance business. British ambulance drivers were killed sometimes. Well, I knew I would not be killed" (37, emphasis mine). The passage indicates Frederic's habit as a recorder: his reactions here arise out of the stream of his recollections rather than being motivated by his conscious artistic purpose. When he thinks of the British gunners at the time of narration, he jumps to his wish of having been with them because it would have been much simpler. But then he catches himself up by thinking of the possible negative consequences of that situation, then he has a short dialogue with himself about whether he would have been killed, then he quickly ends that by giving his view that the war was not real to him. To say that Frederic has planned all these shifts for some artistic purpose of his own is to make an interpretive leap for which the narration provides no spring.

The paradoxical consequence of these three features of the narration can be effectively illustrated by returning to my reading of the sentences ending the first chapter. "At the start of the winter came the permanent rain and with the rain came the cholera. But it was checked and in the end only seven thousand died of it in the army." The rub in seeing Frederic as the victim rather than the source of the irony is that if unselfconscious Frederic has learned about the war and the world at the time of the action, then this knowledge should always be a part of his perspective as he retells the story. In other words, Frederic writes as if he does not know what he in fact knows—and he is not deliberately suppressing his knowledge or manipulating our understanding of his knowledge for any conscious artistic purpose of his own.

Genette has noticed and named this phenomenon of homodiegetic narration, calling it a *paralipsis,* a narration in which less information is given "than should presumably be given in terms of the focalization code governing the narrative," as Gerald Prince describes it in his *Dictionary of Narratology*.[9] But neither Genette nor Prince has analyzed the rhetorical logic of paralipsis's paradoxical nature—as I now propose to do for the case of *A Farewell to Arms.*

Although there is a sense in which Frederic's paralipsis *seems to violate* the conventions of mimesis, it does not actually destroy the mimetic illusion. Why? First, because the narration makes artistic sense and, second, because it makes sense in such a way that there is no reason for the reader to register the paradox during the actual temporal experience of the narrative. Hemingway, in effect, wants to write a Bildungsroman with a tragic twist. If he were to do that from a heterodiegetic perspective, there would be no problem in showing that the protagonist started out in ignorance and ended in knowledge. The narrator and the audience would start out ahead of the character, but eventually he would catch up to and perhaps surpass the audience. But to tell such a story from the perspective of a protagonist who would unselfconsciously record his experiences and some of his judgments and beliefs at the time of the action would have some significant advantages. Such a narration would allow the audience to have a deeper, more intimate relationship with that protagonist, and such a relationship might be necessary for the audience to maintain partial sympathy for him in the early stages of the narrative. Such a narration would also necessarily involve the audience in a great deal of inferential activity that would in itself be a source of the narrative's pleasure. Furthermore, although this procedure would entail the paradoxical situation described above, it would not be noticed. It would not be noticed because as the audience reads the early chapters—and indeed, the middle and later chapters—it does not know whether the narrator will attain any more knowledge than he has at the time of the narration. Thus, when we read the last sentence of chapter 1 in the temporal progression of the novel, we are not aware of the paradox because we do not know that Frederic comes to an understanding of the war and the world that would make it impossible for him to utter such a sentence without being ironic.

If the analysis of this chapter has been at all persuasive, then I think it suggests several noteworthy conclusions about Frederic's narration. First, it indicates the subtlety and skill with which Hemingway handles that narration. As Hemingway carefully constructs a progressive action in which Frederic works through his unstable relations with the war, with Catherine, and finally with the destructive world, he also develops a highly nuanced but clearly discernible progression of voice. Though Frederic's style does remain recognizably the same from beginning to end, his voice does not. Instead, as Frederic takes on features of Passini's voice and Catherine's, he is gradually moving closer to the values of the Orchestrator of the voices, Hemingway himself. Second, in showing that the technique has limits as well as powers, the analysis offers an account for some of the interpretive disagreement about the novel that accuses neither Hemingway nor his critics of being butchers. The disagreements stem not from sloppiness but from divergent inferences that naturally arise as Hemingway bumps up against the limits of his technique. Third, in showing that according to the standards of naturalistic probability Frederic could not logically tell his story as he does, the analysis suggests something about the conventions of homodiegetic narration. We will overlook the mimetic impossibility to allow Hemingway to tell the story in the most effective way—provided that the awareness of the impossibility is not foregrounded by the narrative itself. Taken together, these conclusions suggest that the smooth surface of Hemingway's prose belies the dynamic interaction of voice, character, and action that we must attend to in order to feel the progression of the narrative.

Part Two

Mimetic Conventions, Ethics, and Homodiegetic Narration

4

What Hemingway and a Rhetorical Theory of Narrative Can Do for Each Other: The Example of "My Old Man"

This essay returns to some previous issues—progression, naive narration, the paradox of paralipsis—and looks at them in the context, first, of trying to solve some interpretive problems in the first short story Hemingway published in the United States and, second, of thinking about how those solutions might shed light on rhetorical theory. In addition, the essay continues some of the concerns of the analyses of voice by explicitly raising the question of the flesh-and-blood reader's response to the ethics of the story.

My attempt to have theory and narrative be mutually illuminating here points to one important relation of theory and practice. More generally, this essay and the others in this volume seek not only to illustrate principles of my approach to narrative as rhetoric and to interpret the set of narratives under investigation but also to stretch my understanding of those principles and to suggest that the analyses of the interpretive issues in these narratives will have implications for our reading of others.

Interpretive Problems in "My Old Man"

Just what happens at the end of "My Old Man"? And just how good is Hemingway's first published story? According to such early commentators as Sheridan Baker, Carlos Baker, and Arthur Waldhorn, the ending reveals Joe Butler's disillusionment with his father when Joe learns that he has mistakenly been admiring a crooked jockey. For them, the story is a rather unexceptional achievement, one derivative of Sherwood Anderson's "I Want to Know Why," another tale of boys and horses in which a naive narrator becomes disillusioned with an adult male whom he has valued above all others.

According to more recent commentators such as Sydney J. Krause, Robert Lewis, Gerry Brenner, and Paul Smith, the ending is more complicated than that; in their view, Hemingway has given Joe's tale a "Jamesian" twist by providing evidence that Joe's disillusionment is unfounded. Brenner, who pushes this line the furthest, maintains that Hemingway asks his reader to see that Joe's father has been acting to reform the crooked world of horse racing and that the bettors' final complaints about "what he pulled" are testimony to his honesty (9). For this group, the Jamesian twist adds to the sophistication and quality of the story; rather than being derivative of "I Want to Know Why," "My Old Man" is a step beyond it.

According to Philip Sipiora, who has offered the most recent extended treatment, the ending suggests that Joe recognizes both that his father was involved in fixing races and that he has reformed, a dual recognition that allows Joe to retain his respect for his father. Although Sipiora does not explicitly address the question of the tale's quality, his treatment everywhere implicitly testifies to his belief that it is a significant achievement.

These divergent views of the meaning and value of "My Old Man" present interpretive problems that constitute a theoretical opportunity. The divergence is sufficient to give me pause before simply going ahead and proposing another contender to the title of Most Perspicuous Reading. Instead, I would like to consider both the meaning and the value of the story in light of my approach to narrative as rhetoric, with special attention to the textual features most involved in the disagreement. At the same time, I would like to make not just the story but also the approach an object of investigation so that theory and story can be mutually illuminating. That is, rather than simply invoke rhetorical theory to "solve" the interpretive problems of the story, I would like the theory itself to be open to revision or complication by Hemingway's story. The traffic flow at this intersection of Theory and Story will become clearer as I proceed. For now, I want to consider the details of "My Old Man" that lead to its interpretive problems.

Two key elements of the tale are the sources of disagreement: Hemingway's choice of a naive narrator, and the suddenness with which Joe's feelings for his father alter at the end. Because the naïveté of Joe-the-narrator matches that of Joe-the-character (and this feature of the story is one that we must come back to), he never fully articulates his understanding of the final events of the story. Consequently, we are left to make our own inferences when we read the concluding sequence: the gamblers' remarks that Joe's father "got his all right"; George Gardner's reassuring words, "Your old man was one swell guy"; and Joe's final comments, "But I don't know. Seems like when they get started they don't leave a guy nothing" (129). We reach different conclusions depending on (1) the emphases we put on these final comments (is "But I don't know" a repudiation of Gardner or an expression of genuine doubt?) and (2) the way we add up the previous evidence about Joe's father's behavior and Joe's understanding of it.

Given these sources of disagreement, the story presents a twofold theoretical opportunity: to explore the nature and functions of naive narration and to investigate endings as the conclusions not just of plots—some sequences of events—but also of progressions: audience's involvement with and response to such sequences. I begin with the larger, more overarching concern, the concept of narrative as a developing progression of readerly engagement. This discussion has some overlap with the account given in chapter 1 before my analysis of *The Waves,* but it has a slightly different emphasis.

Character, Progression, and Narrative as Rhetoric

In using a phrase such as "developing progression of readerly engagement," I am calling attention to the way my rhetorical approach focuses on the text as an invitation to an experience that is dynamic in at least two ways. First, the experience is crucially influenced by the movement of the narrative through time. Second, the experience is multilayered, one that engages a reader's intellect, emotions, judgments, and ethics simultaneously. As noted in chapter 1, the general term I use to refer to the concept of narrative-as-dynamic-experience is *progression*. Since the discussion in chapter 1 began with character and moved toward progression, it will be helpful here to begin with progression and focus on response.

Progression refers to the way in which a narrative establishes its own logic of forward movement (and thus addresses the first sense of narrative as dynamic experience), and it refers to the way that movement carries with it invitations to different kinds of responses in the reader (and thus it addresses the second sense of narrative as dynamic experience). The structuralist distinction between story and discourse helps explain the way the logic of narrative movement can develop. Progressions can be generated through what happens with the elements of story, that is, through the introduction of *instabilities*—conflictual relations between or within characters that lead to complications in the action and sometimes eventually to resolution. Progressions can also be generated through what happens with the elements of discourse, that is, through *tensions* or conflictual relations—relations involving significant gaps in values, beliefs, or knowledge—between authors and readers or narrators and readers. Unlike instabilities, tensions do not need to be resolved for narratives to achieve closure. One typical consequence of naive narration is that it establishes some tension between the narrator and the reader.

For example, in the beginning of *A Farewell to Arms,* as I argued in chapter 3, Hemingway generates the movement of his narrative, first, by creating a tension between Frederic's unreflective beliefs about the war and the ones Hemingway asks us to adopt and, second, by placing Frederic in the unstable situation of war and in his complicated relationship with Catherine. The progression then develops from the complications arising from the instabilities, and those complications eventually alter the tension so that, as Frederic's beliefs gradually change, the tension is gradually resolved.

To account for the multiple layers of our responses to narrative, I suggest that as we follow the movement of instabilities and tensions, we respond to the text's—and especially to the characters'—mimetic, thematic, and synthetic components. That is, we respond to the characters as human agents, as representing some ideas, beliefs, or values, and as artificial constructs playing particular roles in the larger construct that is the whole work. In *Farewell,* we respond to Count Greffi, for example, as an individual with specific traits, as representing a set of attitudes that illustrate how to deal with the world's essential emptiness, and as a device for instructing Frederic and the reader in those attitudes. These responses to Greffi become part of our larger experience because they interact with the dynamic sequences of responses we have been making to Frederic from the first page. That larger sequence influences our response to Greffi. Our judgments of his attitudes, for example, depend in part on the judgments we have made about the attitudes espoused by Frederic, Rinaldi, the priest, Catherine, and others. Furthermore, our response to Greffi becomes a new part of the whole sequence, one that adds further nuances to our complex experience of the whole narrative, and then influences our response to later events such as Frederic's final action in the narrative.

Count Greffi's role in *Farewell* illustrates another significant point: not every character or scene will *directly* contribute to the introduction, complication, or resolution of an instability or a tension, yet everyone will have some role in the progression. Nothing Greffi does affects the sequence of events, and nothing he does increases or resolves the tension between Frederic's views and Hemingway's. Nevertheless, his appearance allows Hemingway to introduce for Frederic and the audience one admirable way of living with the knowledge of the world's destructiveness. Greffi thereby contributes to the progression by contributing to the audience's understanding of Frederic's eventual response to his own knowledge of that destructiveness.

To avoid the trap of a priori analysis, I make no claims either about the kinds of progressions that narratives must follow or about the most effective or most frequent relationships among a text's mimetic, thematic, and synthetic components. Each progression will establish its own relationships, and different successful narratives can establish very different relationships.

The Progression of "My Old Man"

Approaching "My Old Man" from this perspective, we can recognize something quite striking about its dynamics. Despite its apparent straightforwardness, the story actually develops from the intersection of two distinct paths: one created by the tensions in Joe's narration and the other created by the instabilities in his father's life as a jockey. The tensions focus our interest very strongly on Joe and his understanding of what he is telling us, whereas the instabilities focus our interest very strongly on Joe's father and what happens to him. Again quite strikingly, the interaction of the tensions and instabilities makes the relationship between father and son a principal interest of the tale, but until the very end of the narrative that relationship is essentially stable: Joe loves and admires his father, and there is no conflict between them.

This understanding of the developing progression already points to some special features of Hemingway's ending. He draws upon the previous tensions and instabilities, first, to make the relationship between father and son the most important focus of the whole story. The resolution of the instabilities in Butler's life becomes subordinated to its effect on Joe's relation to him. Second, Hemingway draws upon the previous tensions and instabilities to transform the father-son relationship from one stable entity into another. Admiration is replaced by some other feeling, which in turn complicates the love. Indeed, understanding more precisely how Hemingway transforms the progression of the whole after Butler's death will not only lead to my proposal about the ending but will also provide the key to seeing what "My Old Man" can do for narrative theory. But before we can analyze that transformation, we need to look more closely at the interaction between the tensions and the instabilities in the beginning and the middle of the tale. I will focus on those elements that are most relevant to our understanding of Joe as naive narrator, of Butler as a moral agent, and of the ending: Joe's opening account of how his father kept his weight down; the juxtapositions of Joe's views with his father's during their time in Milan; Joe's commentary on George Gardner after the fixed Kzar-Kircubbin race at St. Cloud; Butler's actions and reactions between that race and purchasing his own horse; and the final paragraphs of the story.

Joe's opening account does not introduce any instabilities, and, with the exception of minor indications of Joe's superior knowledge about what has happened to his father, it does not introduce tensions until its end. Instead, the account strongly establishes the initial stable situation between Joe and his father. It also introduces us to Joe as an unselfconscious narrator. His references to what he can "guess, looking at it now" and to what his father was like "toward the last" (151) indicate that he has a story to tell, but Joe does not begin that story at the beginning or explain why he begins with this account of how his father kept his weight down. Indeed, because he plunges into the narrative by telling us about habitual actions that do not lead to other actions in the story, he seems less interested in composing a narrative than in just talking about his father. But Hemingway, we realize, is using Joe's apparently unsophisticated narration in some sophisticated ways. To explain those uses more fully, it will be helpful to introduce another element of the rhetorical approach.

Implicit in the discussion of Joe as unsophisticated narrator and Hemingway as sophisticated implied author is a distinction between two audiences, between what Peter J. Rabinowitz has called the authorial and the narrative audiences. On Rabinowitz's account, which I shall examine more closely in chapter 7, the narrative audience is the one implicitly addressed by the narrator; it takes on the beliefs and values that the narrator ascribes to it, and in most cases it responds to the characters and events as if they were real. Joining the narrative audience is crucial for our experience of the mimetic component of the text and sometimes for the thematic and synthetic components as well. The authorial audience takes on the beliefs and knowledge that the author assumes it has, including the knowledge that it is reading a constructed text. Joining the authorial audience is crucial for our experience of all the invitations offered by the different components of the text. Engaging with the text involves entering both of these textually signaled audiences simultaneously; engaging also means that we bring our individual subjectivities, our flesh-and-blood selves to bear on our experience, a point I will pursue further when I discuss the evaluation of "My Old Man."

In the opening pages of Joe's narration, we respond strongly to Joe's voice and immediately start reading mimetically. At the same time, as members of the authorial audience our covert awareness of the synthetic component of Joe's character helps us recognize how Hemingway uses Joe's talk as a brilliant beginning to the story, a beginning that performs four important functions.

First and most obviously, as Joe's narration establishes the initial stable situation, it reveals the strength and importance of his feelings for his father: "When I'd sit watching him working out in the hot sun I sure felt fond of him. He sure was fun and he done his work so hard" (116). Second, the account validates Joe's feelings—and contributes to the establishment of the audience's very positive initial evaluation of Butler. Joe's narration casually reveals how Butler included Joe in what he was doing, and it shows the way the two of them shared the pleasure of the workout: "I'd help him pull off his boots. . . . 'Come on, kid,' he'd say, 'let's get moving.' Then we'd start off jogging around the infield. . . . when he'd catch me looking at him, he'd grin and say, 'Sweating plenty?' When my old man grinned, nobody could help but grin too. We'd keep right on running out toward the mountains" (115). Third, the account reinforces this positive evaluation by linking Butler's workout with the elements of nature that surround it. (Roadwork has never sounded so appealing.) Joe and his father would start out "with the dew all over everything and the sun just starting to get going" (115). They'd be "running nice, along one of those roads with all the trees along both sides of them that run out from San Siro." They'd run out "toward the mountains" until Butler would decide to rest against one of the trees before beginning to skip rope in the sun (115–16).

Fourth, the account implies an equivalence between Butler's working out and his working, and at the end it suggests that the working out is superior to the working. In Joe's description, his father's jumping rope is very much like riding: he'd move "up and down a patch of road" with "the rope going cloppetty, cloppetty, clop, clop, clop" (116). As he jumped, he'd often draw spectators. Most important, the running and jumping would produce for Butler the effect that riding produced for other jockeys. "Most jocks can just about ride off all they want to. A jock loses about a kilo every time he rides, but my old man was sort of dried out and he couldn't keep his kilos down without all that running" (116).

David Lodge's way of talking about metaphor and metonymy in his essay on "Cat in the Rain" provides a helpful first step in understanding this last point. At the level of story, the running has a metonymic relation to the riding: Butler runs in order to be fit to ride. The discourse, however, makes the running equivalent to—and hence puts it in a metaphoric relation to—the riding: Butler's running resembles and produces the same (or better) effects than his riding. The second step is recognizing that the shift from metonymy to metaphor highlights the narrative's first significant instability and tension—located in Joe's remark that his father was "sort of dried out." Joe has repeatedly stated that Butler sweats profusely when working out: Joe describes "the sweat pouring off his [father's] face" (116) and says that Butler would finish jumping with a "whirring that'd drive the sweat out on his face like water" (116). In the authorial audience we cannot take Joe's remark about Butler's being dried out at face value, and so we begin to separate ourselves from Joe's perspective. At the same time, the odd physiological reaction to the riding—as well as the implication that the running and jumping rope are a better substitute—suggests that there is something unstable in Butler's relation to his work, that the psychological dimension of that relation is far more complicated than Joe knows.

This suggestion is immediately reinforced by the next several moves of the narrative. First, Joe reports the way his father, "looking tired and red-faced and too big for his silks," stared at the "cool and kid-looking" Italian jockey, Regoli, as if Regoli had just bumped him and then in reply to Joe's question "What's the matter?" said, "Oh, to hell with it" (117).[1] Second, Hemingway juxtaposes Joe's perspective with his father's in a single sentence: "San Siro was the swellest course I'd ever seen but the old man said it was a dog's life" (117). Third, Hemingway juxtaposes Joe's disquisition on how "nuts" he was about the horses with his father's statement, "None of these things are horses, Joe. They'd kill that bunch of skates for their hides and hoofs up at Paris" (118).

These tensions between Joe's understanding and the authorial audience's and the corresponding hints at instabilities in Butler's work situation prepare the way for our understanding of the first major instability in Butler's life story: the events surrounding his winning the

Primo Commercio. We see that Butler has been going along with the fixing of races and has agreed to participate in the fix at this race, too. But going along with the system means going against his basic nature—it is drying him out and leaving him dissatisfied with his situation. Unable to take it anymore, he rebels and rides to win. The rebellion, however, gives him no satisfaction because it gives him no power. After the argument with Holbrook and the unnamed Italian, "his face was white and he looked sick as hell" (118) because he realizes that by rebelling he has jeopardized his livelihood. Every other event in Joe's father's life is a consequence of the resulting unstable situation.

As we infer the instabilities in Butler's situation, we also begin to complicate our evaluation of his character. He is not the crook that early interpretations of the story have assumed, nor is he the crusading hero that Brenner depicts. Instead, he is a fundamentally decent man caught in a corrupt system, a man who has been complicit with that system but who also rebels against it. He tries not to undo the system but just to get out from under it.

When his flight to Paris does not prove to be an effective escape because he remains blackballed and unable to make a living, Butler uses the system to his own advantage, taking George Gardner's inside information and betting heavily on the Kzar-Kircubbin race. This incident contributes to the progression by eventually making possible Butler's effort to ride without being controlled by the fixers, when he uses his winnings to buy his own horse. I will discuss that development shortly, but for now I will focus on the more immediate effect of the incident itself on the progression: the further development of the tensions between Joe and the authorial audience, a development that has important implications for the ending. The development arises from Joe's response to his first clear look at the corruption of horse racing.

When Butler reminds Joe that the race was fixed by saying that George had to be a "great jock" to keep Kzar from winning, Joe remarks: "I thought, I wish I were a jockey and could have rode him instead of that son of a bitch. And that was funny, thinking of George Gardner as a son of a bitch because I'd always liked him and he'd given us the winner, but I guess that's what he is, all right" (124). By expressing his conclusion this way, Joe reveals his value system: a jockey who would hold back a horse as magnificent as Kzar is a "son of a bitch," regardless of whatever redeeming features he might have. Hemingway, however, has written the scene so that in the authorial audience we recognize the limits of that value system. Joe's last sentence about Gardner indicates that he thinks he is admitting a difficult truth, but in the authorial audience we recognize that Joe's conclusion is based on his partial view of the situation, a recognition that largely depends on the way the story builds a link between Gardner and Butler.

Hemingway links Gardner and Butler, first, by giving them a common voice: as Joe records their dialogue, he unwittingly shows how much knowledge the two men share—when Butler asks, "What's the dope, George?" Gardner simply answers, "He won't win" (121)—and how attuned they are to each other. Butler's first question is asked "in an ordinary tone of voice," and then when George replies in a low one, Butler asks his second question, "Who will?" in an equally low voice (121). Furthermore, they are comfortable enough with each other and with what they are doing to joke. In addition to linking them through voice, Hemingway also links them through action: once Butler uses George's information to make his bet, he is again as complicit in the fixed system as George is. What Joe doesn't see is that if Gardner is a son of a bitch, his father is, too. But just as we depart from Holbrook's evaluation of Butler as a "son of a bitch," we also depart from Joe's judgment of Gardner. Gardner, too, is a man caught in the system. He is acting as Butler has acted many times in Milan, except that he is now also trying to help his friend beat the system. Above all, what we see is that Joe's condemnation is misdirected. His moral sense rightly tells him that he should feel angry, but he understands the system so dimly that he condemns the jockey rather than those like Holbrook who control him. At the same time, neither Gardner nor Butler is off Hemingway's hook: complicity is complicity, not necessity.

Butler's actions after collecting his winnings further shade our evaluation of him. Brenner suggests that Butler's motive has been noble: he takes advantage of Gardner's information to buy his own horse and battle the corrupt system. Had the progression been such that Butler's next act was the purchase of Gilford, then Brenner would be right on target. But Butler's winnings seem to create another variation of the basic instability established after the Primo Commercio: what will he do with his life now? Joe describes their days: "We'd sit at the Cafe de la Paix, my old man and me, and we had a big drag with the waiter because my old man drank whisky and it cost five francs, and that meant a good tip when the saucers were counted up. My old man was drinking more than I'd ever seen him, but he wasn't riding at all now and besides he said that whisky kept his weight down. But I noticed he was putting it on, all right, just the same. . . . he was dropping money every day at the track. He'd feel sort of doleful after the last race, if he'd lost on that day, until we'd get to our table and he'd have his first whisky and then he'd be fine" (125).

Butler's taking advantage of Gardner's information is the flip side of Butler's winning the Primo Commercio. There he asserted himself against the system of fixing by refusing to go along with it. Here he asserts himself against it by taking advantage of it. But each rebellion is an isolated act, and each one leaves him dissatisfied. He cannot take satisfaction in the first act because of its consequences for his work, and he cannot take satisfaction in the second because it has again made him complicit in the system. Buying his own horse, however, is clearly a step toward a positive resolution of these instabilities. Not only does Butler start his "running and sweating again," but when he stands in the place stall after his first race, he is "all *sweating* and happy"—as he is after working out (126, my emphasis). Now that he is outside the system of fixing, Butler is no longer dried out.

When Butler's brief happiness ends in the Prix du Marat, Joe is left to deal with the consequences, and like the situation after the Kzar-Kircubbin race, he assesses his situation as a result of the perspective offered by someone else, this time the bettors. But the situation—and our relation to Joe—is more complicated here. As I noted earlier, the ending suddenly and completely transforms the stable relationship between Joe and his father. It remains unstable only for as long as it takes Joe to assimilate the bettors' harsh words and react to George's comforting ones; then it takes a new—and apparently permanent—stable shape.

Hemingway is able to effect this transformation because the source of the tensions between narrator and authorial audience has also always been a potential source of instability between Joe and his father: the gap between the complex reality of Butler's life and Joe's limited understanding of it always had the potential to affect the relationship between the two of them, either through the misunderstanding itself or through the consequences of its diminishment. Hemingway uses the bettors' words to activate the potential. In a sense, then, the question about the ending is whether the activation and resolution of this instability also resolve the tensions between Joe and the authorial audience.

The analysis I've offered so far points to an answer. Joe reacts to the bettors' words the way he reacts to his father's words after the Kzar-Kircubbin race, that is, he believes that he now sees something that he had been blind to before. To be sure, the bettors' harshness is directed at "the stuff he's pulled"—at his not always going along with the fix. What Joe sees is that his father was, in some way or other, part of the corrupt world of horse racing. Thus, he finds no solace in George's words—"your old man was one swell guy"—because George only repeats Joe's old truth and because Joe believes that George himself is a son of a bitch. Although Joe stops short of fully repudiating Gardner's words and adopting the bettors' views, his "But I don't know" in combination with his final words does indicate that his admiration for his father is completely undermined—and that he has a new, deeper sense of the harshness of the world: "Seems like when they get started they don't leave a guy nothing."[2]

In the authorial audience we recognize that Joe's understanding is still limited. The nuanced evaluation of Butler that we have developed through the course of the progression now functions as the standard against which we measure Joe's conclusions. In that measuring, we see that the tension is altered but not resolved. Joe rightly understands that there was more to his father than he knew, but he gets stuck on his father's participation in the crooked world of horse racing, blinding himself both to his father's rebellion and to his genuine love. Furthermore, following a point made by Robert Lewis, we can see that Joe's failure to appreciate Gardner's kindness to him here is itself a sign of Joe's occluded vision.

Strikingly, the tension between Joe and the authorial audience gives his final sentence, which he uses to thematize his experience, an added twist. We are deeply moved by Joe's devastation. In losing his father, he has essentially lost his world. Although he is now an adolescent, he has made only the smallest of steps toward establishing his independence—occasionally going off bumming with other kids and once showing interest in a girl. But Butler's acquiring Gilford brought Joe completely back within the orbit of his father's life. Now that life is gone and so is his sense of who his father was. Accompanying this loss is a new awareness of the world's capacity for inflicting pain. Furthermore, the gap between Joe's understanding of Butler and ours gives the loss an additional poignance. We see that although Joe has lost all his admiration for his father, there is still much about Butler to be admired. Thus, we agree with Joe's last sentence because it captures something about the world's potential for cruelty, but we also disagree with Joe's needless overgeneralization: "Seems like when they get started they don't leave a guy nothing."

Ethics, Evaluation, and the Flesh-and-Blood Reader

Even as we participate in the authorial and narrative audiences, we never lose our identities as flesh-and-blood readers, and that fact adds a further layer to our experience. Just as the authorial audience evaluates the narrator's values, so too does the flesh-and-blood audience evaluate the author's. Entering the authorial audience allows us to recognize the ethical and ideological bases of the author's invitations. Comparing those values to the ones we bring to the text leads us into a dialogue about those values. Sometimes our values may be confirmed by those of the text, sometimes they may be challenged, and sometimes they may be ignored or insulted. When our values conflict with those of the text, we either will alter ours or resist those of the text (in whole or in part). The ethical dimension of the story involves the values upon which the authorial audience's judgments are based, the way those values are deployed in the narrative, and, finally, the values and beliefs implicit in the thematizing of the character's experience.

Some of the values underlying "My Old Man" are time-honored ones in our culture: the importance of love between father and son, the superiority of honesty to dishonesty. Some indicate a more modern view: individual actions such as the jockeys' participating in the rigged system cannot be judged without regard to the whole context in which they occur. Yet none of the values represents a major departure from or a major challenge to the values that most readers are likely to bring to the story. The values are deployed with considerable skill and sophistication. I believe that this recognition partially underlies the claims that "My Old Man" is less an homage to Anderson than a demonstration of Hemingway's superiority to him. The deployment of the values leads the authorial audience to carefully nuanced judgments of Butler and of Joe. In responding to Butler, we are responding to a man who senses what is right but cannot always act according to that sense. In responding to Joe at the end, we are responding to a boy who is understandably devastated, yet devastated in a way that his fuller understanding would have prevented. Consequently, we are asked to respond in complex ways, asked to draw upon our own experiences with complicity, with undue admiration of a revered figure, and with undue disillusionment. In short, I think Hemingway's deployment of the basic values involves us in a progression whose ethical quality is rich and satisfying. In that sense, "My Old Man" is a very fine achievement, one whose quality has not been fully appreciated.

The values and beliefs associated with the thematizing are likely, I think, to evoke more variation among flesh-and-blood readers. For some, they may be very problematic or even harmful: a person trying to recover from an experience that has left him or her feeling stripped of everything may be seriously set back by experiencing Joe's account of how he came to conclude that "once they get started they don't leave a guy nothing." On the other hand, someone who is further along in such a recovery may find something to build on in recognizing that Joe's conclusion is severely limited. Other readers will resist the general negativism of the thematizing. Nevertheless, to the extent that the resistance leads them to an honest reexamination of their alternative beliefs, their reading will be a positive experience. Those who already agree with Joe's conclusion will have their belief reinforced by reading the story, and they may either engage very powerfully and productively with the story or minimally and unfruitfully.

A second step here is to recognize that the values and beliefs implicit in the thematizing in "My Old Man" are part of Hemingway's larger set of values and beliefs. Although that set has often been too easily summarized and made systematic, two of its important elements are that the world is a destructive place and that men should face that truth with toughness and dignity and strength. Flesh-and-blood readers again vary in their responses to these truths. Some readers build from them a code to live by. Some accept the belief about the world but refuse the stipulation about how best to respond. Others vehemently argue about the problems with Hemingway's focus on men, asserting that his so-called truths are themselves undermined by his failure to represent women acting in accord with them. Still others refuse the initial characterization of the world. And in each case, Hemingway's success in pulling readers into his authorial audience will have consequences for the depth of one's engagement—positive or negative—with his values, just as the outcome of each reader's engagement will have consequences for the way he or she reacts to Hemingway's next invitation.

From Text to Theory

If "My Old Man" works something like the way I have claimed, then it provides three insights into our general understanding of the way narratives, when viewed rhetorically, work—and all three are related to Hemingway's use of the naive narrator. The first insight depends on taking one step further my discussion of the deployment of the narrative's values. The rich ethical quality of the transaction is intimately tied up with Hemingway's handling of Joe's narration: the ethical quality depends not just on our seeing the complexity of Butler's and Joe's situations but also on how we see it. Because the tensions in Joe's narration so strongly activate our powers of inference, we become strongly engaged in the characters' situations, mimetically and ethically. Since our inferences are directed by Hemingway, we rely very heavily on both his craft and his moral vision—and on his way of revealing the vision through his skill with the naive narration. Hemingway's tale is far from the first to show us this potential in naive narration, but "My Old Man" should, I think, deepen our appreciation of the ways in which technique and vision function interdependently as we read.

Second, Hemingway's management of the ending gives "My Old Man" a progression unlike any other that I know, even as it teaches us something about the categories of our analysis. Structuralists distinguish between story and discourse in order to be able to specify the different bases of a narrative's construction, and structuralists such as Chatman go to great lengths to keep the two parts of narrative distinct.[3] I follow the structuralist distinction because separating tensions from instabilities enables me to identify distinct sources of narrative movement. Unlike the structuralists, however, I do not regard the distinction as absolute, and "My Old Man" provides evidence that it is not: Joe's unreliable narration indicates that the same element of a narrative can function simultaneously as discourse (the unreliability creates a tension) and as story (the unreliability simultaneously generates an instability—or at least the potential for an instability). In other words, Hemingway's story suggests that, from a rhetorical perspective, the story-discourse distinction is better seen as a heuristic than as an absolute.

The third insight is more complicated. Even more than *A Farewell to Arms,* the story exposes the paradox of this kind of paralipsis, in which a naive narrator apparently sheds his naïveté. Joe Butler narrates the tale of his disillusionment at some unspecified point after he has experienced that disillusionment. Logically, his new attitude toward his father should permeate his narration. But it does not.[4]

If Joe's new attitude did permeate his narration, the ending would lose all its power. Yet we feel neither that Joe is being insincere nor that he is deliberately withholding his knowledge from us for his own artistic purposes (if he were, then he would not be a naive character but a highly sophisticated narrator). In this respect, the story exposes the inescapably synthetic nature of apparently mimetic naive narration, and it points to one difference between fictional and nonfictional homodiegetic narration. In nonfiction, the homodiegetic or autodiegetic narrator can employ paralipsis, but such employment will always reflect some self-consciousness. A real-life narrator cannot tell a story of self-enlightenment and simultaneously be unaware of that enlightenment until it occurs in the action. (The other alternative, of course, would be that the real-life narrator would have his knowledge inform his narration.)

In the case of "My Old Man," however, Hemingway is able to have the paralipsis and Joe's unselfconsciousness peacefully, albeit paradoxically, coexist: as with *A Farewell to Arms,* the story retains its mimetic power, even after the paradox is exposed.

There are two related reasons for this effect. First, mimesis is always a matter of conventions, and one convention of mimetic narrative is that narration from the time of the action enhances the mimetic effect.[5] Such narration creates the impression that the action is unfolding before us rather than being told after the fact. Second, as in *A Farewell to Arms,* we experience the progression. We do not know that the narrator will lose his naïveté and so are not aware that the logic of mimesis rules out the kind of narration we are reading. It is not until our experience of the narrative is over that mimetic logic steps in and says that we can't have experienced what we just experienced. But that mimetic logic must yield to the commonsense logic that points out we have already experienced it.

Just what happens at the end of "My Old Man"? And how good is the first story Hemingway published in the United States? In answering these questions by saying, in effect, "something complicated and subtle" and "very good indeed," I have also tried to sketch one approach to answering similar questions about other narratives. For now, I want to stand by these answers, but just as Hemingway's story has something to offer narrative theory, I am very much aware that other critics and theorists may lead me to revise them. Progression ought not be a concept limited to narrative dynamics.

5

Reexamining Reliability: The Multiple Functions of Nick Carraway

In a sense, this chapter follows out the logic underlying my analysis of the paradox of paralipsis in the two Hemingway narratives. It starts with a look at an instance of paralepsis. If that paradoxical situation is rhetorically effective, then perhaps an author may also create an effective homodiegetic narrator who fluctuates between being unreliable and being (apparently) omniscient. The key to recognizing such possibilities is to recognize that although any homodiegetic utterance simultaneously brings into existence both a narrator and a character, the narrator functions and the character functions need not coincide or even be complementary. Nick Carraway is a very instructive case in point. The general point in these two chapters about the conventional nature of mimesis is also a feature of my analysis of the simultaneous present-tense narration in J. M. Coetzee's Waiting for the Barbarians *in* Understanding Narrative, *edited by James Phelan and Peter J. Rabinowitz (Columbus: Ohio State University Press, 1994).*

In chapter 8 of *The Great Gatsby,* Fitzgerald has Nick narrate the events that occur in George Wilson's garage the night after Myrtle Wilson is killed by the driver of Gatsby's automobile. Here is the first sentence of this five-page section and a short excerpt from the middle:

> Now I want to go back a little and tell what happened at the garage after we left there the night before. . . .
>
> The effort of answering broke the rhythm of [Wilson's] rocking—for a moment he was silent. Then the same half knowing, half bewildered look came back into his faded eyes.
>
> "Look in the drawer there," he said, pointing at the desk.
>
> "Which drawer?"
>
> "That drawer—that one."
>
> Michaelis opened the drawer nearest his hand. There was nothing in it but a small expensive dog leash made of leather and braided silver. It was apparently new.
>
> "This?" he inquired, holding it up.
>
> Wilson stared and nodded.
>
> "I found it yesterday afternoon. She tried to tell me about it but I knew it was something funny."
>
> "You mean your wife bought it?"
>
> "She had it wrapped in tissue paper on her bureau."
>
> Michaelis didn't see anything odd in that and he gave Wilson a dozen reasons why his wife might have bought the dog leash. But conceivably Wilson had heard some of these same explanations before, from Myrtle, because he began saying "Oh, my God!" again in a whisper—his comforter left several explanations in the air. (165–66)

This section of the narrative is striking for several reasons. First, although Nick announces that he is going to "go back a little and tell what happened at the garage" after he, Jordan, and Tom left, Fitzgerald never bothers to have Nick explain how he learned what happened. We might suppose that either Fitzgerald made a mistake or assumed that he did not need to include any such explanation. Second, the narration is not summary but scene: Nick is a New Journalist *avant la lettre* as he not only gives a verbatim report of a conversation he did not overhear but also includes numerous small dramatic details. Notice, for example, Nick's careful description of Wilson's look as "half knowing, half bewildered" and his drawing out the identification of the drawer Wilson wants Michaelis to open—"Look in the drawer there." "Which drawer?" "That drawer—that one" (165). Indeed, at first glance, the only sign in this excerpt that Nick may be anything other than an omniscient heterodiegetic narrator is the word *conceivably* in the final sentence: "But conceivably Wilson had heard some of these same explanations before, from Myrtle" (166).

In a sense, Nick's narration represents the flip side of Joe Butler's: where Joe's is marked by the *absence* of knowledge and opinion that we eventually learn he should have, Nick's is marked by the *presence* of knowledge that he presumably should not (because he could not) have. Genette, again, has noticed and named this variation of homodiegetic narration, calling it a *paralepsis,* but he does not address its effects. In attending to these effects in *The Great Gatsby,* I want to focus on three questions: (1) Has Fitzgerald violated the terms of his own novel by introducing this paralepsis, by converting Nick from witness-narrator to nearly omniscient narrator? (2) What bearing, if any, does Nick's function here have on our understanding of his much-debated reliability?[1] If Nick's near omniscience can be shown to be legitimate, then perhaps we have evidence to support the view that he is fundamentally reliable. If, however, Nick's near omniscience suggests some violation of the terms Fitzgerald wants to be working within, then perhaps we should conclude that Nick is not merely unreliable but incoherent.[2] (3) How does answering these questions about Nick's narration illuminate other features of Fitzgerald's narrative?

In light of my argument about the paralipsis in Joe Butler's narration, it will come as no surprise that my hypothesis about the first question is that the paralepsis in Nick's narration is no violation. Furthermore, although understanding why the paralepsis fits the logic of the narrative will not directly answer the question about Nick's reliability, it will offer some ways to rethink the reliability/unreliability distinction. These ways, in turn, will then help us recognize the diversity of potential functions a character-narrator such as Nick can be asked to perform within the space of single narrative. Finally, by seeking to understand why Fitzgerald needs Nick to serve multiple functions, we should learn something about the larger workings of Fitzgerald's narrative.

Let us return to the narration of the scene between Michaelis and Wilson. For the most part, Fitzgerald has Nick render the scene in his own voice but through Michaelis's vision. That is, the diction and syntax of the narration are Nick's: descriptions such as "The effort of answering broke the rhythm of his rocking—for a moment he was silent. Then the same half knowing, half bewildered look came into his faded eyes" (165) are perfectly consistent with the voice we have been hearing throughout the narrative. The visual perspective of the scene, however, is Michaelis's. Wilson is always seen from the outside as he would look to Michaelis. Furthermore, Michaelis is occasionally seen from the inside: we are told that "Michaelis didn't like to go into the garage because the work bench was stained where the body had been lying" (165); that Michaelis "*believed* that Mrs. Wilson had been running away from her husband" (167); that he had a "forlorn hope" that Wilson had a friend whom Michaelis could telephone (167); and that he "saw with a shock" (167) that Wilson seemed to be equating God and the eyes of Dr. T. J. Eckleburg. Fitzgerald's technique makes Nick function as a kind of invisible witness positioned over Michaelis's shoulder with the additional privilege of occasionally being able to offer brief inside views of him.

The way Fitzgerald is in violation of the terms of his narrative can be succinctly expressed in the following question: How can a witness-narrator narrate what he didn't witness? Indeed, even if we supply an explanation that seeks to preserve the mimetic illusion Fitzgerald seems to be working within, for example, that Michaelis related these events at the inquest following Myrtle's and George's deaths or that Nick interviewed Michaelis a few days after these events, we still must recognize that the scene gives Nick a kind of privilege that his reporting of someone else's report could not have. As long as we are operating with the logic of strict mimesis, we would have to acknowledge that Michaelis's account could not have been as careful, detailed, and precise as Nick's narration is. Finally, if Fitzgerald were concerned about strict mimesis, he could have easily indicated that Michaelis was the chief source for Nick's knowledge and that Nick's imagination supplied the rest.

Obviously, Fitzgerald was not so concerned, and it is my contention that he was right not to be. What matters at this point in the narrative is not how Nick knows what he narrates but that this scene be narrated and that the information it contains come to us as authoritative. After the excerpt I have quoted, the passage continues this way:

> "Then he killed her," said Wilson. His mouth dropped open suddenly.
>
> "Who did?"
>
> "I have a way of finding out."
>
> "You're morbid, George," said his friend. "This has been a strain to you and you don't know what you're saying. You'd better try and sit quiet till morning."
>
> "He murdered her."
>
> "It was an accident, George."
>
> Wilson shook his head. His eyes narrowed and his mouth widened slightly with the ghost of a superior "Hm!"
>
> "I know," he said definitely. "I'm one of these trusting fellas, and I don't think any harm to *no*body, but when I get to know a thing, I know it. It was the man in the car. She ran out to speak to him and he wouldn't stop."
>
> Michaelis had seen this too but it hadn't occurred to him that there was any special significance in it. He believed that Mrs. Wilson was running away from her husband rather than trying to stop any particular car. (166–67)

This information, of course, is crucial to the reader's inferences about the death of Myrtle Wilson and about the deaths of Gatsby and Wilson himself, which Nick will report very shortly—indeed, within a few pages. If Fitzgerald does not present this information scenically, it will interfere with the reader's inferential activity in piecing the story together, in coming to our own understanding of how neatly Wilson ends up serving Tom Buchanan's purposes. If Fitzgerald calls attention to how Nick learned what he tells us, Fitzgerald will also call attention to the limits of Nick's knowledge, since Nick's research could never give him the full knowledge that his account presumes. In that way, if Fitzgerald tried to supply the source of Nick's knowledge, he would very likely weaken the authority of the scene. By having Nick narrate the scene in his own voice as if he were there on Michaelis's shoulder, Fitzgerald both gives the narration some continuity with Nick's other reporting and invests the scene with full authority. One small sign of his success is that most readers do not even register the paralepsis as anomalous.

If this analysis is correct, it suggests two other important conclusions: (1) as with the paralipsis in Joe Butler's narration, the paralepsis is not violating the conventions of mimesis; those conventions are somewhat elastic and the criterion "what is probable or possible in life" can sometimes give way, even in otherwise realistic narrative, to the criterion "what is needed by the narrative at this point." In other words, mimesis is not a matter of faithfully imitating the real (whatever that is) but is rather a set of conventions for representing what we provisionally and temporarily agree to be the real. In this larger view, Joe's paralipsis and Nick's paralepsis violate a *narrow* standard of mimesis, one based only on imitation-of-the-real ("knowledge alters perception"; "you can't narrate authoritatively what you haven't witnessed"); but Joe's paralipsis and Nick's paralepsis are consistent with a broader standard of mimesis, one that looks both to the real and to conventions for imitating it. Judgments about whether violations of the narrow standard of mimesis are problematic or not depend in part on what they make possible: both "My Old Man" and *The Great Gatsby* are more rhetorically effective as a result of their violations of the narrow mimetic logic. (2) Although a character-narrator's functions as character and as narrator typically influence each other, sometimes these functions operate independently. Both of these conclusions have a significant bearing on the debate about Nick's reliability.

Though Wayne C. Booth was not the first to comment upon the phenomenon of an untrustworthy narrator, his treatment of reliable and unreliable narration in *The Rhetoric of Fiction* remains the chief source of the distinction. Booth defines a reliable narrator as one who shares the norms of the implied author and perceives the facts of the narrative as the implied author does; Booth defines an unreliable narrator as one who deviates from the implied author's norms and/or from the implied author's perceptions of the narrative's facts. The widespread adoption of Booth's distinction has led to two important interpretive habits. First, the distinction is seen as most often relevant to homodiegetic narration. George Eliot's narrator in *Middlemarch* can be distinguished from the implied author by regarding the narrator as a wise, ironic, and gender-neutral persona that the implied Eliot adopts, but almost no one questions whether this narrator shares Eliot's norms. However, any time we have a character-narrator, whether that character is protagonist, witness, or reporter at several removes from the action, the question of reliability is inevitable.

Second, Booth's distinction assumes an equivalence, or perhaps better, a continuity between narrator and character, and so critics look at the character function to shed light on the narrator function and vice versa. That is, the narrator's discourse is assumed to be relevant to our understanding of his or her character, and the character's actions are assumed to be relevant to our understanding of his or her discourse. Thus, interpreters will examine the homodiegetic narrator's character—including such aspects of character as motives, values, beliefs, interests, psychology, race, class, and gender (to the extent these matters can be inferred from events and descriptions)—for clues to the narration and the character's narration for clues to the character. Kent Cartwright's complaint about Nick's narration in the final chapter shows how this assumption operates in practical criticism: "In the novel's final chapter, a peculiar dislocation or reorientation of the story's direction takes place which again connects Nick's personal limitations with his blurred narrative judgment" (227).

The assumption is significant because it means that once we have evidence of some unreliability it is possible (though not necessary) to argue for unreliability all the way down. The debate about Nick provides a wonderful example of this reasoning in Ernest Lockridge's tour de force 1987 essay, "F. Scott Fitzgerald's *Trompe l'Oeil* and *The Great Gatsby*'s Buried Plot." Lockridge uses a small amount of evidence of Nick's unreliability as a warrant for finding in Fitzgerald's novel a plot in which the following events occur: (1) Daisy uses Gatsby to win back Tom; (2) Daisy finishes off her artful scheme by deliberately running over Myrtle Wilson; (3) Wolfsheim, worried about what Tom's investigation of Gatsby will turn up, has his men murder Gatsby; and (4) these men, seeing Wilson arrive on the scene, kill him, too, and make it look like a murder-suicide.[3]

Nick's narration of the events in Wilson's garage suggests that the assumption of continuity between character and narrator may not always be warranted: regardless of the biases and flaws Nick as character has previously revealed, in this segment of the narrative his character is all but irrelevant. Recognizing the possibility of divergence between the character's functions and the narrator's functions also entails recognizing that sometimes the reliability of a homodiegetic narrator can fluctuate wildly throughout the progression of a narrative. Fluctuations that depend on the variable distance between the narratorial and the character functions are different from the gradual movement toward reliability we have seen in Frederic Henry because in Frederic's case the change in narratorial function is directly tied to alterations in his character. These fluctuations are also different from anything that we have seen in Joe Butler, a character-narrator where the effect of the whole narrative depends on the continuity between the two functions.

When the narratorial functions are operating independently of the character functions, then the narration will be reliable and authoritative. Indeed, at such junctures, the narration will be so authoritative that the question of reliability is no more likely to arise than it does in relation to the narrator of *Middlemarch*. When the character and narratorial functions are operating interdependently, the narration may be either reliable or unreliable and the degree of the narrator's privilege will vary depending on his or her relation to the action being reported. Because a particular narrative may require a homodiegetic narrator's functions to vary over the course of a particular narrative, the narrator may, without violating the conventions of mimesis, fluctuate between being highly unreliable, being reliable with a limited privilege, and being fully reliable and authoritative.

Furthermore, recognizing the varying relations between the character and narratorial functions of a homodiegetic narrator facilitates our recognizing two other important relations: (1) the homodiegetic narrator's retrospective perspective may drop out and the character's action may be presented for the reader's judgment in much the way that a dramatic scene works in heterodiegetic narration. That is, the implied author leaves the reader to infer the appropriate conclusions from the scene, regardless of whether the narrator makes the same inferences. Such moments can occur even when the homodiegetic narrator is, like Nick, fairly self-conscious.[4] (2) The character may function as a mask through which the implied author speaks. That is, a narrator's character may be functional to the extent that it provides a persona through which the implied author can express his or her beliefs about the world. In some cases, the persona may actually be less important than the character's experiences, but again the same effect is achieved: the implied author's beliefs take on a particular significance because they are expressed through this particular consciousness at this particular point in the narrative.

These conclusions suggest that it would be helpful to subsume the question about Nick's reliability within a larger account of the relationships between his narratorial and his character functions. All five of the relationships I've just described occur in Fitzgerald's novel: authoritative narration with character backgrounded, limited privilege based on location relative to the scene, effaced narration with character foregrounded, unreliable narration, and mask narration. Before I demonstrate this point by analyzing specific instances of Nick's narration, it will be helpful to consider the rhetorical task Fitzgerald has set for himself in *The Great Gatsby*.

Consider some of the novel's distinctive features. The story is about a self-made man, not long on scruples, who tries to recapture the love of a woman from a higher class, seems to be on the verge of success, but then fails. His effort entangles him in the lives of the woman's husband, his mistress, and the mistress's husband. This entanglement leads to the self-made man's murder at the hands of the mistress's husband through the betrayal of the woman he loves. The narration is by a young Midwesterner, distantly related to the woman, living, for much of the story, next door to the self-made man and trying to find his own way in the world. The narrative begins with a short, though somewhat cryptic, summary of the narrator's conclusions about the events he is to narrate: "No—Gatsby turned out all right at the end; it is what preyed on Gatsby, what foul dust floated in the wake of his dreams that temporarily closed out my interest in the abortive sorrows and short-winded relations of men" (6–7). But then this Gatsby remains a shadowy presence until the narrative is almost one-third complete, and our perceptions of him are almost always filtered through the narrator's consciousness. The events surrounding Gatsby's death are not rendered directly but are rather pieced together after the fact by the narrator—or simply presented as speculation. The narrative closes with the narrator's philosophical meditation linking Gatsby's quest and the dream underlying it to the quests and dreams fueling the exploration of the New World.

This combination of features, I submit, is not a very promising package: the action is tawdry, the central characters neither admirable nor sympathetic, the narration puzzling, and the ending bordering on the ludicrous. Yet, though the narrative is not without its problems (nor its detractors), Fitzgerald designs *The Great Gatsby* according to a logic that is not evident in my list of its unpromising central elements. This logic is to move the audience's understanding of Gatsby along two parallel but quite different tracks. The first track is one that asks the audience to recognize the serious limits—indeed, the social and ethical deficiencies—of Gatsby's actual dreams: to be the self-made man who by force of wealth and personal charm will win back the heart (and body) of Daisy Fay Buchanan. The second track is one that asks the audience to recognize that there is a potential in Gatsby, rooted in the grandness and audacity of his dream and his way of pursuing it, that remains in its way an object of wonder, despite the limits of the actual dream. If the narrative works for us, it works because we feel the pull between these two tracks of our engagement with Gatsby. This narrative logic and the experience it offers readers clearly partakes of the American ideal of individualism that is so bound up with the myth of the American dream and that is therefore subject to serious ideological critique.[5] I share many of the reservations of those who find the novel's ideology problematic, but my interest here is on how Fitzgerald seeks to make the narrative logic work. The answer, I think, lies in the multiple functions of Nick.

There are two main features of Nick's functions within the novel that provide the key to the effectiveness of the narrative logic. First, although the beginning establishes him in a fixed position after the events he is about to narrate, the rest of the narrative shows him in a developing relationship to the ongoing events. Consequently, part of the significance of Gatsby's quest can by seen by Fitzgerald's audience in how it affects Nick as character. Indeed, some such effect is absolutely necessary if the audience is going to recognize that there is something in Gatsby beyond the particular form of his dreams. For this part of the narrative, it makes sense that occasionally Nick's function as narrator will be effaced and his function as character will be foregrounded.

Second, as noted above, Nick performs a wide range of narratorial functions. Some facts about Gatsby's life must be solid and indisputable so that he can be a genuine presence for the audience; for this reason,

Nick needs to be able to offer authoritative narration. At the same time, some parts of Gatsby's life need to be left in shadow so that he can seem, at times, to be larger than life and so that the audience's focus can shift from the specific facts (did he help Wolfsheim fix the World Series?) to the larger picture: he has gotten all his money, regardless of the means, in order to win back Daisy. For this reason, Nick's privilege must frequently be limited. Furthermore, if Nick is to be affected by Gatsby's life, then one way to show that effect is to show how Nick moves from occasional unreliability, in the sense that he expresses norms that are not in accord with Fitzgerald's, to reliability. Finally, given the difficulty of making Gatsby seem greater than his particular dreams, Fitzgerald occasionally wants to be able to use Nick as a mask that he can speak through. To flesh out these points, let me turn to specific examples of each of these narrator-character relationships.

As I have argued above, the authoritative narration in the scene in Michaelis's garage is crucial. Without this scene, we do not have the information necessary to piece together either the events surrounding Myrtle Wilson's death or those leading to George Wilson's murder of Gatsby and subsequent suicide. But Fitzgerald's employment of the paralepsis presents all that information with marvelous efficiency. This process, furthermore, draws us further into the drama of Gatsby's final hours. But its effect also needs to be seen in combination with Fitzgerald's shift back not just to Nick's limited-privilege narration when he tells of Wilson's movements before Gatsby's murder but to a passage of paralipsis: "By half past two he was in West Egg where he asked some one the way to Gatsby's house. So by that time he knew Gatsby's name" (168). We learn later that Nick is withholding his knowledge that Wilson has learned Gatsby's name from Tom Buchanan, a delayed revelation that makes Daisy's betrayal of Gatsby and Tom's callousness toward Wilson, Myrtle, and Gatsby all the more chilling. This revelation deepens the gulf between Gatsby's actual dreams and the potential in his capacity for dreaming. And all these effects are a result of Fitzgerald's realization of the protean possibilities of a witness-narrator such as Nick.

Nick is unreliable—indeed, perhaps *most* unreliable—in his statement that "I am one of the few honest people I have ever known." The statement itself seems to invite doubt: what are you trying to hide by professing your honesty? Nick offers it as a way to explain why he doesn't move faster in his relationship with Jordan Baker: he cannot, he says, get seriously involved with Jordan when he still has a "vague understanding" with a woman back home. Yet in describing his relationship with that woman, he tells us that he is far from honest with her: "I'd been writing letters once a week and signing them 'Love, Nick,' and all I could think of was how, when that certain girl played tennis, a faint mustache of perspiration appeared on her upper lip" (64). Furthermore, Nick's declaration about his own honesty comes after his testimony about Jordan's dishonesty not making "any difference" to him (63). This hardly seems like a logical preliminary to his own declaration.

In addition to showing that Nick does not know himself as well as he thinks, this unreliable narration requires us to puzzle over his relationship with Jordan, the way that he is both strongly attracted to her and simultaneously reluctant to get involved. We can see, in a way that he cannot, that Jordan represents for him the life of the wealthy Easterner and that he is both attracted to and frightened by what that life represents. As the narrative develops, Nick gives in more and more to the attraction—until he sees what happens to Gatsby. By ending his relationship with Jordan, Nick signals the end of his interest in succeeding in New York, the end of his desire to move in the same circles with the Buchanans. Gatsby has no effect on anyone except Nick, and the effect is not exactly heroic. But Nick's admission to himself of his own problematic values is based largely on his recognition of the gap between Gatsby's potential and his actual life. This effect of Gatsby's life is crucial for the audience's acceptance of the view that he is potentially better than his particular dreams.[6]

Nick's visit to Wolfsheim provides an excellent example of a scene where Nick the narrator recedes into the background and Nick the character becomes all-important.

> "Now he's dead," I said after a moment. "You were his closest friend, so I know you'll want to come to his funeral this afternoon."
>
> "I'd like to come."
>
> "Well, come then."
>
> The hair in his nostrils quivered slightly and as he shook his head his eyes filled with tears.

> "I can't do it—I can't get mixed up in it," he said.
>
> "There's nothing to get mixed up in. It's all over now."
>
> "When a man gets killed, I never like to get mixed up in it in any way. I keep out. When I was a young man, it was different—if a friend of mine died, no matter how, I stuck with them to the end. You may think that's sentimental but I mean it—to the bitter end."
>
> I saw that for some reason of his own he was determined not to come, so I stood up. (179–80)

Fitzgerald presents the scene without Nick's commentary, and it is not at all clear that Nick makes the inferences about himself and Wolfsheim that Fitzgerald invites the audience to make. Nick sees that Wolfsheim is determined not to come, but we see that Wolfsheim cries crocodile tears. Nick acknowledges his investment in doing something for Gatsby after his death, but we see that this investment is deeper than he admits. If Gatsby represents everything for which he has always had unaffected scorn, what does Wolfsheim represent? Yet here he is, trying to convince Wolfsheim to do the decent thing and attend the funeral. Again the scene testifies to Gatsby's effect on Nick, to Nick's desire to have someone recognize something important about Gatsby's life, and in this sense, it points to Nick's motivation for telling the tale. Paradoxically, then, the semi-erasure of Nick's narrational filter and the foregrounding of his actions as character in this scene also link up with his larger role as narrator of Gatsby's story.

Finally, the famous last paragraphs of the novel provide the best example of Nick functioning as Fitzgerald's mask.

> gradually I became aware of the old island here that flowered once for Dutch sailors' eyes—a fresh, green breast of the new world. Its vanished trees, the trees that had made way for Gatsby's house, had once pandered in whispers to the last and greatest of all human dreams; for a transitory enchanted moment man must have held his breath in the presence of this continent, compelled into an aesthetic contemplation he neither understood nor desired, face to face for the last time in history with something commensurate to his capacity for wonder.
>
> And as I sat there, brooding on the old unknown world, I thought of Gatsby's wonder when he first picked out the green light at the end of Daisy's dock. He had come a long way to this blue

> lawn and his dream must have seemed so close that he could hardly fail to grasp it. He did not know that it was already behind him, somewhere back in that vast obscurity beyond the city, where the dark fields of the republic rolled on under the night.
>
> Gatsby believed in the green light, the orgastic future that year by year recedes before us. It eluded us then, but that's no matter—tomorrow we will run faster, stretch out our arms farther. . . . And one fine morning—
>
> So we beat on, boats against the current, borne back ceaselessly into the past. (189)

It matters that Nick, who has witnessed the last days of Gatsby's life and whose own life has been changed in the process, speaks these words. But like Frederic Henry's "If people bring so much courage to this world" utterance in *A Farewell to Arms,* this passage is given its shape and point more by the beliefs of the implied author than by the character of the narrator. What is striking about these beliefs is their mixture of romanticism and cynicism. Although the object of the sailors' dream is far more exalted than Gatsby's, although it is, indeed, "commensurate" with man's capacity for wonder, the sailors' dream has much the same outcome as Gatsby's: despite its intensity and magnificence, it is doomed to disappointment. In this passage, then, Fitzgerald speaks through Nick in an effort to convey his authorial vision of the strange amalgam of wonder and futility that defines the romantic dreamer. Fitzgerald leaves us to contemplate this mixture as a final reflection on Gatsby, on Nick—and, if we have been caught by the narrative, on ourselves.

6

Sharing Secrets

This chapter foregrounds the ethical dimension of reading through a meditation on reading "The Secret Sharer" as an experience of sharing secrets. This meditation leads to the hypothesis that the captain's narrative about his secret relationship with Leggatt itself contains a further secret, an implicit communication "whispered in the interstices of the narrative." I consider how an awareness of this secret transforms the understanding of the narrative, leading us to reconfigure the events the captain narrates. By looking for the secret in the captain's discourse, I am again postulating that discourse can simultaneously be story, that discourse can function not just as an important angle of vision on the action but also as part of the action itself. But determining the captain's secret and recognizing how its presence transforms the story he tells is only part of my concern here. I am even more interested in accounting for the ethics of entering the captain's and Conrad's audiences. If to read this narrative is, both metaphorically and literally, to become a secret sharer with the captain, then how does this secret sharing influence the ethical dimension of our reading experience? In answering the question, this essay also reconsiders the relations among authorial agency, textual phenomena, and readerly subjectivity. Rather than emphasizing the authorial audience's position in reconstructing an author's purpose, I argue for a more dynamic, synergistic model, one in which the lines between authorial agency, textual phenomena, and readerly subjectivity are not easily distinguishable.

> "As long as I know that you understand. . . . But of course you do. It's a great satisfaction to have got somebody to understand. You seem to have been there on purpose. . . . It's very wonderful."
>
> —Leggatt to the captain (135)

Reading Secrets: Ethical Questions

"The Secret Sharer": Conrad's alliterative title plays peekaboo with any reader who pauses to puzzle over its meanings. Pondering matters of event and character, we can see the following significations emerge: a secret shared; a sharer who is secret; and a sharer who reveals a secret.[1] As a title, "The Secret Sharer" creates for the reader the expectation that the secret, the sharing, and the sharers will all be identified before story's end.[2] Pondering matters of telling and listening, we can glimpse other, less immediately apparent significations: "The Secret Sharer" names the narrator, the narratee, and, indeed, Conrad and each of his readers. To narrate is to tell secrets; to read narrative is to share in them. "The Secret Sharer," c'est moi—et lui et vous.

These significations about telling and listening (or writing and reading) in turn call attention to the ethical dimensions of Conrad's narrative, both in its events and in its telling and reception.[3] Secrets may be about matters honorable, shameful, or indifferent, may be revelations of virtue, vice, or mediocrity, but, regardless of their content, secrets always have some ethical valence. Furthermore, the keeping or telling of secrets also always has an ethical dimension. We keep or tell secrets to inform or mislead, to titillate or ingratiate, to submit or dominate, repel or seduce, protect or hurt.

In the case of Conrad's narrative, the ethical dimensions of the action are everywhere apparent: the reader's involvement in "The Secret Sharer" is built on the conflict between the captain's responsibility to his crew and his decisions to keep Leggatt's existence a secret and to help him escape. The ethical dimensions of the telling, by contrast, are not so immediately evident. Strikingly, the occasion of the captain's narration is left unspecified. Conrad does not have him indicate any motive for his telling, identify his narratee, or locate himself in space. Even the one marker of the narrative situation Conrad supplies—its temporal location—lacks precision: the narrator comments that "at this distance of years" (123) he cannot be sure that "Archbold" was the name of the *Sephora's* captain, but the distance is not measured by a specific number. Furthermore, although the narrator is very aware of himself as an actor and frequently comments on his behavior, that commentary almost never comes from his vantage point at the time of the narration.[4]

The unspecified occasion of narration is all the more noteworthy because Conrad has, by 1909,[5] already created several works in which the occasion and audience of the first-person narrator are explicitly defined—and made crucial to the effect of the whole narrative. To take just the two most celebrated cases, in *Heart of Darkness* and *Lord Jim,* Conrad includes information about Marlow, Marlow's audience, and the occasions of Marlow's narrations in order to influence substantially the reader's understanding of Marlow's investment in the experiences of Kurtz and Jim. Indeed, our overall response to these texts involves the interaction of our responses to Marlow's narratives about Kurtz and Jim with our responses to Conrad's narratives about Marlow. In other words, by the time he is writing "The Secret Sharer," Conrad has already demonstrated that the technique of specifying narrative situations can extend the meaning and power of some narratives far beyond the meaning and power attendant upon the straight narration of their primary sequences of events.

The material of "The Secret Sharer" certainly seems ripe for such treatment: a young and uncertain captain, trying to establish himself with a suspicious crew, harbors and protects a fugitive from justice because the fugitive seems to be his second self; through his determination to help the fugitive escape and through a surprising assist from the fugitive, he manages to establish his authority with the crew, the ship, and himself. If Conrad had, say, employed Marlow to pass on the captain's story to a group of veteran British seamen, Conrad could have made this tale *Lord Jim Revisited,* with Jim's traits split between the captain and Leggatt, with Marlow once again posing the ethical questions about what it means to be "one of us" and with Conrad's audience attending to the interaction between the captain's narrative and Marlow's quest for its meaning.

Why, then, would Conrad eschew the approach that he had employed so successfully before? What effects and purposes are likely to be guiding his choice of this different technique, which leaves the occasion and audience of the narration unspecified? More particularly, in this narrative of secrets, what is the relationship between the ethical dimensions of the captain's story and the ethical dimensions of his telling? How does a reader's effort to participate in sharing the secrets of "The Secret Sharer" implicate him or her in the ethical dimensions of the story and its telling? Just what is at stake for us when we try to be for Conrad what the captain is for Leggatt—the wonderful somebody who understands?

Detecting Secrets

Let us begin to answer by looking at Conrad's structuring of the action. Conrad evokes and guides the authorial and the narrative audiences' initial interests through his intertwining of two main instabilities: (1) The uneasy relationship between the captain and the crew. In command of his first ship, the young captain must prove both to his older, initially suspicious crew and to himself that he is a capable commander. As he says early in his account, "I wondered how far I should turn out faithful to that ideal conception of one's own personality every man sets up for himself secretly" (107). (2) The uncertainty of whether he will be able to keep Leggatt's presence a secret from the crew, from the captain of the *Sephora,* from everyone.

Conrad's intertwining of these instabilities heightens the suspense we feel in the narrative and authorial audiences, because they pull in opposite directions. The more the captain devotes himself to setting the crew at ease by working closely with them and otherwise following the conventions of command, the more he increases the chances for Leggatt's exposure. The more he gives in to his desires to protect Leggatt and his secret, the more he increases his crew's doubts about his ability. Reading the final episode is so intense partly because the two instabilities fully converge there, raising the conflict to its highest point. As the captain brings the boat near the shore of Koh-ring, he simultaneously risks the two things he has been struggling mightily to maintain: Leggatt's secret existence and the effective command of the ship. Conrad's resolution is wonderfully efficient and—to the authorial audience—satisfying. The captain chooses to endanger the crew, the ship, and his own future for the sake of Leggatt; when he manages, with the assist from the hat he had given Leggatt, to turn the ship in time and to pick up the land breezes, the very dangerous course he has taken becomes, in the eyes of the crew, incontrovertible evidence of his ability and his courage.

Even as Conrad's structuring of the action evokes this sequence of instability, suspense, and satisfaction, his narrative discourse deepens and complicates our involvement in the captain's story. As noted above, although Conrad indicates that the captain is looking back on his earlier experience, the captain only rarely speaks from his perspective at the time of the narration. As we have seen in chapters 3 and 4, this method of autodiegetic narration frequently accompanies unreliable narration, that is, a telling in which a significant gap exists between the values and/or the understanding of the narrator and narrative audience and those of the implied author and authorial audience. Although Conrad does not leave any clear signals that his norms are markedly different from the captain's,[6] both the narrative method and the focus on secrets invite us to ask whether there is more to this narrative than initially appears. More specifically, the technique and the subject matter encourage us to look for an important subtext, some secret whispered in the interstices of the narrative, perhaps even one that the captain himself may not be fully aware of. In other words, the technique and the subject matter authorize the authorial audience to search for a subtext.[7]

The search yields two possibilities I want to consider here: (1) the captain has been having hallucinations, and Leggatt exists only as his fantasy; (2) the captain's fellow feeling for Leggatt arises less from their common background and values than from their mutual sexual attraction.[8] The first possibility, hinted at in the captain's question of whether Leggatt is "visible to eyes other than mine" (134), is intriguing because it suggests a way of rereading the captain's psychology. Rather than a reasonably healthy man facing a difficult set of circumstances, he becomes a seriously unhealthy one whose anxieties about his new command lead him to invent an imaginary friend whom he fully understands and whom he can shelter and protect. On this view, then, the narrative is a study in the development, complication, and final resolution of this anxiety.

This hypothesis, however, is difficult to sustain because it must explain away too much recalcitrant evidence. The greatest recalcitrance is provided by Archbold's visit with its independent confirmation of Leggatt's existence and of the main lines of his story. Other, more minor, evidence includes the steward's hearing Leggatt's movement at a time when the captain is away from his cabin and the appearance of the captain's white hat floating in the sea after Leggatt leaves. Of course, it would be possible to argue that these events are all part of the captain's fantasy, that the captain has used Archbold's visit as the basis for his creation of Leggatt, and that after the event he has imaginatively re-created the version of that visit—and virtually everything else—that we get. In a reader response criticism that emphasized the reader's role in creating the meaning of texts, these arguments might be sufficient to allow the hypothesis to stand. Within a rhetorical approach, however, some significant problems arise. Since the technique gives us the captain's experience as he felt it at the time of the action, how do we explain—without even a covert clue from Conrad—that the captain encounters Leggatt before he encounters Archbold? More generally, the problem with this hypothesis is that it makes the subtext almost a complete secret, something that is pointed to only by the captain's single moment of doubt, a moment which on other accounts is explained as a vivid sign of the strain the captain is feeling.

By contrast, the hypothesis that the authorial audience is supposed to recognize the secret of the homosexual attraction is quite persuasive. The text abounds in evidence—some covert, some not so covert—that invites us to catch on to the secret. The captain's very first glimpse of Leggatt is charged with a sexual electricity: "I saw at once something elongated and pale floating very close to the ladder. Before I could form a guess a faint flash of phosphorescent light, which seemed to issue suddenly from the naked body of a man, flickered in the sleeping water with the elusive, silent play of summer lightning in the night sky" (110). Other elements of the scene also invite attention to its sexual undertones, even as the surface of the text attends more to Leggatt's apparent rising from the dead, his transformation from corpse into living man. The captain's gaze follows the line of Leggatt's naked body from foot to neck: "With a gasp I saw revealed to my stare a pair of feet, the long legs, a broad livid back immersed right up to the neck in a greenish cadaverous glow" (110). When the captain thinks that the naked man is a "headless corpse," he involuntarily drops the cigar he is smoking out of his mouth: a loss of potency and heat. When he realizes that the man is still alive, the heat returns: "the horrid, frost-bound sensation which had gripped me about the chest" passed off (110).[9]

More generally, the captain's consistent gazing upon Leggatt's body suggests that a likely source of their "mysterious communication" is their mutual, unspoken recognition of their attraction: "I, . . . coming back on deck, saw the naked man from the sea sitting on the main hatch, glimmering white in the darkness, his elbows on his knees and his head in his hands" (111). Later the captain says of Leggatt that "with his face nearly hidden, he must have looked exactly as I used to look in that bed. I gazed upon my other self for a while" (120). Furthermore, the captain arranges matters so that he must bathe before Leggatt's gaze: "I took a bath and did most of my dressing, splashing, and whistling softly for the steward's edification, while the secret sharer of my life stood drawn up bolt upright in that little space" (122). After this description, we may feel compelled to ask: If he did *most* of the dressing, splashing, and whistling for the steward's edification, for whom did he do the rest of it?[10]

This evidence speaks strongly of the captain's attraction, but what of Leggatt's? The narrative perspective necessarily limits our access to his thoughts and feelings, but his part in the "mysterious communication" between the two, especially his confidence that the captain would understand everything, suggests that he too feels the unspoken bond. And one of his early speeches strongly suggests that the attraction is mutual: referring to his naked arrival at the ladder of the *Sephora,* he tells the captain, "I didn't mind being looked at [by you]. I-I liked it. And then you speaking to me so quietly—as if you had expected me—made me hold on a little longer" (119).

As the story continues, the evidence for the secret becomes less covert. The first night, the captain reports that "we stood leaning over my bed-place, whispering side by side, with our dark heads together and our backs to the door" (115). Later, he tells us that at night "I would smuggle him into my bed-place, and we would whisper together, with the regular footfalls of the watch passing and repassing over our heads. It was an infinitely miserable time" (131). Why "infinitely miserable"? Perhaps because of sexual frustration. Perhaps their intimacy stopped at whispering, for fear that other expressions of it might become loud enough to alert the watch and expose them both. The ellipsis in Leggatt's comment about the captain's wonderful understanding that I use as my epigraph contains this description: "And in the same whisper, as if we two whenever we talked had to say things to each other which were not fit for the world to hear" (135): what is this but the love which dare not speak its name? Finally, the captain's overt description of their final communication—significantly nonverbal—is charged with the language of desire: "our hands met gropingly, lingered united in a steady, motionless clasp for a second. . . . No word was breathed by either of us when they separated" (140).

The hypothesis encounters no significant recalcitrance, and attending to this subtext has significant consequences for our response. As flesh-and-blood readers, we have our own, sometimes highly charged, responses to representations of homosexuality, responses that range from homophobia to celebratory identification. Second, as members of the authorial audience, attending to this secret alters our understanding of the action. Part of the captain's anxiety about his acceptance by the crew now becomes anxiety over whether they will suspect his sexual orientation. Archbold's talk about why he never liked Leggatt can now be seen as rooted in—may even be a coded way of voicing—Archbold's suspicion that Leggatt was homosexual. The captain's initial negative response to Leggatt's request that they maroon him on one of the islands becomes the response of the selfish, unfulfilled lover. His need to take the ship as close to Koh-ring as possible then becomes his way of atoning for this selfishness. Leggatt's words about knowing that the captain understands come to encompass the whole situation—why Leggatt decided to come on board, why he confided in the captain, why their bond is so strong, why they don't speak about it overtly or act on it differently, why he must leave. The captain's giving Leggatt his hat becomes a substitute for giving him a ring or any other token of remembrance and identification that one lover gives to another. Leaving the hat in the water becomes

Leggatt's way of giving the ring back and a powerful symbol of their unconsummated relationship: the good that they do each other does not depend on possession.

The ethics of attending to the secret of homosexual attraction are fairly complex.[11] The narrative's treatment of the relationship certainly valorizes it: the action is structured so that the authorial audience's pleasure and satisfaction in the story depend on acceptance and approval of the bond between the captain and Leggatt. Furthermore, the uncharacteristically triumphant ending sends a strong signal about how this story endorses that bond and the actions to which it leads. And, as I suggested earlier, Conrad makes the authorial audience yet another "secret sharer"—in the sense of sharing in the secret and in the sense of sharing it secretly. That is, we not only share the secret but do so without any explicit revelation of it. It is debatable whether the captain realizes that his narration reveals the secret. This point is worth dwelling on not for the sake of trying to settle the question but for the sake of assessing the captain's self-understanding after the events. If he is deliberately conveying the secret to readers astute enough to hear it, then he becomes more self-aware and sophisticated as a narrator than his silence about the narrative occasion suggests. If, however, he is inadvertently revealing the secret, then we recognize that although he may have passed a critical test of his captaincy, he still needs to face other fundamental questions of identity.

Conrad's relation to the homosexual secret is even harder to pin down. If we opt for the understanding of the captain as in control of his narrative, we will also see Conrad as carefully in control behind the captain. If, however, we see the captain's revelation as unwitting, we may decide that Conrad has planned it that way or that Conrad himself is not fully aware of the homosexual subtext. In fact, articulating the secret and specifying the evidence for it helps to illuminate one of the fault lines in rhetorical reader response: the one running between the authorial and the flesh-and-blood audiences. On the one hand, the evidence points to a design on Conrad's part that the authorial audience needs to discern; indeed, without such a pattern of evidence, I would not suggest that this secret is a plausible one. On the other hand, I can't help wondering how much my perception of this secret is a consequence of my historical moment, in particular, the way in which the gay studies movement has made me and numerous other academic readers especially attuned to representations of same-sex desire. Is the secret constructed by the implied Conrad or the flesh-and-blood critic? I don't fully know. Furthermore, there is a sense in which, within the rhetorical approach, it is not all that important to know. When the situated subjectivity of the reader encounters the otherness of the text, the analyst cannot always definitively locate the boundaries that mark off flesh-and-blood and authorial audiences—or more generally, reader, text, and author—from each other. The synergy among these different elements of the rhetorical transaction is precisely what the rhetorical approach wants to acknowledge.

In any case, Conrad's strategy of suggesting that there is a secret in the captain's narration without calling explicit attention to any particular secret can be seen as a sign of his confidence in his readers. On this view, Conrad is not only complimenting his audience but subtly collaring us to share his positive view of the captain and Leggatt.

Nevertheless, even this very positive construction of the ethical dimension of reading this story is complicated by the very reliance upon secrets. If homosexuality must remain secret, how can it be genuinely valorized? To participate, as the story asks us to do, in the secretiveness surrounding homosexuality is to be complicit with the forces who would repress homosexuality entirely. For this reason, I find it hard not to become a partially resistant reader of Conrad's text. But the nature of that resistance is itself further complicated by other responses that arise from Conrad's technique for representing the dynamic between the captain and Leggatt.

Guilty Secrets

As some readers have no doubt already noticed, there has been a conspicuous absence from my discussion to this point: I have not said anything about Leggatt's taking the life of another man. I use the phrase "taking the life" rather than "murdering" because Conrad's treatment of the event allows for our reasonable doubt. Leggatt tells his own story, making it clear that the man died at his hands, but he does not take full responsibility for the death:

> We closed just as an awful sea made for the ship. All hands saw it coming and took to the rigging, but I had him by the throat and went on shaking him like a rat, the men above us yelling, "Look out! look out!" Then a crash as if the sky had fallen on my head. They say that for over ten minutes hardly anything was to be seen of the ship. . . . It was a miracle that they found us, jammed together behind the forebits. It's clear that I meant business, because I was holding him by the throat still when they picked us up. (113)

The most striking feature of Conrad's handling of this event is that the captain never explicitly says how he thinks about it and never directs the narratee how to think about it. In reading the report of his conversation with Archbold, we can infer that he has been unwilling to admit Leggatt's role in the man's death. "Don't you think," he suggests, "that the heavy sea . . . might have killed the man?" But Archbold is having none of that: "Good God! . . . The sea! No man killed by the sea ever looked like that." And to demonstrate, "he advanced his head close to mine and thrust his tongue out at me so suddenly that I couldn't help starting back" (124). Though the captain starts back here, he never reaches the place where he assesses Leggatt's conduct for himself or the reader.

Instead, he assumes that the narratee will share his acceptance of it, his willingness to think that Leggatt's ending another man's life is less important than Leggatt's current plight and less important than Leggatt's bonding with him. Since the narratee is unspecified and since Conrad does not clearly depict Leggatt as murderer, we are also likely to feel—as both flesh-and-blood and authorial readers—the pull of the captain's assumptions. To be the secret sharer of this narrative is to adopt these assumptions, at least for the moments when we project ourselves into the narratee's position; to be the secret sharer of the narrative is also to endorse the captain's plan to protect Leggatt. It is, I find, a rather uncomfortable ethical position.

It is uncomfortable because even while we feel the pull of the captain's assumptions as we read from the narratee's position, we remain aware of other complex considerations in the authorial audience position. On the one hand, the captain's assumptions are defensible: Leggatt's plight is serious and the mutual understanding he and the captain share is impressive. On the other hand, the assumptions are questionable: Leggatt may be a murderer, and the captain's efforts to keep him hidden clearly interfere with the captain's performance of his primary responsibilities. In this way, hiding Leggatt's existence becomes the captain's *guilty* secret, a guilt made all the more complicated by the captain's unspoken homosexual attraction. Indeed, Conrad is presenting us with a situation in which the two main internal threats to a "proper" company of sailors—homosexuality and murder—become located, albeit not clearly realized, in the captain's second self. Once we recognize this dimension of the situation, the captain's identification with Leggatt puts the captain in an even greater conflict with his responsibility to the crew. Although the captain seems in one way to have no trouble with the ethics of his behavior, he and we also know that the captain could not successfully defend himself to his crew on ethical grounds. As readers, we become the sharers of the captain's guilty secret, with the added burden of not being sure we can justify it to ourselves. Moreover, once Conrad makes us such secret sharers, once we are in this position of reading guilty secrets, we are at least temporarily in the uncomfortable position of living with them, carrying guilty secrets in our consciousnesses.

The increasing intensity of the narrative, then, depends not just on Conrad's skillful complication and then convergence of the instabilities, not just on our increasing recognition of the subtextual secret, but also on the complication of the reader's feelings of sharing and living with guilty secrets. Conrad's handling of the visit from Archbold and the crew of the *Sephora* nicely illustrates the point. The key instability in the scene is whether the captain can successfully protect Leggatt, and the captain's narration is primarily concerned with that. At the same time, details such as the exchange between the captain and the first mate emphasize that Leggatt is, indeed, a secret to feel guilty about. The mate comments that the story he has heard about Leggatt "beats all these tales we hear about murders in Yankee ships" (128). He also reports the crew's reaction to the idea that Leggatt might be hiding on the ship: "Our chaps took offense. 'As if we would harbor a thing like that,' they said. 'Wouldn't you like to look for him in our coal hole?' Quite a tiff" (128). At this point, the tension is running high between our efforts to read from the narratee position, where we remain sympathetic to the captain, and from the authorial audience position, where we recognize the responsibility to the crew. If the suggestion that Leggatt is on the ship provokes this reaction among "our chaps," we can only imagine what actually discovering him would provoke. Even as we recognize that the crew's position is problematic in its assumption of Leggatt's guilt, the mate's comments also function to underline the captain's need for secrecy and to deepen the guilt associated with the secret.

By the time the captain is bringing the boat to the shore of Koh-ring, we are being pulled in different directions: toward compassion for Leggatt and hope for the captain, toward complicitous guilt that the captain is recklessly endangering the ship, putting his own concerns above those of the crew and the ship. These feelings are mingled with the fear that he will end up grounding the ship. Fear, hope, guilt all come together in the moment where the captain violently speaks to and shakes the first mate—a moment that, as many critics note (see especially Leiter), puts the captain in essentially the position occupied by Leggatt during the crisis on the *Sephora.* As the captain shouts at the mate, our feelings may move us to be shouting to ourselves: Shake some sense into the mate; no, don't touch him at all; bring the ship all the way in; how can you value the secret over the ship; listen to the mate; forget the mate.

In this context, Conrad's successful resolution of the instabilities brings a welcome release from the conflict of our feelings. The release seems all the more satisfying when we reflect that the captain now never has to reveal his secret; the torment that made him feel as if he "had come creeping quietly as near insanity as any man who has not actually gone over the border" (134) is permanently over. But further reflection brings back some uneasiness. For some reason, the captain has decided to reveal the secret—and to some extent relive the torment—by telling the story. Our release is not thereby ruined, but the fragility of the captain's release is underlined. So, too, is the captain's great good fortune in having events work out this way: the ending could so easily have been different. But after such a reading experience, after such discomfort and such welcome release, that is a conclusion we may want, at least for a while, to keep secret.[12]

Part Three

Audiences and Ideology

7

Narratee, Narrative Audience, and Second-Person Narration: How I—and You?—Read Lorrie Moore's "How"

This chapter is the most technical one in the book, focusing on clarifying the concepts of audience I have been using. More particularly, the essay uses the complex addresses of second-person narrative (Lorrie Moore's "How" is my example) as the framework within which to examine the relation between rhetorical theory's concept of narrative audience and narratology's concept of narratee. I argue that the two concepts are not competing but complementary, and I suggest a way of redefining narrative audience to reflect this complementarity. The multiplication of distinctions in this essay does raise the broader practical question of when the terministic screen of rhetorical analysis may become too thick, may, that is, become less of a visual aid and more of an obstruction. Do we always need to distinguish among narrative audience, narratee, ideal narrative audience, authorial audience, and flesh-and-blood audience, when we are focusing on questions of address? No, because in many narratives the differences are nonexistent or negligible. At the same time, however, an awareness of the different roles and of the different kinds of relations between them does provide an important means of explaining the complexity of some narrative discourse, especially in second-person narrative, which typically plays with these audience roles.

How Are You?

A voice addresses you. Not from clouds, a mountaintop, or a burning bush. From this page. It asks how you are and what you're up to. It is a friendly voice, though not immediately recognizable. You are unsure how to react. You have an impulse to shout out that you're fine, you're reading, you'd be grateful not to be disturbed. But you also don't want to be rude, so you just say, "OK" and "Studying second-person narration." The voice wants to know if you've read Lorrie Moore's *Self-Help*. Oh yes, you say—in fact, you've just begun reading an essay about it. The voice asks what the essay's about and if it's any good. You can't tell yet; so far the critic seems more interested in showing off his cleverness than in saying anything about Moore's book. If he doesn't quit, you'll quit reading. OK, says the voice, fair enough; I'll go mute, if you promise to stick around. In fact, to erase the sound of my voice, let's listen to Lorrie Moore's at the beginning of her short story "How":

> Begin by meeting him in a class, a bar, at a rummage sale. Maybe he teaches sixth grade. Manages a hardware store. Foreman at a carton factory. He will be a good dancer. He will have perfectly cut hair. He will laugh at your jokes.
>
> A week, a month, a year. Feel discovered, comforted, needed, loved, and start sometimes, somehow, to feel bored. When sad or confused, walk uptown to the movies. Buy popcorn. These things come and go. A week, a month, a year. (55)

Who Are You?

Perhaps this question would be better phrased as "Who are the YOUs?" to indicate that it refers to the second-person addressees in the two texts of the previous section (i.e., the text of this chapter and Moore's text) rather than to you who are now reading the words of this sentence. The rephrasing does sharpen the question, but, as we shall soon see, trying to answer it will call the logic that motivates the sharpening into doubt. The rephrased question depends on a clear and stable distinction between an intrinsic, textual "you"—a narratee-protagonist—and an extrinsic, extratextual "you"—a flesh-and-blood reader. Both texts, however, undermine the clarity and stability of the distinction. In the first text, the you addressed by the voice "from this page" is both textual and extratextual; it refers not only to the narratee-protagonist but also to you the actual reader.[1] The you who is unsure how to react may or may not be both narratee and actual reader—at that moment, the discourse is blurring the boundaries between them. At the end of the paragraph, the you addressed by the voice is again textual and extratextual, and the shift to homodiegetic narration (from "the voice" to "I") foregrounds that dual address.

Moreover, this play with the location (textual and/or extratextual) of the addressee is only part of the text's story of reading. When we read, "You are unsure how to react," and recognize that the you who is narratee-protagonist need not coincide with you the actual reader, another audience position becomes prominent: the observer role familiar to us in reading homodiegetic and heterodiegetic narration, the position from which we watch characters think, move, talk, act. In fact, what happens as we read "You are unsure how to react" is frequently an important dimension of reading second-person narration: When the second-person address to a narratee-protagonist both overlaps with and differentiates itself from an address to actual readers, those readers will simultaneously occupy the positions of addressee and observer. Furthermore, the fuller the characterization of the you, the more aware actual readers will be of their differences from that you, and thus the more fully they will move into the observer role—and the less likely that this role will overlap with the addressee position. In other words, the greater the characterization of the you, the more like a standard protagonist the you becomes, and, consequently, the more actual readers can employ their standard strategies for reading narrative. However, as recent commentators on second-person narration have consistently observed, most writers who employ this technique take advantage of the opportunity to move readers between the positions of observer and addressee and, indeed, to blur the boundaries between these positions (Fludernik, Kacandes, McHale, Richardson).[2] In short, it's not easy to say who you are.

The same difficulty is present in the opening section of Moore's story. Because Moore begins by narrating an event in which the actual reader is not directly involved—girl meets boy[3]—the observer role is initially more prominent. But in the second paragraph, where the gender of the you is not specified and the general trajectory of the you's experience is widely recognizable, the actual reader is likely to feel the pull of the addressee role. In fact, by showing the movement from observer to addressee rather than from addressee to observer, the passage illustrates how second-person narration almost always retains the potential to pull the actual reader back into the addressee role. Again, with Moore's text, the question "who are you?" does not have a clear and simple answer.

Although it is not easy to say who you are, watching you read can be highly instructive. In the rest of this essay, I would like to pursue that instruction by attending to the way in which the dynamics of second-person narration invite a reexamination of concepts of audience from two distinct but related traditions of narrative study: narratology's "narratee" and rhetorical theory's "narrative audience." My contention will be that each tradition has something to teach the other and that both concepts are necessary to understand the complexities of reading second-person narration. I shall then illustrate the usefulness of the two concepts in a rhetorical analysis of Moore's "How."

Narratee and Narrative Audience

Perhaps the most striking thing about the widely circulating concepts of narratee and narrative audience is that no one has carefully considered their relationship to each other. Are the concepts synonyms and the terms interchangeable? Does one concept subsume the other? If so, which is the more encompassing? Alternatively, are the two terms complementary, overlapping, or incompatible? What does their relationship tell us about the similarities and differences of structuralist narratology and the rhetorical theory of narrative? Second-person narration will help us answer these questions, but it will be helpful first to review the essays in which these two concepts were first formalized, Gerald Prince's "Introduction to the Study of the Narratee" (1973) and Peter J. Rabinowitz's "Truth in Fiction: A Re-examination of Audiences" (1977).

Prince's purpose is to call attention to a previously neglected link in the chain of narrative communication and to demonstrate that "narratees deserve to be studied" (8). He argues, in effect, that the logic of differentiating between authors, implied authors, and narrators applies as well to readers (or receivers), implied readers (or addressees), and narratees (or enunciatees).[4] The author addresses actual readers (receivers); the implied author the implied reader (addressee); and the narrator the narratee (enunciatee). Prince shows that a narrator's discourse frequently reveals evidence of the narratee's identity, even in narratives where there is no explicit address to the narratee. In characteristic structuralist fashion, Prince seeks to find the underlying commonality of diverse narratees and, as a result, proposes the idea of a "zero degree" narratee, an enunciatee with minimal positive traits: knowing the narrator's language, being able to infer presuppositions and consequences as they are reflected in that language, having an excellent memory. Different narratives will then assign further traits to their different narratees. In "The Narratee Revisited" (1985), however, Prince acknowledges that the approach through the zero degree violates Ockham's razor because, in effect, it describes virtually all narratees as deviations from a nonexistent standard. He therefore proposes to "specify all and only classes of signs particularizing any narratee, all and only signs of the 'you' in narrative discourse" (300).

More generally, Prince's structuralist narratology assumes that the narrative text is an object with a communicative purpose. In "Introduction," he attempts to locate the presence and delineate the functions of the narratee within that object. These functions, tellingly, are all instrumental, all part of the narratee's possible role in the communication: the narratee "constitutes a relay between the narrator and the reader, he helps establish the narrative framework, he serves to characterize the narrator, he emphasizes certain themes, he contributes to the development of the plot, he becomes the spokesman for the moral of the work" (23).

Rabinowitz, as his title suggests, frames his discussion of audiences as part of a larger inquiry into "truth in fiction," specifically an inquiry into how certain "facts" of a fictional narrative may be true at one level of reading but not at another. Indeed, my phrase "level of reading" turns out to be a synonym for "kind of audience." Rabinowitz posits four: (1) the actual or flesh-and-blood audience—you and me in both our idiosyncratic particularity and our socially constructed identities; (2) the authorial audience—the hypothetical ideal audience for whom the author designs the work, a design that includes assumptions about what that audience knows and believes; (3) the narrative audience—the "imaginary audience for which the narrator is writing" (127), an audience upon whom the narrator projects a set of beliefs and a body of knowledge; and (4) the ideal narrative audience—the audience "for which the narrator wishes he were writing" (134), the audience that accepts every statement of the narrator as true and reliable.

Rabinowitz emphasizes that readers take up places in the four audiences simultaneously and that this simultaneity is largely responsible for readers' complex relations to truth in fiction. When we enter the authorial and narrative audiences of, say, *Jane Eyre,* we find that there is no significant difference between the narrative audience and the ideal narrative audience and that there is some significant overlap in what the authorial audience and the narrative audience take to be true. Both of the latter two audiences, for example, operate with the same world maps; both attach the same social significance to a marriage between a master and a governess; both have some faith in the power of romantic love. But the audiences' beliefs also significantly diverge. Most obviously—and importantly—in the authorial audience we know that Jane is a fictional character narrating fictional events, whereas in the narrative audience, we assume that a historical personage is recounting her autobiography. Furthermore, it is arguable that each audience has a different view of the narrative's supernatural events, for example, Jane's hearing Rochester call her name, despite being miles away from him. In the authorial audience, we recognize that this event is possible only in fiction.[5] In the narrative audience, we accept the event as Jane does—wonderful and strange, but true. Indeed, the very fact that Jane does not try to convince skeptics in her audience is evidence that she assumes her audience will accept its truth.

Since the publication of "Truth in Fiction," rhetorical theorists have not found much practical use for the concept of "ideal narrative audience." In the afterword to the second edition of *The Rhetoric of Fiction* (1983), Wayne C. Booth adopts Rabinowitz's model minus the ideal narrative audience. Rabinowitz himself drops the category from his discussion of audiences in *Before Reading* (1987). In *Reading People, Reading Plots* (1989), I claim that "although the ideal narrative audience is a logical category of analysis, it has insufficient analytical payoff for me to want to invoke it" (141). Studying second-person narration and trying to understand the relation between the concepts of narratee and narrative audience has made me rethink that conclusion.

As the essays in this book indicate, the rhetorical approach is very concerned with the relation between narrative strategies and the activities of readers—in the way that what occurs on the levels of both story and discourse influences what readers know, believe, think, judge, and feel. In the case of, say, an author who employs an unreliable narrator, one important readerly activity is the rejection of the narrator's assumptions, knowledge, or values. (Many other activities will follow from this rejection, but those activities will vary from one narrative to the next.) In explaining the relation between narrative strategy and readerly activity, the rhetorical critic focuses on how an actual reader can recognize the signs of unreliability and infer the author's different assumptions, knowledge, or values. The key to the rhetorical transaction, then, is the gap between the narrator's assumptions about her audience and the author's assumptions about hers. In explaining the transaction, the rhetorical critic focuses on the way in which an actual reader can recognize that gap and the way in which that recognition is itself a part of the authorial audience's understanding of the narrative. In this way, the activity of the narrative audience is subsumed by the activity of the authorial, and differentiating between the narrative audience and the ideal narrative audience has seemed less important than attending to this subsumption. For example, in "Haircut," answering the question of whether Whitey's customer is Whitey's narrative or ideal narrative audience seems less important than recognizing that Whitey assumes he is an ideal audience and that Lardner assumes readers will recognize Whitey's moral obtuseness. By focusing on the difference between what Whitey expects his audience (ideally) to believe and what Lardner expects his audience to do with Whitey's expectations, the rhetorical critic erases the distinction between the narrative and the ideal narrative audiences. And, as this example of "Haircut" suggests, erasing the distinction means that all narrative audiences are ideal narrative audiences. So while the term *ideal narrative audience* has dropped out of use, the concept has not; it is more accurate to say that, in practice, Rabinowitz's third and fourth audiences have been conflated into the single category of narrative audience. As I turn to look more closely at the relation between this concept and Prince's concept of the narratee, I will suggest why I think it is useful to separate the two audiences once again.

Having seen all this about narratee and narrative audience, what can we conclude about the relationship between them? Rabinowitz, who naturally wants to distinguish his concept from Prince's, offers two answers in "Truth in Fiction." First, the "*narrataire* . . . is someone perceived by the reader as 'out there,' a separate person who often serves as a mediator between narrator and reader. The 'narrative audience,' in contrast, is a role which the text forces the reader to take on. I think that my analysis, centering on an activity on the part of the reader, more successfully explains *why* certain texts evoke certain responses" (127n). Second, the default position of "narrative audience" is not zero degree; instead, it is much closer to "actual audience." Rabinowitz puts it this way: the "narrative audience is much like ourselves, with our beliefs, prejudices, our hopes, fears, and expectations, and our knowledge of society and literature—unless there is some evidence (textual or historical) to the contrary" (128–29n).

These answers initially do more to sharpen the differences between the rhetorical approach and the structuralist one than to distinguish narratee from narrative audience. The key difference in the approaches is encapsulated by Rabinowitz's claims that his model "center[s] on an activity on the part of the reader" and that the narrative audience is "a role the text forces the reader to take on" (127n). *Activity, force,* and *experience* are key terms for the rhetorical theorists. Prince's model, by contrast, sees the text as a message and wants to identify the structural properties of that message. *Component, relay,* and *framework* are key terms for him and other narratologists. The rhetorical and the narratological approaches are not entirely incompatible—a text that exerts a force upon its reader is a communicative object of a certain kind. But the approaches are not exactly the same suit traveling under two different designer labels, and it is not surprising that they view the narrator's audience differently. As Rabinowitz says, Prince's narratee remains "out there," distinct from the actual reader; a narrative audience, by contrast, occupies some part of the actual reader's consciousness and, given the default position, the actual reader also gives traits to the narrative audience.

Confronting this difference, we might be tempted to decide that each concept is adequate within its own theoretical framework—that is, that the concepts overlap but are ultimately neither interchangeable nor in conflict. Consequently, such a response might go, when we want to do structuralist analysis, we should talk about narratees, and when we want to do rhetorical analysis, we should talk about narrative audiences. I would yield to this temptation if it were not for my reading of second-person narration. Second-person narration shows that the two concepts are ultimately complementary—and that both structuralist narratology and rhetorical theory need to recognize that complementarity. It shows further, as I mentioned above, that there are good reasons for reintroducing the distinction between the narrative and ideal narrative audiences.

Let us return to the basic definitions: a narratee is "someone whom the narrator addresses" (Prince, "Introduction," 7). A narrative audience is "the imaginary audience for which the narrator is writing" (Rabinowitz, "Truth," 127). An ideal narrative audience is "the audience for which the narrator wishes he were writing" (Rabinowitz, "Truth," 134). Let us also return to the beginning of Moore's story:

> Begin by meeting him in a class, a bar, at a rummage sale. Maybe he teaches sixth grade. Manages a hardware store. Foreman at a carton factory. He will be a good dancer. He will have perfectly cut hair. He will laugh at your jokes.
>
> A week, a month, a year. Feel discovered, comforted, needed, loved, and start sometimes, somehow, to feel bored. When sad or confused, walk uptown to the movies. Buy popcorn. These things come and go. A week, a month, a year. (55)

Is it adequate to say, as structuralist narratology would, that the unnamed you addressed by the narrator is the narratee and the protagonist, that the narrative's implied reader is different from this narratee, someone who infers from the narrator's address a larger cultural story about female-male relationships? Although this account gets at a good part of the communicative structure of the text, it is not fully adequate. It leaves out the way that the second-person address exerts pressure on the actual reader—even the male reader, as in the second paragraph—"to take on the role" of the narratee-protagonist as "you" experience(s) the ups and downs (especially the downs) of the relationship. In other words, continuing to assume that the narratee is a distinct character who is "out there" will mean not just that we prefer the structuralist to the rhetorical framework; it also will mean that the structuralist analysis will neglect a significant aspect of how the text attempts to communicate.

Perhaps, then, the rhetorical approach will be more adequate. It would say that in Moore's text the unnamed you addressed by the narrator is the narrative audience and the protagonist and that the authorial audience needs to infer the larger story about female-male relationships that Moore is telling.[6] This approach does enable us to account better for the effects that follow from "taking on the role" of the "you," but again the account is unsatisfactory according to its own criteria of explanatory adequacy. Equating the narrative audience with "you" leaves out the way in which we take on an observer role *within the fiction,* the way in which we recognize our difference from "you" and regard her as a person "out there" being addressed by the narrator. This observer role is different from the role we adopt as implied readers (or members of the authorial audience) because in the observer role we believe in the reality of the events. Some of "what happens to us" when we read "How" depends on our dual perspective inside the fiction, on the way that we step into and out of the enunciatee position, while we remain in the observer position and discover what the narrator assumes about our knowledge and beliefs in the enunciatee role. Furthermore, moving into the enunciatee role means that we move into the ideal narrative audience—the narrator tells us what we believe, think, feel, do—while in the observer role we evaluate our position in the ideal narrative audience.

If this analysis is correct, then structuralist narratology needs the concept of "narrative audience" to complement its concept of "narratee," and rhetorical theory needs the concept of "narratee" to complement its concept of "narrative audience." And both approaches need the further concept of "ideal narrative audience." For the sake of clarity and consistency, I propose that we adjust the definitions to reflect the complementarity. Let Prince's definition of narratee stand: the audience addressed by the narrator (the enunciatee). Let Rabinowitz's definition of narrative audience be modified: the actual audience's projection of itself into the observer role within the fiction. In taking on that role, we will always become believers in the reality of the fictional world; consequently, much of our emotional response to narrative derives from our participation in this role. Furthermore, let Rabinowitz's definition of the ideal narrative audience stand: "the audience for which the narrator wishes he were writing" ("Truth," 134). The ideal narrative audience may or may not coincide with the narratee, and the narrative audience may or may not find itself in accord with the assumptions of the ideal narrative audience. In "How," as in most second-person narration, the ideal narrative audience and the narratee coincide in the figure of "You," while the narrative audience fluctuates in its relation to "You"—sometimes coinciding (and feeling addressed), sometimes observing from some emotional, ethical, and/or psychological distance. In *Tristram Shandy,* however, Sterne orchestrates the relationships between narratee, ideal narrative audience, and narrative audience in a different way: he has Tristram correct the responses of particular narratees, thereby indicating the beliefs of the ideal narrative audience and offering the narrative audience the pleasure of observing Tristram's corrections without being implicated in them.

The situation of watching traditional drama clarifies the distinctions. For the mimetic illusion and the emotional force of a play to work, we must enter the observer position of the "narrative" ("dramatic"?) audience and believe in the reality of, say, Othello, Iago, and Desdemona. Indeed, the oft-discussed instances of people leaping upon the stage to stop the action are, in these terms, examples of what happens when we enter so deeply into the narrative audience position that we fail to maintain our simultaneous participation in the authorial audience. This role is clearly distinct from that of an enunciatee or "narratee," someone addressed by a speaker. However, in a soliloquy or aside addressed to (rather than overheard by) the audience, the roles of observer and enunciatee, of "narrative audience" and "narratee," are likely to overlap. But again, the degree of overlap will depend on the relationship between the narrative audience and the ideal narrative audience. In a soliloquy addressed to the audience, the narratee and the ideal narrative audience will coincide; these roles will converge with that of the narrative audience to the extent that the observer can share in the assumptions the soliloquist makes about the audience's beliefs, knowledge, and values. The soliloquies of Shakespeare's villains, for example, create distance between the audience as narratee (or ideal narrative audience) and the audience as observer within the fiction.

In narrative, where we always have narrative audiences and narratees, one of the variables in narrative discourse will be how much the narratee and the narrative audience overlap. As I suggested earlier, what second-person narration shows is that the more fully the narratee is characterized, the greater the distance between narratee and narrative audience; similarly, the less the narratee is characterized, the greater the coincidence between the two.[7] If we return again to the two texts with which I opened this essay, we can see that in the first the identity boundaries between narratee and narrative audience are blurred and that the blurring depends on the lack of characterization of the narratee. In Moore's text, on the other hand, the narratee is designated as female and as moving in a certain kind of social milieu, and these designations allow individual readers to differentiate themselves from her, even as they remain in the observer position.[8]

How I—and You?—Read "How"

Before turning to a rhetorical analysis of "How," I want to consider once again the kind of claims about reading that the rhetorical approach wants to make. By focusing on the text's designs on its reader, the rhetorical approach seems to promise an account not just of the structure and form of the text but also of the experience of reading. But in that promise also lies the problem. Recall Rabinowitz's description of the difference between narrative audience and narratee: the "narrative audience is much like ourselves, with our beliefs, prejudices, our hopes, fears, and expectations, and our knowledge of society and literature—unless there is some evidence (textual or historical) to the contrary" ("Truth" 128–29n). In the mid-1990s, after many years of work on the difference that difference makes in reading, Rabinowitz himself would, I am confident, be among the first to ask, "Who are 'we'?" and to point out that attention to difference suggests that the text will not necessarily exert its force on all readers in the same way.

Rabinowitz's distinction between the actual and the authorial audiences is helpful for negotiating between the force of the text and individual difference, though I do not believe it completely solves the problem. The concept of authorial audience has the advantage of positing a hypothetical reader addressed by the implied author who is able to discern a text's intended force (just as you might be my hypothetical reader who fully understands all my points). The concept of actual reader enables Rabinowitz to acknowledge that many readers will not feel that intended force—and that those who do may have widely different responses to it. The model, then, seems as if it can stand as a heuristic for reading, a delineation of various roles available to the actual reader. As long as the model does not say that authorial reading is the best or only worthy kind of reading, it seems not entirely incompatible with the recognition of difference.

If we probe more deeply, however, the consequences of difference reemerge. If we are a diverse group of readers, then our different cultural experiences and the resulting differences in beliefs, hopes, fears, prejudices, and knowledge will lead us to hypothesize different authorial and narrative audiences as we infer these positions from the details of any given narrative. Consequently, I propose that the model be taken as a helpful heuristic in a different way. It describes the experiences of reading: an entry into a narrative audience, a recognition of a narrator's ideal audience and narratee, an effort to step into the author's intended audience, a relation of those positions to our actual beliefs. It does not, however, judge those experiences according to their proximity to some single standard. Instead, the model invites a sharing of experiences, especially sharing that involves discussion of the textual grounds for those experiences, so that different readers can continue to learn from each other.[9]

In "How," the functions of the narratee and narrative audience cannot be separated from the authorial audience's knowledge of the story's dialogic relation to three especially significant intertexts: (1) the common cultural narrative (especially among young to middle-aged adults of the middle and upper-middle classes) of developing an unsatisfactory relationship and trying to disentangle from it; (2) the standard narrative in self-help books (especially of the kind that end up on the *New York Times* best-seller list); and (3) the previous short stories in *Self-Help,* especially "How to Be an Other Woman." As I noted above, "How" identifies the narratee as female, but the second-person address blurs the separation of narratee and narrative audience frequently enough for the observer of either sex to be pulled into the narrative's subject position: you fall in love, become part of a couple, meet your partner's family, feel uneasy about the relationship, try—unsuccessfully—to find a good time to leave, try being with someone else, have your partner need you because of illness (or weakness), feel a renewed tenderness, discover that it is not enough, slowly resolve to leave, feel very guilty, finally muster the courage to say good-bye, survive the partner's anger but find that you are unable to escape the sadness of the whole experience.[10]

Even as Moore uses the second person to make the narrative audience feel the pull into the subject position, she uses the narratee to put a distinctive spin on the general narrative by switching the standard gender roles: not only is the "you" female but the male expresses stereotypical female desires: "The touchiest point will always be this: he craves a family, a neat nest of human bowls; he wants to have your children" (57). In this way, Moore is reclaiming a subject position for women in this general cultural narrative. But it is hardly a position to be envied, as the interaction with the other two intertexts reveals. Where the standard narrative in the self-help genre always leads its audiences (actual and authorial) onward and upward toward Self-Fulfillment and the Better Life (if genres had official songs, self-help's would be "Nearer My God to Thee"), Moore's narratee-protagonist is on a slow course to nowhere. Moore's critique of the self-help genre combines with the very generality and even triteness of the narrative to underline the story's satiric strain and mitigate the narrative audience's involvement with the narratee-protagonist as a mimetic character. Strong emotions for the narratee seem less appropriate than knowing laughter about modern relationships and self-help books. Yet the story's relationship to "How to Be an Other Woman" and Moore's skill with the second-person address result in the knowing laughter itself existing alongside—and in some uneasy tension with—the narrative and authorial audiences' genuine feeling for the narratee's situation.

"How to Be an Other Woman" is a companion piece to "How" because it places the female narratee in a different relationship. In that story, the narratee-protagonist desires a deeper, more reliable relationship with the man she loves but must face the frustration of always being of secondary importance to him and the pain of his ultimate rejection. Together the stories paint a very bleak picture of women's chances for satisfying relationships. When you want him, he's married (or otherwise committed; one twist in "How to Be an Other Woman" is that the man is separated from his wife and cheating on the woman he lives with, a twist that certainly expands the circle of hurt women). When you decide that you don't want him, you are too kind and too weak to be able to leave. And when you finally do, you do not escape to happiness. This effect of the intertextuality invites the authorial audience to entertain multiple ways of completing Moore's laconic title—yet these ways seem to point back to the wisdom of her choice. She leaves it at "How" because what else is there to say? Adding "It Usually Goes" or "It Hurts" or even an interrogative that cuts off the last part of the earlier title—"to Be?"—seems redundant. "'How?'" you ask. This is "How."

Even more than this intertextuality, Moore's specific modulation of the narrative discourse enables her both to flaunt the triteness of her narrative and to generate genuine feeling with it. I will look once more at the opening paragraphs and then at just two more of the story's many highly nuanced passages.

> Begin by meeting him in a class, a bar, at a rummage sale. Maybe he teaches sixth grade. Manages a hardware store. Foreman at a carton factory. He will be a good dancer. He will have perfectly cut hair. He will laugh at your jokes.
>
> A week, a month, a year. Feel discovered, comforted, needed, loved, and start sometimes, somehow, to feel bored. When sad or confused, walk uptown to the movies. Buy popcorn. These things come and go. A week, a month, a year. (55)

I have already discussed the way that this passage begins the fluctuation for the actual reader between the positions of the narratee and the narrative audience; now I would like to focus on some features of the narrative discourse that are characteristic of the whole story. First, the presentation of various alternatives, which goes along with the story's relation to the self-help genre, establishes a separation between the narrator and the narratee; unlike the case of Jay McInerney's *Bright Lights, Big City,* where the protagonist uses second person to narrate his own story, Moore uses an external narrator to address her narratee-protagonist. Second, although many of the sentences have the surface form of imperatives ("Begin by meeting him," "walk uptown," "buy popcorn"), the very fact that the story is about the desire for love also gives the sentences another effect. They are not just imperatives but also descriptions of the narratee's willing actions. At the same time, the imperative tone and the consistency of the second-person address make it clear that the narratee and the ideal narrative audience will coincide in this story: the narratee is always doing the bidding of the narrator. Third, this dual-directed quality of the verbs is continued by the frequent but not ubiquitous use of the future tense, a technique that allows the narrator simultaneously to predict and to report the events of the story. Thus, on the one hand, the story appears to remain within the confines of a self-help book: rather than being the account of one person's actual experience, it is a primer on how one might behave in a relationship. On the other hand, the story appears very much to be an account of one person's experience as it unfolds. Through these techniques and effects, Moore invites us to attend both to the satiric and to the mimetic elements of the story.

The second passage I want to consider occurs just after "you" have met an actor, who can quote Coriolanus's mother, and with whom you go to bed or from whom you run as fast as you can:

> Back at home, days later, feel cranky and tired. Sit on the couch and tell him he's stupid. That you bet he doesn't know who Coriolanus is. That since you moved in you've noticed he rarely reads. He will give you a hurt, hungry-to-learn look, with his James Cagney eyes. He will try to kiss you. Turn your head. Feel suffocated. (57)

The narratee-protagonist/ideal narrative audience here remains clearly distinct from the narrative audience. The narrative audience in the observer position recognizes how much is going on beneath the surface of the narratee's actions. Her complaints are stand-ins for her larger unhappiness. The problem is not that this man does not know Coriolanus or does not read enough; the problem is that he is not someone else. The narratee is cranky because she is not as forthright as Coriolanus, not able to say what is really on her mind. Thus, though her complaints apparently point to ways that he might change his behavior to please her, these changes will not be enough. So, his "hurt, hungry-to-learn look" is not a response that offers her any real hope. He can learn all he wants, but he will still be himself. That is what is suffocating.

All this takes on a special cast because of the second-person narration. While the clear distinction between the narratee and the narrative audience allows us to infer so much about the narratee's behavior and situation, the "you" address also invites us to project ourselves—as narrative audience, authorial audience, and actual readers—into the narratee's subject position. Consequently, the inferences we make as we occupy the narrative audience position lead us to a complicated vision that mingles narratee and self in the narratee's position. We both occupy the position and know what the position is like in a way that the narratee herself does not. In this way, we feel addressed by the narrator but not fully coincident with the narratee. Different flesh-and-blood readers will then respond differently to this complicated positioning: some may empathize more fully with the narratee, some may grow impatient or indifferent or condemnatory, and others may turn away from this involvement and refocus on the story's mockery of its own triteness and of the self-help genre. If Moore had employed a standard homodiegetic or heterodiegetic narration, she could have built the same inferences into the passage, but it is difficult to see how she could have also retained the effects resulting from this complicated mingling and separation of narratee and narrative audience.

The third passage I would like to examine more closely is the story's last three paragraphs:

> You will never see him again. Or perhaps you will be sitting in Central Park one April eating your lunch and he will trundle by on roller skates. You will greet him with a wave and a mouth full of sandwich. He will nod, but he will not stop.

> There will be an endless series of tests.
>
> A week, a month, a year. The sadness will die like an old dog. You will feel nothing but indifference. The logy whine of a cowboy harmonica, plaintive, weary, it will fade into the hills as slow Hank Williams. One of those endings. (64)

Again the narratee/ideal narrative audience and narrative audience are clearly distinct. This time, however, there is much less of a gap between the two audiences' understandings of the events and the discourse. The first paragraph here reminds the authorial audience of the narrative's triteness: you might see him, you might not, it happens both ways. In either case, though, it won't make much difference. Instead, "There will be an endless series of tests." This sentence is ironic for both narratee and narrative audience. The narrator has previously employed the same sentence in discussing the man's illness. Here it glosses the previous paragraph and extends its meaning: whether the narratee never sees him or sees him functioning fine without her, life after the relationship will be an endless series of tests to diagnose what is now *her* illness, the lingering sadness of the whole experience. And the last paragraph underscores the endlessness by suggesting that even the apparent end, the death of that sadness, does not bring renewal. Stretched out over yet another of the story's many spans of "a week, a month, a year," the dying gives way to the emptiness of indifference, "one of those endings." Narratee, ideal narrative audience, and narrative audience all nod their heads in understanding here. This close positioning of the complementary audiences strengthens the second person's general invitation for the narrative, authorial, and actual audiences to project themselves into the narratee's position. Despite the triteness of the narrative, underscored by the allusion to country music and then one last time by "One of those endings," that position contains real pain. By keeping the narratee, the ideal narrative audience, and the narrative audience closely aligned here, Moore is able to build genuine emotion into her ending. Again, as actual readers we may choose to turn from this emotion or critique it as sentimental. But Moore's ending can be usefully compared to Umberto Eco's example of how to generate sincere emotion within a postmodern consciousness that is aware of language as already worn out, overloaded with meaning from other contexts: the man who wants to tell a woman that he loves her madly but worries that romance novels have turned a direct expression of love into cliché can say, "As Barbara Cartland would put it, I love you madly" (227). Even as Moore's narrative flaunts its triteness and engages in the send-up of the self-help genre, it also invites its readers to respond as we do to traditional mimetic fiction.

You, Me, and Lorrie Moore

Having focused so much on the relations between narratee, ideal narrative audience, and narrative audience in second-person fiction, I would like to close with a comment on those between authors, actual or implied, and actual readers. Brian McHale has suggested that one of the metathemes of postmodernism that is apparent in second-person narration is love, since the mode depends on violating traditional ontological boundaries (between the fictional and the nonfictional realms) in such a way that reading and writing themselves take on an erotic charge (227). I believe that McHale's point is sound, though I also find applying it wholesale to the reading of *Self-Help* runs the risk of violating the thematic spirit of Moore's book. What I would like to propose instead is that the complexities of the reading-writing transaction in "How" and the other second-person stories add another layer to Moore's undermining of the self-help genre. In using the second-person address to invite her actual readers to adopt multiple positionings, Moore implicitly comments on the simplistic assumptions about readers operating in the self-help books. In extending her invitations, Moore compliments her readers' intelligence by implicitly expressing confidence that we can find our ways. When we summon the requisite intelligence and we experience the satisfactions that follow from accepting the invitations, we also turn *Self-Help* into mutual-help, with author and reader once again affirming the value of their activities for themselves and for each other.

In other words, the voice from this page offers you testimony about the value of rhetorical transactions. One of those conclusions.[11]

8

Narrating the PC Controversies: Thoughts on Dinesh D'Souza's *Illiberal Education*

This essay takes a different subject from the others: neither a fictional narrative nor a canonical text but an entry in the so-called culture wars being conducted in the early 1990s: D'Souza's Illiberal Education. *For that reason, the essay runs the risks of dealing with dated material and giving D'Souza's text more prominence than it deserves. I want to emphasize that the essay is interested in D'Souza's book as a representative case: as D'Souza's new book,* The End of Racism, *illustrates, narrative continues to be used in the day-to-day political and ideological battles over the nature of our institutions, and ideologically committed partisans continue to employ at least some of the tactics found in* Illiberal Education. *If the analysis I offer is persuasive, then it has relevance for current and future situations. Furthermore, the essay engages the more general theoretical question of how ideology influences interpretation by reflecting on how my own commitments influence my discussion of D'Souza. Finally, I think it is important for those who disagree with books such as* Illiberal Education, *which have achieved a certain cultural influence, not to ignore them but to take them seriously.*

Narrative, Narrative Theory, and the Case of *Illiberal Education*

Although the media storm swirling around the term *political correctness* has now abated, universities and their publics are still debating such important issues as affirmative action, multiculturalism, speech codes, and faculty accountability to students and taxpayers.[1] As these debates continue, I want to consider Dinesh D'Souza's *Illiberal Education* from the perspective offered by my approach to narrative as rhetoric, because I believe that the book shows—both in its own strategies and in the reception that made it a best-seller—how much the debates are influenced by the narratives that surround them. Indeed, my first reaction to D'Souza's heavily documented book[2] is to echo E. M. Forster: "*Illiberal Education* tells a story. Yes—oh dear, yes—it tells a story." For out of the book's welter of statistics, interviews, case studies, and discursive analysis arises D'Souza's tale of the decline and fall of the contemporary American university. The villain of the piece is what D'Souza calls the "victim's revolution," the efforts by leftist academics to do such things as promote affirmative action, revise the traditional canon, and curb so-called hate speech—in short, to take race and gender into account in admissions, in the curriculum, and in the conduct of campus life. According to D'Souza's narrative, these efforts have undermined the ideal of a liberal education: the university, rather than being a place for open, unfettered inquiry in which students are taught values of toleration and fairness, has become a place beset by a rigid and constricting ideology of victim's rights, a place in which students get "an education in close-mindedness and intolerance, which is to say, illiberal education" (229).

Clearly, much of the attention, both positive and negative, *Illiberal Education* received rests on the perception that its story is important and/or well told. Here I will take the story's importance as a given and focus on its telling. Indeed, my primary interests are *how* D'Souza tells the story, *how* he views his own narrative—and *why*, after studying these matters, I remain unconvinced by the story. I shall employ tools of rhetorical analysis to move both inside and outside D'Souza's ideological and narrative perspectives—in other words, both to listen carefully to his story and to question it seriously. More particularly, I shall, first, analyze the powerful claims D'Souza implicitly makes for his narrative by examining the way he views the relationships between facts, interpretations, and that narrative. Second, I shall argue that many of D'Souza's local narratives do not make—at least as straightforwardly as he thinks—the points that he presents them as making. Third, I shall interrogate my own interested relation to D'Souza's narratives as a way of considering the role of ideology in his construction of those narratives and in my analysis of them. Finally, I shall consider some general conclusions that follow from this exploration of narrative, narrative analysis, and the debates over the university.

Facts, Interpretations, and Narratives

> Here the reader will find a wealth of concrete information and specific detail that has withstood the most searching factual scrutiny. It is possible to come up with varying interpretations, but while people are entitled to their own opinions, they are not entitled to their own facts. What it is important to recognize is not horror stories or excess but the fact that these are the logical consequences of a set of principles, indeed of an ideological world view.
>
> —Dinesh D'Souza, introduction to the Vintage edition, xx

D'Souza's statement proposes a very strict connection between fact, interpretation, and narrative: solid fact provides the firm foundation on which (proper) interpretation and narrative should be built. Although the statement gives lip service to the variability of interpretation, it actually works to control and close off interpretation by claiming that interpretation follows directly from fact. If facts are given, not chosen, and if they point directly to conclusions (as "horror stories" point to an underlying ideological view of the world), then alternative interpretations of the facts, though possible, are finally wrong. D'Souza tightens the link between fact and interpretation through the rhetorical moves of his last sentence: "What it is important to recognize is not horror stories [about the way Political Correctness is ruining campus life] or excess but the fact that these are the logical consequences of a set of principles, indeed of an ideological world view."

The first half of the sentence graciously denies any interest in sensationalism ("horror stories are not important"), but the second half reclaims sensationalism's importance by subsuming it in its alleged underlying cause ("a logical consequence of a set of principles"). More significantly, in light of D'Souza's seemingly commonsensical assertion that you can't choose your facts, the otherwise inelegant phrase "the fact that" raises the stakes of his claim here. That "horror stories" have a dangerous ideological perspective as their underlying cause is not just D'Souza's opinion or interpretation—this is a matter of fact. And just as we cannot choose to accept or reject this fact, we cannot choose to accept or reject the narrative that follows from it, because this narrative is now also rooted in the indisputable.

If we look more closely at the passage, however, we can see that, despite D'Souza's skillful rhetoric (and to some extent, because of it), this passage actually indicates that facts and interpretations are much less tightly connected than it overtly claims. D'Souza's confident assertion in the last sentence indicates that he regards the close link between facts and interpretations as fairly straightforward and unproblematic. The rhetorical strategy of the whole passage tells a different story, however. D'Souza is worrying here about those readers who have disputed his evidence and especially those who have tried to interpret it differently. So he makes his assertion about the indisputability of his facts, and then tries to make this tight link between fact, interpretation, and narrative. But he must also deal with the inconvenient *fact* that his evidence has been—and will be—used as the basis for different interpretations. As we have seen, he tries to acknowledge this fact and then gloss over it. But the glossing over does not work. If it is a fact that people are entitled to their different interpretations, then it cannot indisputably be a fact that the "horror stories" are a logical consequence of an "ideological world view"—unless, of course, there is only one correct interpretation of the facts. But if there is only one correct interpretation, people are not entitled to their own (differing) interpretations—unless, of course, they are entitled to ignore the truth. And if they are entitled to ignore the truth, they are entitled to ignore the (indisputable) facts. In other words, they can choose their own facts. If D'Souza is serious about people being able to form differing interpretations, then his conclusion about the link between fact and interpretation does not follow. If he is serious about the link between fact and interpretation, then people cannot choose their own interpretations.

To come at this point about the gap between facts and interpretations from another direction, let us imagine a reader who believes that the horror stories are not "a logical consequence" of an underlying set of principles but rather a consequence of some people's overzealousness. According to this reader, these well-intentioned people become so committed to one principle (e.g., speech that mocks minority groups should be discouraged) that they ignore other equally important principles (even distasteful speech deserves First Amendment protection because otherwise all unpopular speech is subject to censorship). Clearly, D'Souza's assertions in this passage will not convince this reader because what D'Souza points at—the "fact" that the horror stories are the consequence of an underlying set of principles—is something this reader disputes. In effect, he says to D'Souza, "You see the wrong thing when you look at the horror stories." Indeed, this reader would be inclined to point to the horror stories and say, "Mr. D'Souza, can't you see that they stem from overzealousness?" To which D'Souza would probably reply, "You see the wrong thing when you look at the facts."

Neither act of pointing to the horror stories will settle the dispute about how to interpret their meaning. The facts of the horror stories are susceptible to more than one interpretation. Indeed, whether a particular incident deserves to be designated as a "horror story" will frequently be a matter of dispute. By insisting on the gap between facts and interpretations, I have only complicated the issue of how the arguments and controversies surrounding the role of the university should be narrated. Insisting on the gap immediately raises two related questions: (1) why does a given observer develop one interpretation rather than another? and (2) how is it possible to adjudicate among different interpretations of the same phenomena? I think I can better address these questions—and the larger issue of narrating the political correctness controversy—after analyzing a few of the many places in *Illiberal Education* where the relations D'Souza finds between facts, interpretations, and narratives seem highly questionable. My purpose is neither to disprove D'Souza's entire narrative (I work with too small a portion of his book) nor to develop a counternarrative; instead, I want to focus attention on the broader question of the role of narrative and narrative analysis in the debate over the university.

D'Souza at Tufts: Narrative Thematizing

In his introduction to the paperback edition, D'Souza recounts an incident during his visit to Tufts University shortly after the original hardcover came out:

> I was berated by a white student who maintained that my defense of academic standards amounted to nothing more than an apology for the "white perspective." Universities needed to give equal prominence in the classroom to black, Hispanic, and non-Western perspectives, he argued.
>
> When I asked him to identify the white perspective, he looked appalled and threw out his arms, as if to say it was so obvious that it needed no elaboration. I insisted, however, that he provide two or three specific examples of a white perspective.
>
> "How about rationality?" he said with a confident grin.
>
> I wrote that down on the blackboard. "What else?"
>
> "How about logocentrism?" That's how they talk on many campuses these days.
>
> "What's that?" I asked.
>
> "The white man's obsession with big words," he maintained, so I wrote down logocentrism, and asked for another example.
>
> "How about sexual restraint?"
>
> "Not in my experience," I said. But I wrote that down too.
>
> For students in the audience, this proved to be an exercise in getting the joke a few minutes after the punch line. There were titters in the crowd, but the laughter came almost in slow motion. Gradually, students realized that the concession to white norms of all qualities of logic, clarity of expression, and decency of behavior—and the implication that such things could not be expected from other groups—was profoundly condescending and ultimately demeaning to the minorities. Angrily, the advocate of race-based knowledge accused me of "insensitivity" and of unconsciously advancing the goals of "white America." (xii–xiii)

D'Souza goes on to give an interpretation of this narrative—and one of another incident at Tufts in which a professor tells D'Souza that, although his speech is racist, he is not because only whites can be racists:

> As my experience at Tufts indicates, the First Amendment remains in force at many American universities, but there is also a pervasive illiberalism of mind. Instead of cultivating in young people those qualities of critical thought and civil argument that are the essence of a liberal education, university leaders have created sham communities where serious and honest discussion is frequently drowned out by a combination of sloganeering, accusation, and intimidation. (xiii)

D'Souza's way of telling the story also implies other features of his interpretation. Because the student is initially unable to give any content to the phrase "white perspective," the narrative implies that it is merely a bit of liberal cant, a phrase devoid of meaning. Even better for D'Souza's purposes, when pressed, the student comes up with meanings that can't be considered the exclusive property of whites—unless one is hopelessly racist. The student is thus caught in self-contradiction, and the concept of a "white perspective" seems fatuous. Furthermore, in making the point about the student's self-contradiction, D'Souza appears to show that he is actually more sensitive about race and racism than the student. All in all, from D'Souza's perspective, it's hard to imagine a better way to begin.

But let's look more closely at how this narrative works. One apparently slippery maneuver D'Souza makes is to leap from rationality, logocentrism, and sexual restraint to "all qualities of logic, clarity of expression, and decency of behavior," but I don't want to make too much of this point because it is possible that the student's other answers justify D'Souza's leap. More central to the narrative's argumentative point is the thematic function of the student. The narrative will work for D'Souza to the extent that we regard the student not as an isolated individual but as a representative of a much larger group of white, liberal-minded undergraduates who share his beliefs. The narrative signals the student's representativeness in large part by the minimal development of his mimetic function, that is, by not individualizing him. D'Souza gives him no name, no physical characteristics; D'Souza refers to the student simply as "he"—until the end of the narrative when "he" is replaced by a clear thematic designation, "the advocate of race-based knowledge." D'Souza gives the student minimal mimetic life in brief descriptions of the student's demeanor and affect at different points of the narrative, but these all highlight a general progression from arrogant confidence to anger, and the narrative implies that both emotions are unjustified.

Is D'Souza's thematizing of the student warranted? Is the student's definition of a "white perspective" widely shared? Do most people who believe that a white perspective on academic standards could be usefully supplemented by the perspectives of other races define the white perspective as rationality, use of big words, and sexual restraint? The answer is clearly no. The link between the facts of D'Souza's narrative and his interpretation starts to loosen. To be sure, the narrative effectively shows that the student does not understand his own position very well, but it does not succeed in discrediting the more general idea about the importance of cultural perspectives.

Furthermore, once we loosen the connection between fact and D'Souza's interpretation, we open the space for another interpretation, one that is less flattering to D'Souza. Once the student confidently says that "rationality" is part of the white perspective, D'Souza must know that he will be easy game. Rather than stepping in at that point and talking about the dangers of making a concept such as rationality the distinctive property of one race, D'Souza strings the student along, makes a joke about one of his answers ("Sexual restraint"/"Not in my experience"), and lets the larger joke gradually dawn on the rest of the audience—a surefire way to humiliate the student. If we adopt this interpretation, then this early narrative has almost the opposite effect of the one D'Souza wants: rather than showing him to be open-minded and tolerant, the narrative shows him to be, well, an intellectual bully; rather than being sympathetic to him, we are inclined to be sympathetic to his opponents. Consequently, rather than being disposed to accept D'Souza's narrative about the way things are on campus these days, we are inclined to doubt it.

D'Souza's Case Studies: The Powers and Limits of Monologism

In chapter 7, "The Tyranny of the Minority," D'Souza offers a long series of "case studies" designed to show the epidemic of abuses committed in the name of the new political orthodoxy accompanying the victim's revolution. D'Souza's strategy of piling up the cases makes good sense because it overwhelms the objection that he is arguing merely by anecdote. The message of quantity is that these stories are the rule, not the exception. But the way D'Souza tells and juxtaposes some of these cases again invites a narrative theorist to loosen the link between fact and interpretation. The following two cases occur consecutively in D'Souza's text.

> *The Case of Murray Dolfman*
>
> Nobody in Professor Dolfman's class in legal studies at the University of Pennsylvania could identify where the term "servitude" could be found in the American Constitution, so Dolfman commented that there were "ex-slaves" in the class who should have an idea. "I don't know if I should have used that term," Dolfman recalled, "but it got students to think of the Thirteenth Amendment right away."
>
> Shortly afterwards, a few minority students came up to Dolfman and accused him of racial insensitivity. A second charge against Dolfman was that he had once told a black student to change his pronunciation from "de" to "the." Dolfman said that he met with the students, and apologized if they had taken offense. "I told them that I understood and shared their concerns, that I am Jewish and during *seder* we pray: When we were slaves unto Pharaoh." Dolfman also pointed out that it would be important for students, in courtroom argument in later years, to speak in a clear and comprehensible manner.
>
> "They seemed to understand," Dolfman recalled, and the matter was dropped for a few months. But after that, during Black History Month, it was brought up again and again, Dolfman said, "to illustrate just how bad things are at Penn."
>
> The adrenalin generated by the Black History Month rhetoric brought about a demonstration of minority students, several dozens of whom occupied Dolfman's class and prevented him from teach-

ing. "They read a document of indictment to my students," Dolfman said. President Sheldon Hackney met with Dolfman and asked him to refrain from public comment, even to abstain from defending himself against accusations. Then Hackney joined the ranks of the accusers, telling the campus newspaper that conduct such as Dolfman's was "absolutely intolerable." Dolfman was pressured to issue what he termed a "forced apology" and to attend "racial awareness" sessions on campus. The university subsequently decided not to renew Dolfman's teaching contract for one year.

Dolfman is now back at Penn, a chastened man. "The message has been driven home very clearly," Dolfman said. "You can't open your mouth on these issues now without fear of being humiliated."

The Case of Pete Schaub

When Pete Schaub, a business major at the University of Washington at Seattle, enrolled in a Women's Studies class in early 1988, he expected to learn about the "history of women and the contributions they have made." Schaub said his mother was a 1960's rebel who divorced his father and moved to rural Washington state to live "close to the land."

"Introduction to Women's Studies," taught by Donna Langston and Dan-Michele Brown, was not what Schaub had expected. On the first day of class Brown asserted that "the traditional American family represents a dysfunctional family unit." Students who protested that their families were functional were shouted down by teaching assistants hired by Langston and Brown. "Denial, denial," they yelled in unison. A few days later Langston brought guest speakers to talk about masturbation. "They said you don't need a man," Schaub said. "They proceeded to show how to masturbate with a feather duster, and they had dildos right there."

When Professor Brown claimed that U.S. statistics showed that lesbians could raise children better than married couples, Schaub asked for the source. "I asked after class," Schaub said. "I wasn't challenging her." But the teacher "wouldn't hear of it. She said: 'Why are you challenging me? Get away from me. Just leave me alone.'" A member of Brown's undergraduate circle called Schaub a "chauvinist goddamn bastard." The next day, Schaub was banned from class. The teacher had two campus police officers waiting in the hall to escort him away.

> Schaub protested to the administration, but nothing happened for several weeks. Finally he was permitted to go back to class, but advised by Associate Dean James Nason to drop the course. (201–3)

On the one hand, I am prepared to believe that here we have two genuine horror stories and that, if I investigated these cases, I would reach conclusions similar to D'Souza's. On the other hand, I am also struck by how D'Souza's narration of each and his juxtaposition of the two actually undermine their force and begin to open each of them up to alternative interpretations. The problem here is not the way D'Souza thematizes the characters but rather the combination of point of view and what Bakhtin calls monologism—D'Souza's strategy of giving weight to only one ideology in the narrative. D'Souza tells each story from the perspective of the protagonist; he asks us to see everything just as Dolfman and Schaub do. In one way, of course, this restricted perspective makes the stories more powerful; there is very little recalcitrant material in them—almost everything points to the interpretation that D'Souza gives them. If one is already convinced of the tyranny of the minority, these narratives will surely reinforce one's conviction. But if one is not already convinced, the restriction to one ideology is likely to seem suspicious. These are narratives about disputes and about the kinds of disputes that many people are now familiar with. It seems reasonable to ask about how the "antagonists" would interpret the facts of these stories.

Once we become conscious of the monologism, the little bit of recalcitrant material in each becomes available as the basis, if not for counternarratives, at least for complications of these two. Dolfman's singling out the African American students as "ex-slaves" who should know what "servitude" means appears to mark them as Other and put them in the role of educating those in the mainstream. Such a judgment does not mean that Dolfman deserved to have his teaching contract suspended, but it certainly alters the sense of "horror" in this story. Schaub's apparent belief that talk of masturbation and lesbian sex is somehow beyond the pale opens the question of whether his teachers, however mistakenly, were picking up signs of homophobia in his behavior. That is, one may legitimately wonder whether the teachers' past experience with genuinely homophobic students might be influencing the dynamics of their interaction with Schaub. Again, raising this question does not justify what happened to Schaub, but it does suggest a more complicated situation than D'Souza's account admits.

Even if D'Souza's narratives by themselves don't give us much sense of a possible other side, the juxtaposition of the two stories makes me wonder about how he handles the narration. In the first story, the professor is without fault and the students are tyrannical; in the second, these roles are reversed. This switch reinforces the desire to know how the African American students in Dolfman's class would tell their story and how Professors Brown and Langston would tell theirs. Surely their interpretations of the same basic facts would not coincide with D'Souza's. The question then arises: why should we accept D'Souza's monological interpretations as final?

D'Souza and Atwater at Howard: Reading Cultural Narratives

In chapter 4 of *Illiberal Education,* D'Souza discusses the efforts of Howard University students to resist the appointment of Lee Atwater to the Board of Trustees. The main reason for the students' resistance was Atwater's role as the man behind the Willie Horton ad in George Bush's 1988 campaign against Michael Dukakis. Through this ad, as D'Souza reminds us, "Atwater helped destroy . . . Dukakis' electoral base in the South by exposing the Massachusetts governor's furlough program, exemplified by black convict Willie Horton, who used a weekend release to assault and rape a white woman in Maryland" (96). The passage I want to focus on here is argument rather than narrative, but matters of narrative and narrative analysis are crucial to understanding and evaluating that argument.

> Atwater's initial claim that Horton's race was totally irrelevant is perhaps a bit much. The students' point that, even if anchored in the crime statistics, Atwater used Horton to play on fears of black crime is probably valid. The irony, however, is that one of the biggest complaints at Howard—if the campus newspaper's reports are any indication—is the crime rate in Washington, D.C., that is hurting

> Howard students. *The Hilltop* echoes this in issue after issue. The April 7, 1989 edition, for instance, coming right after the Atwater controversy, reported as its lead story, "Donald Hatch, the AIDS rapist, who terrorized the Howard community in the fall of 1987, was sentenced last week." It turns out that Hatch "raped and orally sodomized a Howard student after threatening her with a hypodermic needle which he claimed was contaminated with the AIDS virus." Hatch was black but got no sympathy; rather, Howard students proclaimed the sentence "marvelous." Alonza Robertson said that burglaries are common at Howard, especially during breaks when students go home, and the campus does not provide adequate security. "A couple of girls were raped here recently," Robertson said matter-of-factly.
>
> In the Horton case, however, both the convict and his crimes were far from home base. Howard students tended to think of Horton as an *issue*, not as a dangerous con who sadistically attacked an innocent couple. The entire moral equation would be changed if Horton attacked a black family. Yet Howard protesters did not find it at all inconsistent that they would protest Atwater's political use of Horton while insisting that the administration bolster campus security to avoid further burglary and rape. (106–7)

The underlying logic of this argument goes like this: if you're an African American who wants protection from crimes by other African Americans, you have no right to call Atwater's Willie Horton ad racist. If you admit that some African Americans have committed rape, how can you object to Atwater's ad? If there are African American rapists, how can Atwater's reference to one be racist? In this case, D'Souza's interpretation seems not just questionable but seriously—even shockingly—inadequate. The interpretation is wanting because D'Souza fails to recognize how Atwater's ad about Willie Horton intersects with a larger cultural narrative of black-white relations, a narrative that is both patriarchal and racist. In this narrative, the white man's fear of the racial Other mixes with his hatred for the black man, and the hatred and fear fuel each other. Because the white man also convinces himself of the black man's inferiority, he does not fear the black man's intelligence or his strength or his spirituality; instead, the white man fears the black man's allegedly unrestrained sexuality, because sexual intercourse between races leads to the contamination or pollution of white blood. Those who intermarry must be ostracized, and black men who rape white women must be severely punished. Atwater's ad appeals to this racist narrative by using Willie Horton's crime as a representation of the racial anarchy threatened by Dukakis's being soft on crime.[3]

Despite D'Souza's acknowledgment that the ad did "play on fears of black crime," his main argument about the inconsistency of the Howard students misses the connection between Atwater's ad and the larger narrative. From the perspective of rhetorical theory, we can say that D'Souza's argument fails to recognize that Horton is not just a person but also a thematic character with this large thematic function. To put the point another way, D'Souza does not recognize how the relations between facts and their symbolic weight change from one discourse to the next. In the Howard students' discourse about safety on campus, an African American rapist is as dangerous—for all races of women—as a white rapist. The symbolic dimensions of the rapist's and the victim's racial identities are less important than the threat the rapist presents. In the discourse of political advertisements, however, when a white politician chooses a black rapist's attack on a white woman as the symbol of another white politician's softness toward crime, the situation is very different. Here race matters and takes on significant symbolic weight precisely because the discourse of the ad intersects with the larger cultural narrative. D'Souza's handling of the local narrative here seems to be the weakest part of the book.

Narrative, Analysis, and Ideology

Let us return to the two questions I raised earlier: (1) what causes a given observer to choose one interpretation rather than another? and (2) how can we adjudicate among different interpretations of the same phenomena? My examination of these few narrative moments in *Illiberal Education* suggests that one (unsurprising) answer to the first question is ideological commitments. D'Souza is clearly interpreting the facts in a way that advances his conservative view of the American university. If he had less of an a priori commitment to this view and its correctness, he would be less likely to overthematize the Tufts student, more likely to allow the other side of the Dolfman and Schaub cases into his narratives, and more likely to recognize the difference between the Atwater ad's use of Willie Horton and the presence of African American rapists in the neighborhood of Howard University.

But if this conclusion is unsurprising, the relation between it and D'Souza's initial claim about facts, interpretations, and analysis is perhaps less immediately evident. The overthematizing of the Tufts student, the monologism of the case studies, and the attention to the "facts" at Howard in the absence of the larger cultural narrative are all consistent with a belief that facts directly point to their own interpretations. Once we see this consistency, we can also see what D'Souza does not acknowledge and would probably deny: his statement about facts and interpretations itself reveals two significant, closely related assumptions: (1) one can unproblematically separate facts from their contexts, the complex situatedness that sometimes makes facts difficult to ascertain, and (2) once abstracted, they will tell their own story. The analysis of D'Souza's narratives suggests not only that these assumptions are highly questionable but also that they function to keep him from recognizing the powerful role ideology plays as he moves from his facts to his interpretations.

As D'Souza would no doubt himself be quick to point out, this attention to ideology needs to be turned on the arguments I have been making about *Illiberal Education.* If ideology plays such an important role in D'Souza's moving from facts to interpretations to narratives, then it follows that ideology also plays a significant role in my evaluation of those narratives. If I shared D'Souza's ideological commitments, I would no doubt praise his book as highly as Roger Kimball does in his review for the *New Criterion* ("indispensable reading"; "D'Souza has chronicled the intellectual and moral degradation of a great liberal institution" [8]). Because my ideological commitments are different, however, I am more inclined to see alternative interpretations of the same facts and, consequently, I end up challenging these local narratives and remaining skeptical about *Illiberal Education*'s global narrative.

Having acknowledged the importance of ideological commitments in both the construction and analysis of these narratives, should we conclude that in these matters ideology finally *determines* interpretation? If so, then any genuine adjudication is impossible, since any judge will simply decide on the basis of her own ideological commitments. Anyone who has spent much time reading the debates about the university is likely to be tempted to answer this question in the affirmative. Anyone who has dipped into Kimball's *Tenured Radicals* will find his praise of D'Souza to be entirely predictable, but Gerry O'Sullivan's negative review seems no less a consequence of his ideological commitments: "In the continuing devolution of the conservative critique of academic life, few have aspired to the depths of Dinesh D'Souza's *Illiberal Education*" (43). To consent to the view that commitments determine interpretations, however, is to deny the existence of facts as anything but the product of interpretation. To do that in this realm is to deny that people on all sides of the debates have experienced pain, oppression, and injustice, while others have experienced profit and pleasure.[4]

Ideological commitments, then, inevitably influence interpretations of facts, and to some extent such commitments help shape facts in one way rather than another—as we have seen in considering the cases of Dolfman and Schaub. But this phenomenon of commitments influencing interpretations that in turn shape facts—let me call this phenomenon a fact—can itself be a reason to question our interpretations. This questioning, of course, will not itself be totally neutral and objective, but it can—and should—come from the commitments of a competing perspective. That is the strategy I have employed with D'Souza's narratives, and I would expect him to employ a similar strategy in assessing my interpretations. If the questioning is serious, then it can have genuine consequences—can make us change our interpretations—because in some cases facts are sufficiently recalcitrant to resist the interpretations that our commitments would encourage us to make. It seems to me that D'Souza's interpretation of the situation at Howard is a clear example of such a case.

At the same time, these very principles mean that I must be open to the possibility that D'Souza will be able to show me that this conclusion about his handling of the Howard situation needs to be revised. This awareness does not, however, prevent me from taking my stand, from claiming that my interpretation of his account should persuade, if not him, then most other readers of our exchange. In other words, because commitments influence interpretations that in turn shape but do not create facts, the narratives we tell about those facts legitimately make truth claims, but those claims are likely to be highly contested. This contestation is one important means by which we can revise the narratives and refine their truth claims, though our reaching the stage where our narratives are beyond contestation is as unlikely as the eventuality that facts will speak their own interpretations. Furthermore, because the narratives we tell about our world themselves reinforce or revise our ideological commitments and our interpretations of that world, we have a very big stake in the ongoing negotiation of those narratives.[5]

For that very reason, narrative theorists in the academy have another lesson to learn from *Illiberal Education:* the importance of telling stories about the university to the larger public in a way that is both engaged and accessible. If we speak only to ourselves or if we speak to our publics without recognizing the importance of adapting our language to our audience, we will not be shaping the public narrative about university life, and we will be left in the position of reacting to the stories told by others. Narrative theory offers us valuable tools not only for the serious analysis of *Illiberal Education, Tenured Radicals,* and other such attacks but also for the task of constructing alternative narratives for the public. Narrative theorists, I believe, have a vital role to play in the ongoing debates about the university; it is time we both recognized and embraced that role.

Postscript

D'Souza wrote a brief reply to this essay when it first appeared in *Narrative,* one in which he makes the general point that he is appealing to liberals "on their own terms" and asking them to combat the way "liberalism is being betrayed by political correctness" ("Response," 268). The only specific analysis he responds to is the one about Murray Dolfman and Pete Schaub, arguing that my discussion offends "what Aristotle has called common sense" because my ability to imagine alternative voices shows that he has, in some sense, included them:

> When Professor Phelan says it is possible to read the record differently, I am not sure whether he means that the facts are not as I describe. (No one, to my knowledge, has demonstrated that.) Perhaps he means that Dolfinan's and Schaub's detractors would see the facts in a different light. "How dare Professor Dolfman use the term ex-slave?" "Pete Schaub is nothing more than a male chauvinist jock." While I do not offer a detailed study of these nuances of assertion and counterassertion, I think they are implicit in the narrative. They are there for the reader to see, which is why Professor Phelan found them.
>
> Thus Professor Phelan's analysis unwittingly exonerates me of the charge of monologism. My narrative, he acknowledges, gives room for more than one interpretation. He seeks out an alternative interpretation. He assumes, wrongly, that I am unaware of or tried to suppress his interpretation. My argument is that the weight of the evidence does not bear it out. ("Response" 268–69)

My reply was also brief:

> I acknowledge the cleverness of D'Souza's rejoinder to my point about the monologism of his narratives about Murray Dolfman and Pete Schaub. As he suggests, however, he and I will continue to disagree about both how he tells his stories and the larger narrative these stories form. On his account, I offend "what Aristotle called common sense" by both accusing him of monologism and claiming to hear other voices or at least "nuances of assertion and counterassertion" in those narratives. "They are there for the reader to see, which is why Professor Phelan found them," and, thus, my "analysis unwittingly exonerates [him] of the charge of monologism."
>
> I find this reasoning similar to D'Souza's narratives: like them, it has a surface appeal, but the more one looks at it the more the appeal fades. The initial appeal here derives in part from D'Souza's tapping into a general truth about narrative: purely monologic narratives are very rare, because the act of narrating almost inevitably involves some implicit communication of alternative ways of telling the story, shifting the emphasis, locating the privileged positions. So I would agree that D'Souza's narratives are not *totally* monologic; nevertheless, I still maintain that they—and D'Souza's defense of

them in his reply—reflect an author with a monologic imagination. That is, the narratives still show that D'Souza's way of telling the stories seeks to exclude or to undermine the alternative voices and perspectives that briefly appear within them.

D'Souza's effort to express those voices in his reply tellingly reveals this monologic imagination. He imagines those he calls Dolfman's and Schaub's "detractors" saying such things as, "How dare Professor Dolfman use the term ex-slave?" "Pete Schaub is nothing more than a male chauvinist jock." The first voice speaks *de haut en bas;* the second engages in an ad hominem attack. Neither voice says anything that might pass for rational argument (or the beginning of one). Consequently, the voices are no sooner heard than they are discredited. A storyteller who imagines the opposition's voices this way seems unable to imagine any genuine merit in them. Such a storyteller, in other words, seems unable to hear alternative voices without first filtering them through an imagination that is already convinced of their error. For these reasons, I find myself slowly beginning to accept D'Souza's claim that he has not "tried to suppress" my alternative interpretations. He has not tried to suppress them, I think, precisely because he has been unable to imagine them.

. . . By telling his stories so that they conform so neatly to his ideology, D'Souza encourages us to accept his larger claim that facts of campus life speak his interpretations of them. By (unwittingly) revealing in his reply that his ideology strongly controls his hearing of alternative voices, D'Souza gives us even greater cause to dispute that larger claim. ("Monologic Imagination," 270-71)

9

Toward a Rhetorical Reader-Response Criticism: The Difficult, the Stubborn, and the Ending of *Beloved*

In this essay, more than any other in the book, I make the case for viewing narrative as rhetoric through an appeal to the phenomenology of reading. In seeking to link the experience of reading with the activity of interpretation, I experiment with the form of the standard critical essay by deliberately employing multiple voices and styles, juxtaposing a somewhat lyrical expression of response with abstract theorizing and a stream-of-consciousness account of reading and responding to the character of Beloved. *Like the other essays in this book, this one is concerned with tapping into the intuitive experience of reading and articulating its bases in order to express cognitively what we experience intuitively. In the fourth section, in particular, I attempt to stay very close to that intuitive experience even as I inevitably move to more abstract cognition.*

The motivation for this experimentation with form arises from the specific hypothesis I want to advance: some textual recalcitrance cannot be fully explained, even though it functions very productively in our reading; the focus on Beloved *tries to get at an instance of that recalcitrance, while the analysis of the narrative's ending seeks to explain the character's productive functioning. In developing the case, I also reflect on the powers and limits of interpretation's desire for mastery.*

> The imagination that produces work which bears and invites rereadings, which motions to future readings as well as contemporary ones, implies a sharable world and an endlessly flexible language. Readers and writers both struggle to interpret and perform within a common language sharable imaginative worlds.
>
> —Toni Morrison, *Playing in the Dark*

Reading *Beloved*

I am in *Beloved* and *Beloved* is in me.

Like Stamp Paid, I enter without knocking. For days I live at 124. I become Sethe. Paul D. Denver. Amy Denver; Baby Suggs; Stamp Paid. The days are intense, difficult, exhausting, rewarding. I reach to understand. Stretching, straining, marveling, I perform Morrison's world.

But *Beloved* also eludes me. Like Stamp Paid on the threshold of 124, I cannot enter. Parts of Morrison's world won't let me in. Especially Beloved herself and the narrative's last two pages. *Who, what is Beloved? Yes, Sethe's murdered daughter. And—or?—a survivor of the Middle Passage.* Labels, not understanding. And why the cryptic ending? Why move away from the intimate scene between Sethe and Paul D to declare "this was not a story to pass on"?

Another label for Beloved—from the litcrit drawer: oppositional character. Spiteful ghost, manipulating lover, selfish sister, all-consuming daughter. But also innocent—and representative—victim. Where is the integration—or the reason for no integration? A label for the ending: confrontational. But why this prose: "In the place where the long grass opens, the girl who waited to be loved and cry shame erupts into her separate parts, to make it easy for the chewing laughter to swallow her all away" (274)?

These questions, I see, are interconnected—answer one and other answers will follow—but something, someone blocks my way. *Morrison? Me? My race? Gender? Something I have locked away in a tobacco tin inside my heart? Some other ignorance or insensitivity? All of these?*

Oppositional character, confrontational ending indeed.

There is a loneliness that reads.

Reading, Response, and Interpretation

Other critics of *Beloved* both relieve and exacerbate the loneliness, especially in relation to Beloved. In particular, Deborah Horvitz, Judith Wilt, Elizabeth House, Barbara Rigney, Ashraf H. A. Rushdy, and Jean Wyatt offer excellent insights about Beloved, perceptions about her or her monologue that substantially advance my efforts to share Morrison's world.[1] At the same time, their work paradoxically increases my loneliness because Beloved still seems to elude explanation and a gap remains between response and interpretation. Beloved is a survivor of the Middle Passage and of a white man found dead in his cabin around the time she shows up at 124 (House). She is both Sethe's murdered daughter and her murdered African mother (Wyatt), a specific character in a specific family and a representative of all the Middle Passage women (Rigney), "and also all Black women in America trying to trace their ancestry back to the mother on the ship attached to them" (Horvitz). She is a figure filled with the psychokinetic energy of the others who then use that energy to act out their needs and desires (Wilt). She is the incarnation of Sethe's guilt (Rushdy). Because the novel supports—indeed, insists on—all these not entirely compatible accounts, it prevents us from resting with any one and makes the struggle to "perform" her part of Morrison's world extraordinarily demanding. Moreover, adding the possibilities together gives us something less than the sum of the parts: Beloved dissolves into multiple fragments.

This gap between the experience of reading *Beloved* and the explanations offered by its interpreters is, in one respect, par for practical criticism's course. Despite the significant work done in reader-response *theory* in the last twenty-five years, including such useful books as those by Iser, Flynn and Schweikart, Rabinowitz, Crosman, and Steig, most interpretive *practice* remains unaffected by this work, rarely taking its starting point from the critic's response.[2] Perhaps the most dramatic example of this general critical habit of separating the experience of reading from the act of interpretation occurs in Robert Scholes's widely read *Textual Power.* Scholes proposes a progression from reading to interpretation to criticism but does not build the act of interpretation on the act of reading. For Scholes, to interpret is to thematize, and to thematize is to divide the text into a series of repetitions and oppositions and to link these repetitions and oppositions to cultural codes. By locating the fundamental interpretive move in the division of the text into binary categories rather than in the identification of a sequence of responses, Scholes effects a divorce between reading and interpretation.[3]

I would like to take a closer look at the activities of reading and interpretation in order to explore further the relations and gaps between them and to highlight significant features of our conventional behavior as practical critics. To do standard academic interpretation (hereafter SAI) is to explain as coherently and comprehensively as possible the how and why of a text's signification. Because SAI has as its goal cognitive explanation, it involves a kind of translation. The text's language is viewed as that which is in need of explanation; the interpreter provides some other context and some other language—in effect, a code—to achieve that explanation.[4] In SAI, the key move in developing the explanatory code is abstraction from the details of the text. My claim about the gap between reading and SAI is that academic interpreters typically do not attend to the multileveled act of reading when they perform this abstraction.

I hasten to add that I consider this situation neither a scandal nor a surprise. Because the numbers and kinds of possible translations are potentially infinite (though at any given juncture in the history of criticism only a finite number will be practiced),[5] there is no *necessary* connection between reading and the endpoint of any one interpretation, and the last thing I want to do is to try to legislate one. Indeed, much of the current valuable work in cultural studies and the New Historicism depends on the interpreter doing such things as finding points of contact between literary and other cultural representations—activities that often appear unconnected to the interpreter's reading experience.[6]

Nevertheless, I believe that our conventional habits leave largely undeveloped one very rich kind of interpretive practice, one that I will call *rhetorical reader-response*. This practice follows from the position I sketched in the introduction and exemplified most fully in the essay "Sharing Secrets," which defines rhetorical reading as the recursive relationship between authorial agency, textual phenomena, and reader response. Thus, it assumes that the text is a sharable medium of a multileveled communication between author and reader, even as it takes the reader's experience of the text as the starting point for interpretation. Its effort is to link response to interpretation by seeking textual sources for individual responses, while also acknowledging that the construal of those textual sources is influenced by the reader's subjectivity. In other words, in its way of linking reading to interpretation, rhetorical reader-response maintains both that the text constructs the reader and that the reader constructs the text, with the result that it does not believe that there is always a clear, sharply defined border between what is sharable and what is personal in reading and interpretation. Furthermore, even as the approach starts with response, it does not regard that response as something fixed beyond question but rather as something that may change and develop in the very effort to link reading and interpretation.[7] All this helps clarify the claims I want to make for what follows: when I speak of the experience of reading *Beloved* here, I am referring to my experience. Nevertheless, I will try to focus on elements of my experience that I take to be not idiosyncratic but sharable. Moreover, in this essay I am not primarily concerned with trying to specify the boundary between textual and personal sources of experience. Instead, I want to explore further the typical gap between reading and SAI in order to reconsider SAI's treatment of textual recalcitrance, a reconsideration that in turn will reveal the desires driving SAI. Finally, both explorations will have significant consequences for the claims I want to make about *Beloved* and about rhetorical reader-response criticism.

The Difficult, the Stubborn, and Interpretive Desire

One of the challenges and pleasures of interpretation is finding the "right translation," uncovering a code that allows us to claim cognitive understanding of the text, to hear the "click" of the numerous signals of the text rearranging themselves into our new system of intelligibility. Virtually all texts, to one degree or another, present some obstacles to the interpreter, some material that initially seems resistant to whatever translation schema the interpreter is employing.

We academic interpreters naturally gravitate toward recalcitrant material, but we typically assume that all recalcitrance can yield to understanding, even if all that is finally revealed is the inevitability of recalcitrance.[8] Indeed, this desire for and faith in explanation is the enabling assumption of some of our best criticism. But by always assuming that everything can be explained, we overlook the possibility that sometimes recalcitrance may not be overcome—that is, may not be overcome without some sacrifice of explanatory power. Saying that Beloved is this and this and this and that and that and that without attending to the difficulty of integrating all those identities explains Beloved in one way, but it does not explain what it is like to read and respond to her in the novel. Reading *Beloved* leads me to propose a distinction between two kinds of obstacles to understanding that result in two kinds of reading experience: *The difficult* is recalcitrance that yields to our explanatory efforts, while *the stubborn* is recalcitrance that will not yield.[9]

The first chapter of Morrison's narrative offers an encounter with the difficult. Morrison herself has offered a response-based account of her strategy, saying that she wanted her readers to experience "the compelling confusion of being there as they [the characters] are; suddenly, without comfort or succor from the 'author,' with only imagination, intelligence, and necessity available for the journey" ("Unspeakable Things Unspoken," 33). Morrison's technique does, indeed, induce a "compelling confusion," one that envelops all the characters and even the setting. Questions about Sethe, Denver, Baby Suggs, the ghost, and Paul D, about their pasts, their presents, and their futures, pile up with each new sentence. Yet, with some work, including rereading, and some patience, this confusion yields to understanding, and we can see how Morrison uses this difficulty to influence our entrance into her "imaginative world." In making us feel off-balance, she highlights many of that world's particular ground rules, including some that not all of her readers will share: in this world, ghosts are not only present but taken for granted; in this world, the past coexists with the present.

As I've already suggested, I believe that Beloved herself is a paradigmatic case of the stubborn. Despite the best efforts of many careful readers, her character escapes any comprehensive, coherent account.

No matter how we arrange or rearrange the information about Beloved, there is always something that does not fit with the experience of everything else. We can solve the problem by following Deborah Ayer Sitter's advice to "regard Beloved as a function rather than a person" (29), advice which in effect says "change your assumptions and your expectations; stop trying to read about a person here and recognize that you are reading about a synthetic construct that Morrison can maneuver as she sees fit." But finally, following this advice seems to require neglecting the way Morrison cues us to read Beloved as both a function and a person. When we read, say, about Paul D's encounter with her in the cold house, we experience him first struggling against and then consenting not just to a function but also to a person—however enigmatic.

In the brief discussion of *Beloved*'s first chapter as an instance of the difficult, I followed Morrison's lead and suggested some positive role, some functionality for that experience. I want to claim a similar functionality for the stubborn, a claim that highlights its paradoxical nature. On the one hand, I am identifying the stubborn as that which resists explanation; on the other, in claiming that it has a positive functionality, I am suggesting that it can yield to one kind of explanation, thereby apparently containing and confining it—and so collapsing it back into the difficult. I will say more about this paradox after trying to clarify the claim about functionality by distinguishing the stubborn and the difficult from a third kind of recalcitrance, one that lacks a positive functionality, *the erroneous*.

Again *Beloved* furnishes an example. Despite Morrison's careful planning, she indicates in the first chapter two conflicting dates for the narrative's present time action: 1873 and 1891.[10] I see no way of resolving this conflict, and apart from specious generalizations about Morrison dramatizing the difficulty of reconstructing history, I cannot find any account of its functionality.[11] The conflict is an instance of the erroneous, a small distraction (if noticed at all) that has no positive contribution to make and no functionality within Morrison's narrative. By contrast, the stubborn is an experienced recalcitrance whose very resistance to explanation contributes significantly to the experience of the larger narrative. In other words, although it cannot be fully comprehended, we may be able to comprehend its effects. Indeed, when the reader encounters the stubborn, the interpretive task shifts from explicating it to explaining the purpose of its recalcitrance.

Articulating the distinction between the difficult and the stubborn invites reflection on SAI's underlying desire for mastery—and articulating the paradox of the stubborn invites similar reflection about the desire of a rhetorical reader-response criticism. Whatever we do with texts, however much we admire their power, and however much we pay lip service to their inexhaustibility, the act of interpretation rests upon a desire to make texts yield up their secrets, to take possession of them. This desire to possess, as I said above, often leads to brilliant interpretive insights, but it also blinds interpretation to its own hubris. Introducing the category of the stubborn into rhetorical reader-response makes possible a recognition of that hubris. The paradox of the stubborn, however, also allows for the repression of that recognition: if we get caught up in explaining the stubborn's functionality, we can erase its elusiveness and turn its stubbornness into the Truth of the text, which we once again possess. Letting the stubborn remain stubborn means that we accept the possibility that "the struggle to interpret and perform" a sharable world is one we cannot entirely win. In this light, the paradox of the stubborn can be seen as its simultaneous effect of enriching that struggle and preventing it from being completely successful.[12]

Encountering the Stubborn: Reading/Interpreting Beloved

A baby ghost. A spiteful, venomous baby ghost. No, a "sad" ghost (8). Or a "lonely and rebuked" one (13)? Still, a powerful baby ghost, who can make the whole house pitch. A tired breathing.

These multiple signifiers attach to her and haunt or brood over her later bodily incarnation(s).

An innocent, needy twenty year old. In need of a mother. With no wrinkles. Who comes when Sethe's water breaks. Who calls herself Beloved. Who has a scar on her neck. Who can't walk but picks up a chair single-handed. Denver's guess about her identity is also mine. But what does Beloved want? None of the previous associations seems exactly apt—she is not spiteful or venomous or powerful and, after a while, not tired.

Self-absorbed and Sethe-obsessed. Thirsty—for mother love. "Tell me your diamonds" (58).

Her appearance is disruptive—Sethe, Denver, and Paul were moving toward some harmony—and exciting. What mysteries does she contain?

Puzzling conversation with Denver. Cross-purpose communications?

> "Why you call yourself Beloved?"
> "In the dark my name is Beloved."
> "What's it like over there, where you were before? Can you tell me?"
> "Dark. . . . I'm small in that place."
> . . . "Tell me, how did you get here?"
> "I wait; then I got on the bridge. I stay there in the dark, in the daytime, in the dark, in the daytime. It was a long time." (75)

Return from the underworld? Survival of Middle Passage? There is a difference, but what is it? As the mystery deepens, my attachment grows.

Return of the spiteful. Why strangle Sethe? Revenge? Seems more like jealousy: Sethe is thinking that she is glad to have Paul D. A warning delivered? So obscurely? But is she the strangler? She denies it when Denver asks her why, but she acts guilty. Still, she claims, "The circle of iron choked her." OK, Sethe as slave. But Sethe never wore the literal iron. Is Beloved a seer then? A haunting, strangely frightening prophet.

The Ghost of Sex. Moving Paul D. Against his conscious will. Finally coming to him in the cold house. "You have to touch me. On the inside part. And you have to call me my name" (117). Motivation? Yes, separate Paul from Sethe. But there's more. She wants him for herself. Why? To be Sethe's rival? Electra? And why does she have power over Paul? Wilt says that Beloved acts out the other characters' psychic needs; suggests Denver's desire to separate Paul and Sethe, and Paul's need to break the lock on his tobacco tin. *Suggestive, but not finally satisfying. Beloved loses her identity in this view. Perhaps the sexual battle is the flip side of their battle when she was a ghost. And now she wins? But why can she break apart Paul's tobacco tin when his loving Sethe hasn't yet done that? Emotions mingle here: touched by her vulnerability, haunted by her power, scared and relieved for Paul.*

More puzzles. Beloved knows one white man. *Perhaps she is not the crawling-already? baby returned.* Beloved disappears when she accompanies Denver to the cold house. *She must be a returned ghost.* Beloved curls up in the dark and points to a face Denver can't see—"her face," which is then "Me. It's me" (124). *A Middle Passage ghost?* Beloved "knows" that she could wake up and find herself in pieces. *More conflicting feelings: tenderness, fear, and always the mystery.*

Sethe comes to believe that Beloved is her daughter come back to her.

Beloved never tells her story the way Denver tells hers or Sethe and Paul D rememory theirs. And Morrison, who employs a remarkably protean narrator, never offers an inside view of Beloved—until the monologue. House and Horvitz each explicate its cryptic discourse admirably. The central story it tells is that of a small girl and her mother being forced to travel on a very crowded slave ship. The girl keeps looking for her mother's face, but she loses it when the mother jumps into the sea. She is eventually put with a man who "hurts where I sleep," but she escapes from there and comes out of the blue water to see "the face that left me"—Sethe's (212, 213). As House says, the monologue supports the view that what we have been reading is a complicated case of mistaken identities. Beloved is not Denver's sister and Sethe's daughter, but a survivor of the Middle Passage. And as Morrison says, the desires of this independent survivor and those of Sethe and Denver meet. Perhaps stubbornness is only difficulty.

Doesn't work. Why privilege the monologue over everything else? Though things like the white man get explained (or more accurately, now have possible explanations), much is still left unexplained: the strangling, the moving of Paul D, the disappearance. Furthermore, so much of the experience of the previous twenty-one chapters depends on the *possibility* that Beloved is Sethe's daughter that transforming the stubbornness into difficulty denies the experience.

BETTER TO THINK OF THE MONOLOGUE AS A COUNTER TO THE POWERFUL RESPONSES TO BELOVED AS SISTER AND DAUGHTER IN DENVER'S AND SETHE'S MONOLOGUES. MONOLOGUE DEEPENS STUBBORNNESS RATHER THAN TRANSFORMS IT. NOW MOVED INSIDE BELOVED'S FEAR AND CONFUSION AND PAIN—ATTACHMENT AND SYMPATHY INCREASE EVEN AS THE MYSTERY DOES.

The stubbornness persists as Beloved fades into the background and

Denver moves up front. *Who is this character draining Sethe of her life?* Rushdy says she is the incarnation of Sethe's guilt. *Makes good sense of some things—Sethe on a hopeless quest of expiation. But Beloved-as-Guilt-Incarnate denies the experience of her monologue and simplifies the complex dynamics between Beloved, Sethe, and Denver. But her childlike selfishness complicates feelings further—understandable yet dangerous; I fear for Sethe, Beloved is too much with her. And me?*

The strange disappearance. How? Where? Is she pregnant?

Who is she in the last two pages?

From Encounter to Formal Interpretation: The Ending of *Beloved*

After concluding the penultimate chapter with an intimate scene of hope and reconciliation between Sethe and Paul D, the narrator suddenly swerves to a very different spatial, temporal, and emotional stance, one that puts considerable distance between that intimate scene and the concerns of the final two pages. In them, the narrator writes a kind of elegy for Beloved that also subtly calls attention to some larger claims that Morrison herself wants to make for her narrative. The effects of attending to Beloved as stubborn are inseparable from the development of these claims as we seek to interpret the difficulties of this chapter. After the opening paragraph, which effectively breaks the mood of the previous scene by discussing different kinds of loneliness (Sethe's loneliness that "can be rocked" and Paul D and Beloved's loneliness that "roams" [274]), the narrator turns her full attention to Beloved.

"Everybody knew what she was called, but nobody anywhere knew her name. Disremembered and unaccounted for, she cannot be lost because no one is looking for her, and even if they were, how can they call her if they don't know her name?" (274).

These sentences complicate our relation to Beloved and to the larger narrative, because they emphasize her stubbornness and begin to introduce the paradox of the reading/writing situation as well as to split the awareness of the authorial and narrative audiences.[13] The characters may forget Beloved, but we do not. Indeed, the narrator's insistence on bringing her back into the narrative and calling her "disremembered" paradoxically emphasizes that she is not entirely forgotten, not entirely disremembered. We cannot, however, escape the assertion of the first sentence. And since we do not know her name, we do not know her origin—and do not, cannot fully know her. The two sentences together deepen the paradox of reading Beloved: unlike the others who knew her name, we do not dismember her by "disremembering" her, but we also do not really know this woman we are remembering.

The shift to the present tense in the second sentence further complicates the reading situation. On the very first page of the narrative, the narrator has made us aware that she and her audience are contemporaries, that we exist together in a present distant from the time of the action. "In fact," she says, "Ohio had been calling itself a state *only* seventy years" (3). Only from a temporal vantage point of considerably later than 1873 would the narrator use that *only.* By employing the present tense here and not clearly indicating that it is the historical present, the narrator subtly includes her contemporary audience among those who are not looking for Beloved. But this very inclusion foregrounds the split between the narrative and the authorial audiences. As members of the narrative audience, we may at one level be among those who are not seeking Beloved, but at another level, by the very act of taking in the narrator's words, we are seeking her and remembering her. As members of the authorial audience, we can initially exempt ourselves from any implication in the "disremembering" or the looking because we know that Beloved is a fictional character rather than a historical person. By using the narrator to call attention to the split between audiences, Morrison is beginning to move toward some larger claims about the *kind* of story she has been telling.

"Although she has claim, she is not claimed. In the place where the long grass opens, the girl who waited to be loved and cry shame erupts into her separate parts, to make it easy for the chewing laughter to swallow her all away" (274).

Again the present tense signals our inclusion. Beloved has claim on our attention, our knowledge. But her stubbornness means that she cannot be contained by our knowledge. The first sentence also conveys an implied challenge to the authorial audience. Will we claim, if not her reality, her story—with all its stubbornness? This question becomes more urgent as the narrator picks up numerous threads from Beloved's monologue—the long grass where Beloved first lost her African mother, her fear of breaking into pieces and being chewed and swallowed—and interweaves them in a metaphorical description of her erasure from history. As the narrator turns elegiac for Beloved here, Morrison also begins to draw upon the stubbornness of the character and the complex emotions the narrative has evoked to proliferate her signification and make a claim about her significance. The erasure of Beloved from history is the erasure of the small African child who lost her mother in the long grass, as well as the African American who feared she would fall apart when she lost her tooth, as well as all the slave women she comes to represent.

"It was not a story to pass on" (274).

The bald statement, after white space and with the vague "It," disrupts our reading because it is so apparently self-contradictory. Hasn't the narrator just "passed on" the story, and haven't we just spent an enormous amount of emotional energy reading it? Of course, one way to naturalize the sentence is to stay in the narrative audience and read it as the indirect discourse of Beloved's community, to interpret it as their response to her appearance and disappearance. But because the white space encourages our attributing the vision and voice of the sentence to the narrator, we become aware of additional readings, even in the narrative audience. "It was not *a story* to pass on" and "it was not a story *to pass on*"—in the sense of "to pass by"—but it was something else, *a reality to be confronted.* Sethe and Denver were not able to read the story of Beloved's possible other identity. Beloved was never able to recognize the difference of Sethe's story from her African mother's. Only we have seen the irreconcilable stories and the character who cannot be contained by either; only we have felt the full range of emotions generated by her narrative. Will we adopt the attitude expressed in the indirect discourse and find the stubbornness of Beloved's character a reason not to pass on her story? Or will we accept the challenge of confronting its multiple, stubbornly shifting realities?

There is yet another layer here, one that we may see more clearly in the light of both the paradox of stubbornness and the underlying desire of interpretation for mastery. In focusing so far on the productive functionality of Beloved's stubbornness, I have in a sense been making that stubbornness the key to the ending—and by extension to Morrison's narrative. I have, in other words, been turning the stubborn into the difficult—and exhibiting once again the power of interpretation's desire for mastery and possession. But even as "It was not a story to pass on" challenges the authorial audience to confront the multiple realities of Beloved, it also challenges our ability to share those realities. More particularly, I must ask how much I, as a privileged white male reader, see and fail to see, share and fail to share in Morrison's vision of the horrors of the Middle Passage, of slavery, of the intensity and desperation of Sethe's mother love—and that of Margaret Garner, the historical figure upon whom Sethe's story is based. To presume mastery here is to move beyond hubris.

> They forgot her like a bad dream. After they made up their tales, shaped and decorated them, those that saw her that day on the porch quickly and deliberately forgot her. It took longer for those who had spoken to her, lived with her, fallen in love with her, to forget, until they realized they couldn't remember or repeat a single thing she said, and began to believe that, other than what they themselves were thinking, she hadn't said anything at all. So, in the end, they forgot her too. Remembering seemed unwise. . . .
>
> It was not a story to pass on. (274–75)

Morrison continues to implicate her audience in the narrator's statements and to press her challenge about what we will do with our reading of Beloved's story. Beloved is a painful memory even for those who knew her, because she reminds everyone of the depths of pain they endured in slavery. A white reader like myself may try to escape the pain—and any responsibility—by confessing, as I just did, the limits of his understanding. But this passage blocks that move. In reading this narrative, we—white readers, black readers, all readers—have, in a sense, lived with Beloved. Will we forget her because it is unwise to remember, unwise because remembering may entail some responsibility to her memory? At this juncture, the repetition of "It was not a story to pass on" continues the challenge in the same vein: to pass on this story is to be unwise because the story is too disturbing and too unsettling, has depths of pain that may never be plumbed. The implication about the cowardice of turning one's back is clear.

> So they forgot her. Like an unpleasant dream during a troubling sleep. Occasionally, however, the rustle of a skirt hushes when they wake, and the knuckles brushing a cheek in sleep seem to belong to the sleeper. . . . They can touch it [an old photograph] if they like, but don't, because they know things will never be the same if they do.
>
> This is not a story to pass on. (275)

The ending takes a significant turn at "however." They may forget/repress—we may forget/repress—but Beloved is not thereby erased from history. She lives on in some way. Furthermore, once we acknowledge her presence in history, "things will never be the same." By having the narrator shift from "It was" to "This is" not a story to pass on, Morrison addresses the authorial audience most directly. Furthermore, the sentence is now loaded with almost as many meanings as Beloved, and it has its force precisely because Beloved has been so loaded with meanings. This is not just a story to tell for amusement; this is not a story to pass by; this is not a story to tell lightly, because once you tell it things will never be the same. But this is also not a story that you will ever fully comprehend.

At this point, then, Morrison has gradually built up to some very significant claims for *Beloved*. Morrison has transformed the historical event that provided the germ of the narrative, Margaret Garner's killing her child in 1855 and expressing serenity afterwards, into an emotionally powerful fiction. In this conclusion, however, she is challenging us to treat the narrative as a species of history. In insisting on Beloved's enduring presence and the power of her story, Morrison is drawing upon the representative quality of all the possibilities that Beloved has come to stand for and be associated with: all the daughters and all the families whose lives were twisted by "the men without skin"; all those who lived under slavery, and who lived with its legacy even after it was outlawed; indeed, the "sixty million and more" who died on the slave ships and to whom Morrison dedicates the book. At the same time, by concentrating the power of all these possibilities within the single character, Morrison points to the depths of each: we can name the multiplicity, but we cannot claim to know it in the sense of mastering it.

> By and by all trace is gone, and what is forgotten is not only the footprints but the water too and what is down there. The rest is weather. Not the breath of the disremembered and unaccounted for, but wind in the eaves, or spring ice thawing too quickly. Just weather. Certainly no clamor for a kiss.
>
> Beloved. (275)

These last two segments of the narrative complete it in an appropriately powerful way. Remaining in the present tense, the narrator details the final disappearance of Beloved, and then employs the negatives to suggest her ineradicable presence beneath all denials of her. More than that, the negatives suggest her need to "be loved." Then finally, the narrator utters her name. The functions of this signifier are now manifold. In the immediate context, "Beloved" signals the return of the repressed. Not just ineradicably there underneath our history, she—and all those she stands for—are now produced for our contemplation and are what this narrative leaves us with. Unable to do justice to all the complex realities signified by "Beloved," we nevertheless end our reading by attending to them. Moreover, this narrative, which takes its title from this word, stands as testimony to the presence and the complexity of those realities.

At the same time, the word breaks the pattern of repetitions. "It was not a story to pass on." "It was not a story to pass on." "This is not a story to pass on." "Beloved." The eruption of the word itself exemplifies the point: not a story to pass on, but a person whose multiplicity transcends any story that can be told about her. And here the importance of the fiction comes back: her story stands in for the millions and millions of other slaves, whose lives and deaths, though not passed on in story, are just as deep, just as emotionally wrenching, just as important and just as stubborn as hers.

The pattern also makes "Beloved" available to be read not just as the narrator's final word but also as Morrison's final address to her readers. Just as the preacher at Beloved's funeral began by addressing his audience, "Dearly beloved," so Morrison ends by addressing us as

"Beloved." The intratextual link makes it a gesture of affection and a reminder of the challenge: we are beloved, not yet Dearly Beloved. This reminder of the character's naming effectively blocks any impulse to romanticize the character even as we keep her story alive: the reminder calls back what Sethe did to get the name on the tombstone, and, indeed, it calls back the knowledge that "Beloved" is the tombstone marker itself. Furthermore, this reminder once again blocks any impulse to master the stubbornness of her character by pointing to the gaps that keep her from yielding to our understanding and then by extension to all the history that we have lost, especially to that of the sixty million and more whose names we do not know. "Everybody knew what she was called, but nobody anywhere knew her name" (274).

Recursiveness and the Limits of Interpretation

Beloved still eludes me, but I feel that I see more of her. I still cannot—and do not want to—transform Beloved's stubbornness into a difficulty to solve, but I comprehend some of the reasons for that stubbornness. Furthermore, just as the effort to attend to the stubborn has helped root interpretation in the experience of reading, so too has interpretation allowed for a clarification, an enrichment of that reading experience. Within this rhetorical reader-response approach, reading and interpretation, like thinking and writing, can be endlessly recursive, each one opening up the possibility of revision in what the other has just done.

Perhaps more significantly, the stubborn helps reveal the limitations of interpretation's desire for mastery, helps remind us that the effort to perform an author's world does not always have to result in a virtuoso performance for the interpretation to be valuable and enlightening. In the spirit of that recognition, I offer the conclusions of this essay not as fixed, frozen, and beyond question but as working hypotheses about complex matters. To claim any more would be to exhibit a decidedly unproductive personal stubbornness.

Appendix

Why Wayne Booth Can't Get with the Program; or, The Nintentional Fallacy

This essay is a rather different experiment with the form of the critical essay from the one undertaken in chapter 9. Its success or failure rides at least as much on the handling of voice as on the specific critical principles being explored. In any event, since the dominant voice here belongs to one Jonathan Allen rather than to the "I" of these headnotes and the "I" of all the previous essays, it might be a welcome change for all of you who have let that "I" speak into your ears for lo, these many pages.

A couple of weeks ago, while I was in the throes of drafting a paper about the significant alterations in Wayne Booth's thinking implied by his developing the concept of coduction in *The Company We Keep,* I received a rather amazing letter. As soon as I read it, I realized that it contained a far more appropriate assessment of Booth's evolving thoughts about the relations between authors, texts, and readers than anything my lugubrious analysis would yield. This letter, as you'll see, is far from unqualified praise of Booth, but I believe it gets at aspects of his work that a more reverential approach would just plain miss.

Ucando Interpretation Schema
1212 Madison Ave.
New York, NY 10101

Dear Professor Phelan:

You probably don't know who I am, though I did receive a little notoriety among members of the MLA back in 1986 when *College English* published the text of a talk I gave to the Executive Council. As president of the Madison Avenue Advertising Board, I proposed that the MLA support the Board's idea of using well-known fictional characters to endorse commercial products. (Becky Sharp for MasterCard and Abel Magwitch for True Value Hardware Stores ["A True Value file is a real pip"] were two of my favorites.) Of course those stodgy Council members weren't, shall we say, buying, so we never launched the campaign. Despite that disappointment, I haven't abandoned my quest to put literary studies in the center of our national consciousness by linking them to popular culture. And just recently, I've had my Breakthrough Insight. Like the Canon automatic camera, my thinking is so advanced it's simple. As one of my humanities professors once said, it's all a matter of formulating the right question. As soon as I asked, what are the hottest things going in literary study and in children's popular culture, I knew how Lily Briscoe felt when she saw how to finish her painting. Theory and Nintendo: revolution via the computer; turn interpretation into a Nintendo game and transform the nation's consciousness. Students of America, liberate that signifier, but beware the mise-en-abyme; explore different levels of signification; uncover the cultural code, find the magic theme, and rescue the princess Meaning. Move over, Super Mario Brothers; here come Nina Baym and Wayne Booth. Move over, Nintendo Entertainment Systems; here comes Ucando Interpretation Schema.

My research and development team—a half-dozen recent Ph.D.s who did dissertations in critical theory but couldn't find teaching jobs—has already developed several schema in the few short months of our operation, including the one that I expect to be our hottest seller, "PC or Not PC?" But the reason that I'm writing to you is that we've gotten stuck with the one based on Booth's theory, tentatively entitled "The Wayne Dance." The research team is getting pretty fed up and one of them has been complaining that Booth isn't worth all the trouble he's been giving us—"he's not, you know, what I'd call poststructuralistically trendy." To be honest, I'm getting pretty frustrated myself—after all, I've got a cultural revolution to get under way here—but I'm not quite ready to give up: I seem to have a soft spot in my heart for the unreliable narrator. I called Booth for advice, but, frankly, he was no help at all. I was shocked to learn that he'd never even heard of Nintendo let alone played it: I guess they don't make Renaissance men like they used to. He did, however, recommend I write to you—"Phelan's weird enough to get into this" was what he said.

Let me describe the basic setup and one of our successes so you can get a better idea of what we'd like to do with "The Wayne Dance." The first screen in every schema shows a figure (or two, if you are playing against someone) at one end of a landscape. The figures, whom we call His and Her Meneut, remain the same from schema to schema but the landscape always varies. In the deconstructionist game, for example, it's a well-planned neighborhood, with carefully tended gardens, symmetrical houses, a well-organized downtown. In "PC or Not PC?" it's the interior of a church: the Meneut figure stands at the back and looks down the aisle at the people filling the pews on the left and the right, shouting back and forth at each other. The object of the game is to advance across the landscape to some designated desirable point. To play, you run the light of a scanning pen over whatever text you select and then answer the questions that appear on the screen. With every question you answer, the Meneut figure advances a few steps into the landscape, and sometimes the landscape itself gets transformed and reconfigured around her.

Let's say that the text is Poe's "The Cask of Amontillado" and you're playing the deconstructionist game, "Always Already Aporia!" The object of the game is to break down the orderliness of the initial landscape until you reach a point where you can no longer tell which way to move because all lines of differentiation between the gardens, roads, houses, suburbs, and downtown get lost. You begin by using the scanning pen to read the first paragraph into the game's memory:

"The thousand injuries of Fortunato I had borne as I best could, but when he ventured upon insult I vowed revenge. You, who so well know the nature of my soul, will not suppose, however, that I gave utterance to a threat. At *length* I would be avenged; this was a point definitely settled—but the very definitiveness with which it was resolved precluded the idea of risk. I must not only punish but punish with impunity. A wrong is unredressed when retribution overtakes its redresser. It is equally unredressed when the avenger fails to make himself felt as such to him who has done the wrong."

Then the following question appears on the screen: "In this text which are the apparently privileged terms, *insult* or *injury; revenge* or *retribution*?" If you select *insult* and *revenge,* then a new screen appears in which His Meneut has advanced a little into a landscape that is losing its order: the gardens are no longer neatly rectangular; the roads now wind and vary in length. To get to the final point of aporia, you have to answer correctly a whole series of questions that lead you to see that the apparently privileged terms are in fact dependent on the subordinate ones: Montresor's vengeful insults to Fortunato have their power because they are prelude to the ultimate injury—murder. Montresor, indeed, has his revenge, but his revenge also has him, and it is his having him that produces this text, a text that simultaneously boasts of his successful revenge and testifies by its very existence to the way retribution has overtaken him. Pretty neat, huh? A few weeks ago I thought a privileged term was what you used to refer to the queen of England; now I'm ready to challenge J. Hillis Miller to a game of "Always Already." Imagine what the Nintendo generation will do with our schema.

Frankly, though, our success with deconstruction makes me more frustrated and impatient with Booth. We had no trouble selecting a landscape—an elegant, albeit somewhat crowded, dance floor. We also decided to introduce a third figure into the schema, one we've named Implied Arthur—A-r-t-h-a for the female version. Our idea was this: at the beginning of "The Wayne Dance" Her Meneut and Arthur would be at opposite sides of the floor; as the scanner read the text, music would start to play and the other figures on the floor would begin to dance. As the player answers questions correctly, Her Meneut and Arthur would start to move around the other figures and objects on the floor, trying ultimately to reach a meeting point in the exact center, where they would then dance together. Their meeting would trigger new music and their dance would go on as long as the player desired. Sounds good, right?

Well, we can't get anything to work. The first trouble we had was developing the schema so that it would differentiate between correct and incorrect answers to whatever questions we formulated. As usual, we used the computer to help develop the schema: we loaded all of Booth's books into the computer's memory and gave it a few instructions about organizing the material. But when we started trying out questions, the computer kept either getting hung up or allowing multiple answers. One of the researchers finally suggested that we erase *Critical Understanding* from the memory—"That pluralist claptrap about multiple validity messes up the computer's binary operations." Then someone else said we should probably also erase *Modern Dogma and the Rhetoric of Assent*—"I'm afraid that now we have a program whose first impulse is to say yes to every answer." Sure, sure, I said, just get me a game that works. But they still haven't.

Take the first paragraph of Poe again. It's easy enough to program the game to recognize the first-person pronoun and then generate the question, "Is the Narrator reliable?" What we can't do is program the game to recognize whether yes or no is a better answer: there just doesn't seem to be anything in Poe's language that settles the matter. We also are at our wit's end with the problem of how to handle irony: there doesn't seem to be any surefire trigger even to produce the question, never mind getting the machine to distinguish between answers. If you don't mind my saying so, I'm starting to suspect that all Booth's work is just rhetorical voodoo. When I came in this morning, I had this memo from one of the researchers on my desk.

"I think I've figured out why we can't do The Wayne Dance. Despite his reputation as an old Chicago School formalist, all Booth's work finally depends on matters that are not actually available in the formal features of texts. Deciding whether a narrator is reliable or unreliable, whether an utterance is ironic or nonironic, whether a third-person narrator is a dramatization of an authorial self or of a different persona—none of these decisions can be made only by pointing to the text. In every case, Booth is talking about the communication of values and beliefs through language—and through what language doesn't say. He's talking about how authors imply their values and how readers infer those values, and though he tries like hell in the *Irony* book and elsewhere to make those processes intelligible, it's clear that in his view there are no immutable rules for understanding them. Amazingly, though, he believes more firmly that this kind of communication occurs than that he or anyone else will be able to explain it adequately. I think his faith is romantic tosh—but I know, I know, mine's not to reason why / mine's just to program and sigh. Anyway, maybe if I just focus on *The Company We Keep,* I can figure out something."

Wait, here's the same guy with another memo. . . . Worse news.

"I thought that junk from *The Rhetoric of Fiction* and *A Rhetoric of Irony* was hard to work with. This stuff in *Company* is impossible. What's more, if we take it seriously we have to redesign the whole game. Coduction changes everything. Booth's reader doesn't just dance with the author anymore. She dances with other readers, too, so we'd have to have all the figures moving in relation to each other. Yet, they shouldn't all be doing the same dance, and indeed, they shouldn't all be hearing the same music. Booth's thinking seems to go something like this: if decisions about understanding are difficult, decisions about values are even more so. But like the effort and the process involved in understanding, the effort and process involved in evaluating are crucial for human life and for the communities in which we live. In *Company,* Booth's own ethical commitment to rhetorical community is even stronger than his commitment to understanding the absent author. In retrospect, his evolution to this position seems inevitable—there are just a few seeds of it in *The Rhetoric of Fiction* and *A Rhetoric of Irony*—but those seeds are developing into roots in *Modern Dogma* and *Critical Understanding.* The rationale behind his recommendation to assent to another's argument until having reasons not to and the rationale behind his choice of a pluralism based on vitality, justice, and understanding are essentially the same: the practices that follow from these commitments will enhance the lives of those who meet in intellectual exchange of whatever kind.

Anyway, in *Company* Booth testifies that his dancing with other readers has made him able to make moves on the floor that he'd never have been able to do with just himself and the author. His dancing is a lot messier than it used to be, and he often doesn't know when to stop, but he seems happier. Less uptight, more willing to be wrong, though oddly also more committed to the questions of ethical evaluation that got him into trouble in *The Rhetoric of Fiction*. Well, I'm glad he's happier, but the whole thing seems crazier and crazier to me: does Booth really live in the postmodern, poststructuralist 1990s? I know, I know, you just care about getting the schema to work. I'm now convinced that there is no way to do that. It's time to stop the music on 'The Wayne Dance.'"

Professor Phelan, is my man right? Is there any way to save "The Wayne Dance," any way to keep Booth part of the coming revolution? Please reply as soon as possible. I'll remember you when the revolution comes.

Urgently,

Jonathan Allen

My reply was short.

Dear Mr. Allen:

I think you have two choices: (1) make "The Wayne Dance" a game for two or more players and have the schema produce the same response at every juncture: "Read this carefully and then talk about it with your partners for as long as you want." (2) Start the revolution without Booth; somehow I don't think he'll mind.

Sincerely,

James Phelan

Notes

Introduction

1. It is perhaps especially significant that this second request comes as a spontaneous interruption to the maid's story: so caught up is Madame Blanchard in the narrative that her impatience to learn what happened next paradoxically leads her to slow down the progress of the narration by her expression of interest in having it move to the next stage.

2. For more on this definition see Barbara Herrnstein Smith and the reply by Seymour Chatman.

3. *Deconstruction* by now is a term whose meaning has widened considerably as it has been disseminated through our culture. It is not only Derridean philosophers and critics who deconstruct but also television personalities and sportswriters—indeed, anyone who questions anything is liable to be called a deconstructor. Within the realm of theory, to deconstruct sometimes now means to demystify or to show that what we thought was natural and immutable is actually constructed and changeable as well as to show how a given logic, when read rigorously, undermines itself. I am concerned with this last meaning of the term not only because I think it is closer to what was originally seen as radical in deconstruction but also because it is the one that bears most closely upon deconstruction's attention to rhetoric.

4. Having offered these generalizations, I hasten to add some important qualifications. Barbara Johnson's work, especially in her recent book, *The Wake of Deconstruction,* shows that deconstruction is neither passé nor incompatible with a politically engaged criticism. Furthermore, her statement—and demonstration—that "the point of a deconstructive analysis is not to treat intentionality as an 'on off' switch but to analyze the functioning of many different, sometimes incommensurable, *kinds* of intentionality" (18) moves deconstructive practice closer to the kind of rhetorical analysis I attempt here, just as, in ways I will discuss below, my shift away from emphasizing intention moves my rhetorical analysis in the direction of Johnson's. In other words, although Johnson remains more interested in incompatibilities among kinds of intentionality and I remain more interested in reconstructing coherences, I also find a greater overlap between the underlying conceptions of rhetorical

reading in her work and mine than I do in the work of the earlier, more widely influential Anglo-American deconstructors such as Paul de Man and J. Hillis Miller, whose conceptions I focus on here.

5. See especially *A Rhetoric of Irony* (1974), where Booth includes "intended" as one of the marks of stable irony and where he employs E. D. Hirsch Jr.'s distinction between meaning and significance throughout his argument; in addition, see the final—and longest—chapter of *Critical Understanding* (1979), where Booth employs different concepts of author as guides to rhetorical reading. In *The Company We Keep* (1988), Booth complicates his previous rhetorical model by introducing into it the concept of "coduction," the way in which readers' interactions with each other help modify their responses (especially their ethical responses) to narratives. With his sights set on the knotty problem of the "ethics of fiction," however, Booth does not directly address the question of how significant an adjustment he is making in his rhetorical model.

6. One recent strong example of the approach is Peter J. Rabinowitz's *Before Reading,* a study of the recursive relationships between interpretive conventions and textual details. Rabinowitz shows how these relations guide readers' efforts to fashion the text, which he metaphorically postulates as an unassembled swing set, into an intelligible whole.

Chapter 1

1. By "implied audience" here I mean what Peter J. Rabinowitz has called "the authorial audience," i.e., the hypothetical audience that possesses the requisite knowledge and interpretive skills to respond as the author intended. Since most readers typically try to join this hypothetical audience, I shall refer to it here as "we." For more on audiences in narrative see Phelan, *Reading People, Reading Plots;* Rabinowitz, "Truth in Fiction" and *Before Reading;* and chapter 7 of this book.

2. Friedman goes on to employ psychoanalytic theory to uncover the gendered dimensions of the opposition she posits and to discuss how elements of lyric in Barrett Browning's "Aurora Leigh," H.D.'s *HER,* and Woolf's *To the Lighthouse* disrupt the traditional sequence of narrative plots. For a later, highly insightful development of Friedman's thought about plots and plotting, see her "Spatialization: A Strategy for Reading Narrative."

3. In what follows I am influenced by the work of Elder Olson and Ralph Rader, who both emphasize that the group of works generally given the label *lyric* needs to be understood as a collection of works that operate by distinctly

different constructional principles. Olson, focusing on the boundaries between what is conveyed in lyric and what conveyed in drama or narrative, describes three kinds: lyrics of expression, which convey a single mental activity or emotional response; lyrics of address, which convey a verbal act; and lyrics of colloquy, which convey an interaction between speakers. Rader, focusing on the relations between poet and speaker in different poems, distinguishes between the dramatic monologue in which the poet creates a character other than himself; the mask lyric in which the poet adopts a persona to speak for him; the dramatic lyric in which the poet re-presents his experience through a dramatic actor; and the expressive lyric in which the poet presents his own cognitive experience. By focusing on the role of character and of judgment in lyric, I am not so much interested in testing Rader's and Olson's distinctions as I am in identifying aspects of the implied audience's relation to lyric that they do not address. For a much different approach to the lyric, one which insists on the difficulty of definition, see Albright.

4. For more on this kind of relation between speaker and author, which eliminates one plank of New Critical dogma, see Rader.

5. The present tense, a feature common to dramatic lyrics, also contributes to maintaining the lyric mode: we find the speaker describing what he sees, not narrating what he did. But this technique itself could be used to great effect in narrative, as Faulkner proves in *As I Lay Dying*.

6. It is also possible for the speaker to be more individualized than Frost's speaker, but it seems to me that once we move to a situation where the primary work of the poem is the creation of the character of a speaker (the dramatic monologue), we leave the territory of the lyric and move into the region of drama.

7. Many critics (see esp. Freedman and Richter) have richly described the characters' traits, and so I am doubly aware that any brief sketch will be reductive. But to illustrate my point about their differentiation, I will risk that reductiveness: Bernard is the storyteller, the adopter of many disguises, the husband and father; Neville, the homosexual poet, is Bernard's opposite who loves order; Louis is the successful businessman who nevertheless remains insecure; Susan is the woman who loves and who hates, who turns her back on the city and finds some contentment in her farm; Jinny is the woman who lives by the energy of her body; Rhoda, an eventual suicide, is Louis's counterpart, uncertain, insecure yet highly imaginative.

Critics such as Richter, Freedman, and Graham who see the characters as part of a single consciousness very astutely point out the ways in which the characters are joined by interlocking motifs or how, taken together, they form an image of a complete, androgynous individual. The trouble with these formulations, however, is that they deny the reading experience of the novel. In entering the lyric perspectives of each speaker, we are responding to them not as fragments of a larger symbolic whole but as individuals with separate perspectives on their experience.

8. Cf. J. W. Graham, who says that Woolf sought to establish a narrative "omnipercipience: a *perception* (not an understanding) of the characters' inner experience fused with a *perception* (not an understanding) of what they do not perceive—the background of time and the sea against which they are set" (204).

9. For a much different view of the thematic component of the novel, see Jane Marcus.

Chapter 2

1. I am acutely aware that in an essay of this length I cannot do justice to the complexity of the Showman's voice—especially when some of the essay is spent on matters other than analyzing the voice itself. I offer what I have developed here as a place to start on that much larger project, a place that offers some foundation in its general discussions of voice and of evaluation but that needs a lot more construction arising from extended analyses of the Showman's discourse, especially in relation to Amelia.

2. In part 2 of *The Rhetoric of Fiction,* "The Author's Voice in Fiction," still probably the most widely read discussion of voice in the Anglo-American critical tradition, Wayne C. Booth never seeks to identify the distinctive features of voice but instead uses the term loosely to refer to the author's *presence* and its overt manifestations through the commentary of a reliable narrator or its covert incorporation through the manipulation of an unreliable narrator. Booth's imprecision with the term does not impede his argument, which is really about authors' uses of different kinds of rhetoric for different ends, but the imprecision is, I think, symptomatic of the way Anglo American critics have thought about the term.

Mikhail Bakhtin's work on "double-voiced" discourse provides the richest source for anyone who wants to delve into the concept of voice more fully, and in what follows I acknowledge an enormous debt to his discussion in the chapter entitled "Discourse in the Novel" in *The Dialogic Imagination.* Nevertheless, to adopt Bakhtin's work entirely means to view the novel only as a site of multiple voices. That principle has its uses, but here I want to retain the notion that voice exists alongside character, style, event, setting, and other distinct elements of narrative.

3. Here my interest in voice diverges from that of Peter Elbow, who wants to investigate what makes a voice distinctive and personal. His interest follows naturally from his purpose of teaching students of writing to develop distinctive voices, and I do not think our difference amounts to a serious disagreement. I would just point out that when a writer develops a distinctive personal voice or idiolect, he simultaneously develops a relationship to one or more sociolects as well. Elbow's voice is distinctive—but distinctive within a broader sociolect of academic critical discourse.

4. For a discussion of how style functions relative to other elements of narrative, see my *Worlds from Words*.

5. Thackeray, *Vanity Fair,* 666. Hereafter references will be given by page numbers in parentheses in the text. The novel was first published serially in 1847–48 and in book form in 1848.

6. There are many exceptions, of course. Frequently, episodes cluster together into larger incidents that make the thematic point. Most noteworthy here is the mininarrative surrounding the end of Becky's intrigue with Lord Steyne. And given the device of following the same cast of characters, Thackeray can, as the narrative progresses, return to material that he has used earlier and give it some new uses. He does this recycling most obviously at the end of the narrative when Becky shows Amelia the letter George wrote her before Waterloo and when Becky reattaches herself to Jos. For a somewhat different account of the pattern of organization, see Burch.

7. This point in a sense builds upon the case that Juliet McMaster has made for the importance of the Showman's commentary.

8. For some worthwhile studies of Thackeray's technique along lines different from the ones I am developing here, see Tillotson, Loofburrow, Wheatley, Sinha, Scarry, and Ferris.

9. In *A Rhetoric of Irony,* Wayne C. Booth has persuasively argued that all irony involves victims—or at least potential victims: those people who don't get it. The difference between Thackeray's ironic one-upmanship and, say, Austen's treatment of Mrs. Bennet is that Austen's narrator, unlike the Showman, never gives us ironic commentary about Mrs. Bennet that also announces her own superiority. Indeed, although Austen's narrator frequently speaks ironically, she rarely gives direct ironic commentary in her own voice about any character but instead uses the irony to establish norms that can undercut a character's speech (quoted or reported) or behavior. She is not showing off at the character's expense the way Thackeray sometimes appears to do.

10. G. Armour Craig argues that in many cases the narrator's coyness about Becky's guilt, e.g., in her relationship with Lord Steyne, adds to the complexity

of the issue. McMaster makes a similar point. As will become clear, I do not think the coyness works that way in this passage.

Chapter 3

1. I borrow the term from Wayne C. Booth, who uses *distance* in *The Rhetoric of Fiction* to denote the relations between unreliable narrators and implied authors.

2. See Reynolds, *Hemingway's First War*, 56; and Oldsey, *Hemingway's Hidden Craft*, 64.

3. Behind this sentence is the assumption, now somewhat familiar to readers of this book, that in reading a fictionalized narrative we are asked to join two distinct audiences—the narrative audience that exists on the same fictional plane as the narrator and the authorial audience that seeks to understand the whole communication from the author, including the functions of the narrative audience. The question about voice here is tied up with a question about how the authorial audience is asked to relate to its simultaneous participation in the narrative audience. For more on these audiences, see Rabinowitz, "Truth in Fiction."

4. For a discussion along different lines of Frederic's "retrospective narration," see Nagel.

5. For more on this point, see Hamburger and Fleishman.

6. There are, of course, a few occasions when Frederic shifts from past to present and speaks with the vision he has at the time of narration: most notably when he talks about the priest knowing what he (Frederic) "was always able to forget" and when he articulates his knowledge of how the world kills everyone. But the vision and voice of these passages do not carry over into the rest of the narration, and they do not indicate that he has become a self-conscious narrator.

7. For further discussion of the passage, see *Reading People, Reading Plots,* 177, 184–85.

8. For another view on chapters 38 to 40, see Robert Lewis, *Hemingway on Love.*

9. The binary opposite of *paralipsis* is *paralepsis,* a narration defined by Prince as one "giving more information . . . than should presumably be given in terms of the focalization code governing a narrative." I consider paralepsis in my discussion of Nick Carraway's narration in chapter 5 below.

Chapter 4

1. One of the more overt elements of this scene and, indeed, of the whole opening is the emphasis on Butler as an aging jockey. But I have chosen to focus on what I see Hemingway communicating just beneath this overt level, things like the discrepancy between the sweating while working out and failing to sweat while riding, which seem to me not fully explainable by Butler's age.

2. Joe's final sentence can also be read as applying to his father: he's lost his life, and now they're taking his reputation from him, too. But the main "guy" "they" have started on and left with nothing is Joe. The bettors' negative words hurt Joe, not his father. Gardner's words are an effort to comfort Joe. Joe's "But I don't know" indicates that he cannot take comfort in these words. Why? Because "they" have started on him and "they don't leave a guy nothing."

3. See especially Seymour Chatman's essays in *Coming to Terms* entitled "The 'Rhetoric' of 'Fiction'" and "A New Point of View on 'Point of View.'" For an argument focused on the limits of the structuralists' interest in sharp divisions between story and discourse, see Harry Shaw's "Loose Narrators."

4. The final sentences are in present tense rather than in the past. But the lack of any bridge in the narration from past to present indicates that the present tense functions to convey Joe's continuing loss of faith in his father rather than an insight that his telling the story has suddenly led him to. That is, if we ask, when does Joe lose his firm belief in his father, the answer is after he has heard the bettors' words. And if we ask, why does Hemingway shift to the present tense, the answer is that he wants to show Joe still feeling the effects of the experience, something he couldn't do as effectively if he had Joe stay in the past: "But I didn't know. Seemed like once they got started they don't leave a guy nothing."

5. For more on mimesis as conventional, see chapter 5.

Chapter 5

1. The trajectory of the commentary on Nick's reliability is itself worthy of analysis. In *The Rhetoric of Fiction,* Wayne Booth cited Nick as an example of a "thoroughly reliable" first-person narrator. But since then, Nick has been seen as more and more unreliable. See, for example, Donaldson, Cartwright, and especially Lockridge. Of these essays, I find Donaldson's to be the most illuminating, though his approach is very different from mine.

2. Although he does not comment on this segment of the narrative, Ron Neuhaus notes Fitzgerald's effort to have Nick speak as an "omniscient I" in

the latter part of the book, and he finds that the split between the ironic Nick and the omniscient Nick creates an incoherent effect.

3. Lockridge, to his credit, is scrupulous enough to acknowledge that Nick's unreliability is such that we cannot know for sure that this buried plot is the real one, and so he thematizes the puzzle in his statement that "*The Great Gatsby* embodies a modern predicament: the belief that it is impossible to see or know anything absolutely" (179).

4. In effect, I am at this point building on Dorrit Cohn's work on consonant and dissonant narration (that is, narration in which the homodiegetic narrator identifies with the character and that in which the homodiegetic narrator judges the character). My point is that the reasons for mixing consonant and dissonant narration may have less to do with the character's ability to view his or her past than with the implied author's need to move between presenting the narrator as self-aware and presenting the character as acting in such and such a way. My discussion of Nick below should clarify this point further.

5. For an excellent recent example of such ideological critique, one that includes a fine discussion of Fitzgerald's representation of Daisy, see Tyson.

6. Again, it is important to point out that the logic of the narrative sets up the female character, this time Jordan, to be the site of evil and temptation.

Chapter 6

1. Mary Ann Dazey points out that the title is doubly ambiguous: the referent of *sharer* might be Leggatt or the captain, and *secret* can be either an adjective modifying *sharer* or a part of a noun-noun compound analogous to such phrases as *Conrad aficionado* or *pizza lover.*

2. For a good discussion of the importance of titles in influencing readers' expectations, see Rabinowitz's *Before Reading,* 47–65.

3. For an extended treatment of the ethical dimensions of writing and reading narrative, see Booth, *The Company We Keep.*

4. It is this feature of the technique, I believe, that leads even such a perceptive critic as Steven Ressler to remark, "There is no retrospective sense, no time gap between the original events and their recounting" (97). In other words, though Ressler's claim runs counter to the narrator's remark about the "distance of years," it does capture the narrator's practice of presenting the events without commentary from his older, seemingly more mature self.

5. Keith Carabine finds documentary evidence to support the view that Conrad wrote the story between December 3 and December 15, 1909.

6. In this connection, it is worth noting that, despite considerable debate about the captain's decision to protect Leggatt, most critics assume that, on the axis of values at least, the captain is a reliable narrator. Noteworthy exceptions are Troy and Murphy.

7. Identifying a subtext always has the attraction of making us feel that we are especially astute readers, the ones who "get it," as opposed to, say, the benighted narrator and those flesh-and-blood readers who remain tied to the view of the narrative audience, unable to join us in the authorial. Before declaring that a possible subtext is part of the authorial design, it is helpful to remember that this attraction is quite strong and that the search for subtexts, if conducted with sufficient ingenuity, can almost always turn up a delicious finding. In other words, we may sometimes decide that some of what we catch as we go fishing under the overt text should be thrown back.

8. Other possible hidden meanings are suggested by Johnson and Garber's wonderful, playful essay exemplifying the strategies of psychoanalytic interpretation.

9. For more on this moment, see Johnson and Garber.

10. The captain himself uses the word *queer* (in scare quotes)—"I don't know whether the steward had told them that I was 'queer' only, or downright drunk" (121)—but, as far as I have been able to determine, this word did not have the associations with homosexuality in 1909 that it does in contemporary usage.

11. In "Betraying the Sender," Peter J. Rabinowitz has argued that some texts that contain secrets—his main example is Nella Larsen's *Passing*—are "fragile" because their appeal depends on their creation of two authorial audiences, one that does not get the secret and one that does. Once the secret becomes generally known, the power and appeal of the texts is, if not entirely lost, then altered. His essay offers a fascinating exploration of the ethics of teaching fragile texts. I do not think that "The Secret Sharer" is a fragile text in Rabinowitz's sense because I think that its power and appeal remain even after the secret is revealed. Furthermore, as will become clearer in the next section of this essay, I also think that this particular secret is only a part of the text's power and appeal.

12. I wish to acknowledge the helpful comments of Elizabeth Preston, Susan Swinford, Mark Conroy, Peter J. Rabinowitz, and Rick Livingston on an earlier version of this essay.

Chapter 7

1. A full analysis of the audience positions would also include some account of how the implied reader's position is part of the text's play with audience, but for purposes of clarity, I have not presented that part of the analysis (and, indeed, the text hardly deserves such attention).

2. For important earlier work on the technique, see Morrissette and Hopkins and Perkins. See also the recent special issue of *Style* (28, no. 3 [1994]), guest-edited by Monika Fludernik, devoted to second-person narrative, in which the present essay initially appeared.

In a sense, the theoretical section of this essay is also a revision of my discussion of the relation between narrative and characterized audiences in chapter 5 of *Reading People, Reading Plots*.

3. Although the sex of the "you" at this point in the narrative is not definitively marked, it soon will be: at a wedding, his mother "will introduce you as his *girl*" (56). For more detailed commentary on this beginning, see Richardson.

4. In "The Narratee Revisited," Prince admits that in the earlier essay, he "too often conflated" narratee, addressee, and receiver (302). To avoid a similar conflation here, I have included the alternative terms for these concepts. As Prince explains, "The narratee constitutes a special case of the enunciatee (to adapt Greimassian terminology): it is the enunciatee—the encoded or inscribed 'you'—in a narrative text and it may or may not coincide with the ostensible addressee of that text and/or with the receiver of it: thus, I might explicitly address a narrative to X but (consciously or unconsciously) inscribe Y as a 'you' in it and (accidentally or not) Z may turn out to be its actual receiver" (302). In *Lolita,* for example, Humbert Humbert explicitly addresses (at least initially) a judge and jury; but by the end, Lolita herself is inscribed as his main audience, and John Ray Jr. turns out to be the actual receiver. Although this delineation of the different readerly roles increases the precision of our analysis, it also runs the risk of creating a terminological tangle around *addressee* when we discuss second-person narration. To avoid the tangle, I shall hereafter follow Prince's model and use *enunciatee* to designate the narratee and reserve *addressee* for the implied reader.

5. Whether this view of the authorial audience's beliefs can be demonstrated or not, the larger point is that our decision about where to locate the belief does have consequences for our understanding of the effects Brontë is after. In *Wuthering Heights,* by contrast, I would contend that Emily Brontë asks her authorial audience to view the supernatural events—the life after death of first Catherine and then Heathcliff—as genuinely possible. This demand on the ac-

tual reader is one reason so many people find the book both powerful and strange. Just how *Wuthering Heights* communicates this demand is a complex matter that would take a separate essay to demonstrate; for now, let me just say that the unreliable Lockwood's commonsense faith in the impossibility of the life after death is one important (though not, of course, sufficient) indicator.

6. Note the similarity between structuralism's implied reader and rhetorical theory's authorial audience. These two concepts are largely interchangeable.

7. This is the insight upon which Robyn Warhol builds her useful study of "distancing" and "engaging" narrative address in nineteenth-century British fiction.

8. Although my primary concern here is with second-person narration, I intend the point about the complementarity of narratee, narrative audience, and ideal narrative audience to be useful when talking about homodiegetic and heterodiegetic narration as well. To take just two examples: in Lardner's "Haircut," Whitey's narratee is the customer in the barber chair; in the narrative audience, we observe the haircut and the storytelling, and we recognize that Whitey assumes the customer is the ideal audience simply because the customer is a man from out of town. This recognition, in turn, helps characterize Whitey and helps distance our position in the narrative audience from the position Whitey attributes to his ideal audience. In *Lord Jim,* the shifting of narratees and the difficulty of determining Marlow's ideal narrative audience are both crucial parts of the narrative audience's experience, because they signify how much the narrative is about Marlow's effort to tell Jim's story in a way that will then enable him to come to terms with it.

In chapter 5 of *Reading People, Reading Plots,* devoted primarily to Calvino's *If on a winter's night a traveler,* I discuss the narratees in "Haircut," *Lord Jim, If on a winter's night,* and a few other texts as examples of what I call a "characterized audience" and distinguished them from the narrative audience. Although I still find that those designations are helpful, I believe that employing the concepts of narratee, narrative audience, and ideal narrative audience as complementary allows for a fuller and more precise account of the narrative discourse of these texts.

9. This formulation has much in common with Wayne Booth's concept of coduction. See *The Company We Keep,* 70–75 and passim. One of the Press readers for this book suggests that I am "overly impressed" with Moore and is not entirely sure that the genuine emotion I find in the story is there to be found. These comments strike me as the basis for a productive coduction; to the case that I make in the body of this essay, I will only add here that my general effort as a flesh-and-blood reader is to adopt an attitude of generosity toward implied authors. Whether I am overly generous to Moore is a judgment

that I will continue to question—and something I hope to get some advice about from other readers.

10. The story is working against the standard "happily ever after" heterosexual romance narrative. Whether gay and lesbian readers will be able to move easily into the enunciatee position is, I think, highly debatable. The lesbian reader, however, may find it easy to join Moore's authorial audience to the extent that they will be inclined to read against the imperatives of the self-help genre ("Begin by meeting *him* in a class").

11. For helpful commentary on this essay, I am grateful to Jane Greer and especially Peter J. Rabinowitz.

Chapter 8

1. One feature of the debates about political correctness that seems to have remained is the practice of referring to these debates as the "culture wars." I have refrained from that practice here because I think that the war metaphor itself helps generate more heat than light; it encourages people to think of themselves as fixed in one camp or another, and it encourages them to demonize those who disagree with them (their so-called enemies). Although I have deep disagreements with D'Souza, I have no interest in making him a demon, and I respect his own efforts to refrain from ad hominem arguments.

2. D'Souza writes 762 footnotes, citing university reports, campus newspapers, university press books, metropolitan dailies, weekly and monthly magazines, and scholarly journals.

3. Atwater's ad also has the important function of combatting George Bush's negative image as a "wimp" by projecting it onto Dukakis—but that dimension of the ad is part of another narrative.

4. Stanley Fish has long promoted the view that in literary criticism there are no facts independent of interpretation, and he has often seemed interested in extending this claim to the world at large. Yet, in one of the essays he wrote for his series of debates with D'Souza, he goes to great pains to argue that there are facts that all interpreters should recognize and that some of these facts refute some of D'Souza's claims. See "Speaking in Code, or, How to Turn Bigotry and Ignorance into Moral Principles," esp. 94–98, in *There's No Such Thing as Free Speech*.

See also Gerald Graff's argument for the way that arguments such as D'Souza's have highlighted problems in theorists' commitments to and understandings of certain elements of poststructuralist theory.

Many antifoundationalist philosophers have been arguing that there are no facts outside of some discursive framework for constituting them. I find that this description does not quite capture the complex relation between facts and interpretations. While I agree that any fact is a fact relative to some discursive framework, it seems to me that the significant larger conclusion is not that there are no facts independent of interpretations (Fish's position) but that there are a plurality of facts, each of which has its intelligibility within its own system. Thus, although it would be possible to redescribe, say, the cases of Dolfman and Schaub within a system of intelligibility that interpreted their behavior as a system of neurons firing, that description would not be in competition with the descriptions that D'Souza offers. The coexistence of different facts demonstrates the plurality of our ways of conceiving of those facts, not their lack of existence.

5. Of course, the ways in which any particular narrative rises above the contestation and achieves a widespread acceptance are many and complicated, involving such things as the relation between one's power to speak, the skillfulness with which one tells the narrative, and the audience's assumptions about the speaker's position. In short, to say that we must make our stands on the truth as we see it is not to suggest that those truths will necessarily prevail. I know that in the marketplace of ideas there is no such thing as the free, disinterested play of the best and truest that has been thought and said.

Chapter 9

1. Morrison's novel, in the short time since its publication, has already attracted a significant number of very fine interpretive essays. In addition to the essays by Horvitz, Wilt, House, Rigney, Rushdy, and Wyatt that I draw upon here because they most directly address the question of Beloved's identity, see also Finney, Holloway, Henderson, Schapiro, and the five essays published together in the autumn 1992 issue of *African American Review* by Bell, Demetrakopoulos, Page, Sale, and Sitter.

2. None of the numerous essays on *Beloved* I have read shows any significant debt to reader-response theory. One of the very attractive features of Steig's fine book is how tightly he connects the experience of reading and the act of interpretation. Rabinowitz, as his title suggests, is primarily interested in the conventions that influence the experience of reading. Crosman is concerned with the different frames that we can bring to the act of interpretation. The contributors to Flynn and Schweikart's collection offer a variety of perspectives on the difference gender makes in reading.

3. That Scholes's book won the NCTE's David Russell Award I would

like to read as a sign of both its excellence and a wide acceptance of its views. In his more recent *Protocols of Reading,* Scholes redescribes interpretation as having both centripetal (in toward the text and its intentionality) and centrifugal movements (out toward the reader and her subjectivity); in making the space for the centrifugal, he allows more play for the reader's response, yet stops far short of locating interpretation in experience. His 1993 essay, "Responsible Extravagance: Reading after Post-Structuralism," calls for an even greater license to the reader's ingenuity. For a fuller discussion of the model Scholes sets forth in *Textual Power,* including some reservations about its heavy reliance on repetitions and oppositions, see my *Reading People, Reading Plots.*

4. The typical code consists of (1) categories that organize the numerous signals in the language of the text into fewer, more general units and (2) rules for combining the categories. Sometimes the categories are provided by the text (e.g., "rememory" or "claiming one's freedom" or "circling" in *Beloved*); sometimes they are provided by an interpretive system the critic brings to all texts (e.g., object relations; gender and power; dialogism); and sometimes they are provided by some combination of text and interpretive system (call and response; maternity and slavery). The critic then employs the rules for combining the categories and seeks to develop a coherent and comprehensive account of how the text's language (or at least some significant subset of that language) can be understood as signifying a particular set of meanings.

Standard accounts of interpretive adequacy such as those in Booth and Hirsch usually include a criterion of "precision" or "correspondence" in addition to comprehensiveness and coherence. I do not include it here because, unlike them, I am not trying to establish the philosophical grounds of interpretive adequacy but to describe what practical critics generally do under the umbrella of interpretation. For the same reason, I will not try to sort out—and create a hierarchy among—different notions of comprehensiveness, coherence, or precision.

For similar and fuller descriptions of interpretation along the lines I've sketched here, see Steven Mailloux's essay on the term in McLaughlin and Lentricchia, and Rabinowitz's discussion in the chapter in *Before Reading* called "Starting Points."

5. Stanley Fish, among others, has argued that at any one time the institution of criticism will sanction only a limited number of translation schemes (or in Fish's language, interpretive communities). Fish's point here, whatever reservations one might have about his larger account of the profession (see Battersby), is descriptively accurate. My point is that interpretation is potentially, not actually, infinite.

6. I recognize that this statement is open to the objection that such critics,

having been trained in a certain way, are in fact basing their interpretations on their reading responses, that, for example, they read with a knowledge of the cultural networks they trace in their interpretations and so respond accordingly. Objection sustained—and indeed, I have tried to account for this possibility in my description of reading. But my point here is that the ground of the appeal in, say, Stephen Greenblatt's interpretation of *King Lear* in *Shakespearean Negotiations,* is not at all to the act of reading or viewing the play, but rather on his work of contextualizing and analogizing. His claim is not at all about how it feels to be in the audience at the Globe, but very much about what the play can be said to mean in its cultural moment. I admire his work, but want to ask a different question: what happens when we ground our interpretations in the act of reading?

7. The approach I am advocating here has links with the reader-response criticism of Iser and Rosenblatt and with the rhetorical poetics associated with Chicago School criticism. But I am more interested in the affective dimensions of reading than Iser or Rosenblatt, and I depart from the Chicago School's treatment of the reader as, ultimately, a property of the text.

8. For a lively argument that recalcitrance itself is the basis of literary form and quality, see Wright. I find much of Wright's argument to be appealing, but I stop short of accepting his strongest claims, which seem to make recalcitrance not just a means but also the purpose of literary form.

9. The category of the stubborn clearly has some affinities with the deconstructive notion of unreadability, especially as it has been developed by Paul de Man's rigorous analyses. But I take the concept of the stubborn in a direction different from the one in which he takes the notion of unreadability. Where his rhetorical concerns focus on the figures of the text, mine move to questions of author-reader relations. Where his unreadability leads to the mise-en-abyme, my stubbornness leads to a paradoxical functionality within a larger system of what can be read (as I try to demonstrate below).

10. The fourth sentence reads, "For years each put up with the spite in his own way, but by 1873 Sethe and her daughter Denver were its only victims" (3), suggesting 1873 as the present. Then, in dating the departures of Howard and Buglar from 124, the narrator says, "Ohio had been calling itself a state only seventy years when first one brother and then the next stuffed quilt packing into his hat, snatched up his shoes, and crept away from the lively spite the house felt for them" (3). Since Ohio became a state in 1803, this sentence puts their departure in 1873, which could still fit with that fourth sentence. On the next page, the narrator says first that "Baby Suggs died shortly after the brothers left" and then that Denver "was ten and still mad at Baby Suggs for dying" (4). So Denver appears to have been born in 1863. Later in the chapter, in

present time, Sethe says to Paul D that Baby Suggs has been dead "Eight years now. Almost nine," which suddenly jumps the present action to 1891. That would fit with our learning that Denver is eighteen, but of course later we learn that Denver was born in 1855 during Sethe's escape from Sweet Home, so the present action must be occurring in 1873. And indeed, after the first chapter all the signals point to 1873–74 as the time of the narrative's present action.

11. Later on Morrison gives inconsistent evidence about how long Sethe was at 124 before schoolteacher arrives: sometimes she says three weeks, other times four. Since these dates often come through a character's stream of consciousness, I believe that this inconsistency can be read as functional in its demonstration of the interaction of history and memory.

12. Introducing this distinction between the difficult and the stubborn or, more precisely, introducing a category called "the stubborn" (the difficult has long been our stock in trade) is not without its own potential problems. One critic's example of stubbornness will be another's instance of mild difficulty. The category of the stubborn could easily become a wastebasket into which tired critics—or those facing deadlines—toss their recalcitrant data. But the abuse of a thing is no argument against it. Like all interpretive hypotheses, claims about the stubborn will be subject to the scrutiny of other interpreters; those that wither under such scrutiny will turn out to be, well, not so stubborn after all. Furthermore, given the pride of place currently accorded to the ability to produce innovative close readings, I doubt that critics will rush to proclaim any given textual phenomenon as an instance of the stubborn. The risks of being wrong are too great. If another critic shows that what I take to be the stubborn is actually the difficult, then I am in the embarrassing position of having to admit that I have not read closely enough. I am less worried about the possible abuses of the concept than I am hopeful about its potential to advance the cause of tightening the connections between the experience of reading and the activity of interpretation.

13. The key difference between narrative and authorial audiences at this juncture of *Beloved* is that the narrative audience believes in the reality of the character and events while the authorial audience knows that it is reading fiction. See Rabinowitz's "Truth in Fiction."

Glossary

This glossary seeks to define, with clarity and concision, the set of terms and concepts fundamental to my understanding of narrative as rhetoric. In most cases, there are fuller discussions of these concepts, including information about their sources, in the preceding essays. It is my hope that opting for leanness here will, in combination with the fuller discussions in the essays, best serve the goal of clarity. My definitions of narratological terms such as *paralipsis* and *paralepsis* are inflected by my commitment to the rhetorical approach; for more formal narratological definitions, see Gerald Prince, *A Dictionary of Narratology*.

addressee the audience to whom an utterance is directed. When the speaker is the narrator, the addressee is the narratee; when the speaker is the implied author, the addressee is the implied reader or authorial audience; when the speaker is the flesh-and-blood author, the addressee is the flesh-and-blood audience.

antifoundationalism the philosophical position that maintains there are no universal or fundamental truths, no bedrock assumptions upon which to base a metaphysics. The version of antifoundationalism I consider in the introduction holds that all truths are constructed by our discourse.

authorial audience the hypothetical, ideal audience for whom the author constructs the text and who understands it perfectly. The authorial audience of fiction, unlike the narrative audience (defined below), operates with the tacit knowledge that the characters and events are synthetic constructs rather than real people and historical happenings. The term is synonymous with *implied reader.*

authorial intention the meaning and purpose of an utterance as designed by its author. It is much easier to define the term than to identify all the different stances critics and theorists have taken regarding the concept.

autodiegetic narration the telling of a story by its protagonist. See also *homodiegetic narration* and *heterodiegetic narration.*

character an element of narrative that has three simultaneous components—the *mimetic* (character is like a person), the *thematic* (any character is representative of one or more groups and functions in one way or another to advance the narrative's thematic concerns), and the *synthetic* (character plays a specific role in the construction of narrative as made object).

coduction the production of interpretation or evaluation through conversation with other readers.

dialogism the presence of multiple voices within a narrative and their relationships. See also *double-voicing*.

(the) **difficult** textual phenomena that initially provide some recalcitrance to interpretation but are designed to be interpreted. See also the *stubborn* and the *erroneous*.

dimensions and **functions** the attributes of a character that create the potential for signification within the progression are dimensions. The realization of that potential creates functions. On the mimetic level, an attribute is a trait; when one trait combines with others to form a portrait of a possible person, that mimetic dimension is participating in a mimetic function. On the thematic level, an attribute is a trait considered as representative (e.g., a character's race) or as an idea (e.g., a character's belief in the supernatural); when the progression turns in some way on the presence of this trait, then it is being thematized or, more formally, the thematic dimension becomes a thematic function. On the synthetic level, dimensions are always functions because dimensions are always already parts of the construction of the narrative. The synthetic functions can, however, be more or less foregrounded; in realistic narrative, they tend to remain in the background; in metafictional narrative, they tend to move to the foreground.

discourse the set of devices for telling a story, including vision (who sees), voice (who speaks), duration (how long it takes something to be told), frequency (whether something is told in singulative or iterative manner), and speed (how much story time is covered by a stretch of discourse). In structuralist narratology, discourse is regarded as the "how" of narrative, distinct from the "what"—character, event, and setting.

distance the relation between the norms of an implied author and those of a narrator. Distance will always be greater in unreliable narration than in reliable narration.

double-voicing the presence of (at least) two voices in one utterance. In unreliable narration, for example, we hear both the narrator's voice and the implied author's voice undermining the narrator's.

enunciatee the audience directly addressed in second-person narration. See also *addressee.*

(the) **erroneous** textual phenomena that fall outside the larger pattern of a text's design (e.g., Morrison's giving two dates for the present time action in the first chapter of *Beloved*).

fabula the "what" of narrative before it is rendered in discourse; the sequence of events in chronological order.

formalism an approach to literature that assumes that its meaning is to be found in the specific features of the text itself rather than in the author's consciousness, the reader, history, or other so-called extrinsic factors.

foundationalism a philosophic position that seeks to ground truth and meaning in some fixed, transcendent concept; Descartes's "cogito, ergo sum" is a classic instance of foundational thinking.

heterodiegetic narration in which the narrator exists at a different level of (fictional) existence from the characters. Omniscient third-person narration, for example, is heterodiegetic.

homodiegetic narration in which the narrator exists at the same level of existence as the characters. *The Great Gatsby* is an example of homodiegetic narration. When the character-narrator is also the protagonist, as in *A Farewell to Arms,* the homodiegetic narration can be further specified as autodiegetic.

ideal narrative audience the hypothetical, ideal audience for whom the narrator is writing. See also *narratee* and *narrative audience.*

implied author the consciousness responsible for the choices that create the narrative text as "these words in this order" and that imbues the text with his or her values. One important activity of rhetorical reading is constructing a sense of the implied author.

implied reader the audience for whom the implied author writes; synonymous with the *authorial audience.*

instabilities and **tensions** unstable situations upon which narrative progressions are built. Narrative moves by the generation, complication, and (sometimes) resolution of instabilities and tensions. An instability is an unstable situation within the story: it may be between characters; between a character and his or her world; or within a single character. A tension is an unstable situation within the discourse, consisting typically of a discrepancy in knowledge, judgments, values, or beliefs between narrator and authorial audience or between implied author and authorial audience.

lyric a genre in which situations, feelings, ideas, or actions are presented as significant in themselves and worthy of the audience's contemplation rather than for the audience's judgment.

mimetic/mimesis mimetic refers to that component of character directed to its imitation of a possible person. It also refers to that component of fictional narrative concerned with imitating the world beyond the fiction, what we typically call reality. Mimesis refers to the process by which the mimetic effect is produced, the set of conventions, which change over time, by which imitations are judged to be more or less adequate.

monologism single-voiced and thus single-minded and single-valued discourse; discourse not open to alternative views.

narratee the audience directly addressed by the narrator; the narratee may or may not coincide with the ideal narrative audience.

narrative in rhetorical terms, the act of somebody telling somebody else on a particular occasion for some purpose that something happened.

narrative audience the observer role within the world of the fiction, taken on by the flesh-and-blood reader in that part of his or her consciousness which treats the fictional action as real. The narrative audience position, like the narratee position, is subsumed within the authorial audience position.

narratology the theoretical movement, rooted in structuralism, whose goal is to define the essence of narrative as a mode of discourse, to describe its fundamental structure and to delineate the nature of its particular elements—author, narrator, narratee, character, event, setting, and so on.

narrator the teller of the story.

paralepsis a device in which a narrator's discourse reflects a greater knowledge than he or she could presumably have; in other words, a device in which the narrator tells more than he or she knows.

paralipsis a device in which a narrator's discourse does not reflect his or her full relevant knowledge; in other words, a device in which the narrator tells less than he or she knows.

poststructuralism a theoretical movement, marked by a general commitment to antifoundationalism, focusing on the instability of language, the cultural constructedness of all categories, including those previously thought to be natural, and the plurality and fragmentation of the subject.

pragmatism/neopragmatism a philosophic position arising out of antifoundationalism, which views truth and meaning as the product of our beliefs and our discourse about the world and its entities.

progression the movement of a narrative from beginning to end and the principles governing that movement. Progression exists along two simultaneous axes: the internal logic of the narrative text and the set of responses that logic generates in the authorial audience as it reads from beginning to end. Though this description focuses on the movement of narrative through time from beginning to end, a concern with progression is more than a concern with narrative as a linear process, precisely because it recognizes the dynamic, recursive relationships among the authorial audience's understanding of beginning, middle, and end.

recalcitrance a resistance by textual phenomena to interpretation. See also *difficult, erroneous,* and *stubborn.*

reliable and **unreliable narration** reliable narration is that in which the narrator's report of facts and rendering of judgments are in accord with the perspective and norms of the implied author. Unreliable narration is that in which the narrator's report of facts differs from the implied author's or in which the narrator's judgments about the events or characters differ from the implied author's. This second kind of unreliability is more frequent.

sjuzhet the fabula rendered in a specific narrative discourse; the synthesis of story and discourse.

story the what of narrative: character, events, and setting are parts of story; the events in chronological order constitute the story abstracted from the discourse.

structuralism the theoretical movement devoted to uncovering the basic structures underlying cultural discourses from literature to fashion. Structuralism took Saussure's analysis of language in *A Course in General Linguistics* as its model and tried to find correspondences between the structures of these other discourses and the structure of language as described by Saussure.

(the) **stubborn** textual recalcitrance designed not to yield to interpretation yet nevertheless contributing to the text's overall design.

synthetic that component of character directed to its role as artificial construct in the larger construction of the text; more generally, the constructedness of a text as an object.

thematic that component of character directed to its representative or ideational function; more generally, that component of a narrative text concerned with making statements, taking ideological positions, teaching readers truths.

voice the synthesis of a speaker's style, tone, and values.

Works Cited

Albright, Daniel. *Lyricality in the English Novel.* Lincoln: University of Nebraska Press, 1985.

Austen, Jane. *Pride and Prejudice.* Edited by Donald J. Gray. New York: Norton, 1966.

Baker, Carlos. *Ernest Hemingway: A Life Story.* 1969. Reprint, New York: Scribner's, 1988.

Baker, Sheridan. *Ernest Hemingway: An Introduction and Interpretation.* New York: Holt, Rinehart and Winston, 1967.

Bakhtin, Mikhail. "Discourse in the Novel." In *The Dialogic Imagination,* translated by Carol Emerson and Michael Holquist. Austin: University of Texas Press, 1981.

Barthes, Roland. *The Pleasure of the Text.* Translated by Richard Miller. New York: Hill and Wang, 1975.

Battersby, James L. "Relativism, Rationality, and Professionalism." *PMLA* 107 (1992): 51–64.

Bell, Bernard W. "*Beloved:* A Womanist Neo-Slave Narrative; or, Multivocal Remembrances of Things Past." *African American Review* 26 (autumn 1992): 7–15.

Booth, Wayne C. *The Company We Keep.* Berkeley: University of California Press, 1988.

———. *Critical Understanding: The Powers and Limits of Pluralism.* Chicago: University of Chicago Press, 1979.

———. *The Rhetoric of Fiction.* 2d ed. Chicago: University of Chicago Press, 1983.

———. *A Rhetoric of Irony.* Chicago: University of Chicago Press, 1974.

Brenner, Gerry. *Concealments in Hemingway's Fiction.* Columbus: Ohio State University Press, 1983.

Brontë, Charlotte. *Jane Eyre.* New York: Norton, 1987.

Brontë, Emily. *Wuthering Heights.* New York: Penguin, 1985.

Burch, Mark H. "'The World Is a Looking-Glass': *Vanity Fair* as Satire." *Genre* 15 (1982): 265–79.

Burke, Kenneth. *A Rhetoric of Motives*. 1950. Reprint, Berkeley: University of California Press, 1969.

Calvino, Italo. *If on a winter's night a traveler*. Translated by William Weaver. New York: Harcourt Brace Jovanovich, 1981.

Carabine, Keith. "'The Secret Sharer': A Note on the Date of Its Composition." *Conradiana* 19, no. 3 (1987): 209–13.

Cartwright, Kent. "Nick Carraway as an Unreliable Narrator." *Papers on Language and Literature* 20 (1984): 218–32.

Caws, Mary Ann. "Framing, Centering, and Explicating: Virginia Woolf's Collage." *New York Literary Forum* 10–11 (1983): 51–78.

Chatman, Seymour. *Coming to Terms*. Ithaca: Cornell University Press, 1990.

———. *Story and Discourse*. Ithaca: Cornell University Press, 1978.

———. "Response to Barbara Herrnstein Smith." *Critical Inquiry* 7 (1981): 802–9.

Claridge, Laura, and Elizabeth Langland, eds. *Out of Bounds: Male Voices and Gender(ed) Criticism*. Amherst: University of Massachusetts Press, 1990.

Coetzee, J. M. *Waiting for the Barbarians*. New York: Penguin, 1980.

Cohn, Dorrit. *Transparent Minds: Narrative Modes of Presenting Consciousness in Fiction*. Princeton: Princeton University Press, 1978.

Conrad, Joseph. "The Secret Sharer." In *The Complete Short Fiction of Joseph Conrad*, vol. 2, edited by Samuel Hynes, 105–43. Hopewell, New Jersey: Ecco Press, 1992.

Craig, G. Armour. "On the Style of *Vanity Fair*." In *Style in Prose Fiction*, edited by Harold Martin, 87–113. New York: Columbia University Press, 1959.

Crosman, Inge. *A Poetics of Reading*. Princeton: Princeton University Press, 1989.

Dazey, Mary Ann. "Shared Secret or Secret Sharing in Joseph Conrad's 'The Secret Sharer.'" *Conradiana* 18, no. 3 (1986): 201–3.

de Man, Paul. *Allegories of Reading*. New Haven: Yale University Press, 1979.

Demetrakopoulos, Stephanie A. "Maternal Bonds as Devourers of Women's Individuation in Toni Morrison's *Beloved*." *African American Review* 26 (autumn 1992): 51–59.

Dick, Susan. "I Remembered, I Forgotten: Bernard's Final Soliloquy in *The Waves*." *Modern Language Studies* 13, no. 3 (1983): 38–52.

Donaldson, Scott. *By Force of Will: The Life and Art of Ernest Hemingway*. New York: Viking, 1977.

———. "The Trouble with Nick." In *Critical Essays on F. Scott Fitzgerald*, edited by Donaldson, 131–39. Boston: G. K. Hall, 1984.

D'Souza, Dinesh. *Illiberal Education: The Politics of Race and Sex on Campus.* New York: Random House, 1991.

———. "Response." *Narrative* 2, no. 3 (1994): 268–69.

Eco, Umberto. "Postmodernism, Irony, the Enjoyable." In *Reflections on "The Name of the Rose,"* translated by William Weaver, 65–72. London: Secker and Warburg, 1985. Reprinted in *Modernism/Postmodernism,* edited by Peter Brooker, 225–28. New York: Longman, 1993.

Elbow, Peter. "The Pleasures of Voices in the Literary Essay: Explorations in the Prose of Gretel Ehrlich and Richard Selzer." In *Literary Nonfiction: Theory, Criticism, and Pedagogy,* edited by Chris Anderson, 211–34. Carbondale: Southern Illinois University Press, 1989.

Faulkner, William. *As I Lay Dying.* New York: Vintage, 1930.

Ferris, Ina. *William Makepeace Thackeray.* New York: Twayne, 1983.

Finney, Brian. "Temporal Defamiliarization in Toni Morrison's *Beloved.*" *Obsidian II* 5 (1990): 20–36.

Fish, Stanley. *Doing What Comes Naturally.* Durham, North Carolina: Duke University Press, 1989.

———. *There's No Such Thing as Free Speech.* New York: Oxford University Press, 1994.

Fitzgerald, F. Scott. *The Great Gatsby.* New York: Macmillan, 1925, 1992.

Fleischman, Suzanne. *Tense and Narrativity: From Medieval Performance to Modern Fiction.* Austin: University of Texas Press, 1990.

Fleishman, Avrom. *Virginia Woolf: A Critical Reading.* Baltimore: Johns Hopkins University Press, 1975.

Fludernik, Monika. "Second Person Fiction: Narrative *You* as Addressee and/or Protagonist." *AAA—Arbeiten aus Anglistik und Amerikanistik* 18, no. 2 (1993): 217–47.

Flynn, Elizabeth, and Patricinio Schweikart, eds. *Gender and Reading.* Baltimore: Johns Hopkins University Press, 1986.

Forster, E. M. *Aspects of the Novel.* New York: Harcourt, Brace, and World, 1927.

Freedman, Ralph. *The Lyrical Novel: Studies in Hermann Hesse, Andre Gide, and Virginia Woolf.* Princeton: Princeton University Press, 1963.

Friedman, Susan Stanford. "Lyric Subversion of Narrative in Women's Writing: Virginia Woolf and the Tyranny of Plot." In *Reading Narrative: Form, Ethics, Ideology,* edited by James Phelan, 162–85. Columbus: Ohio State University Press, 1989.

———. "Spatialization: A Strategy for Reading Narrative." *Narrative* 1 (1993): 12–23.

Genette, Gérard. *Narrative Discourse: An Essay on Method.* Translated by Jane Lewin. Ithaca: Cornell University Press, 1980.

Graff, Gerald. "Paradoxes of the Culture War." *Narrative* 1 (1993): 66–68.

Graham, J. W. "Point of View in *The Waves:* Some Services of the Style." *University of Toronto Quarterly* 39 (1970): 193–211.

Greenblatt, Stephen. *Shakespearean Negotiations.* Berkeley: University of California Press, 1988.

Hamburger, Käte. *The Logic of Literature.* Translated by Marilynn J. Rose. Bloomington: Indiana University Press, 1973.

Hemingway, Ernest. *A Farewell to Arms.* New York: Scribner's, 1929.

———. "My Old Man." In *In Our Time,* 115–29. New York: Scribner's, 1925, 1958.

Henderson, Mae G. "Toni Morrison's *Beloved:* Re-Membering the Body as Historical Text." In *Comparative American Identities: Race, Sex, and Nationality in the Modern Text,* edited by Hortense J. Spillers, 62–86. New York: Routledge, 1991.

Hirsch, E. D., Jr. *Validity in Interpretation.* New Haven: Yale University Press, 1967.

Holloway, Karla. "*Beloved:* A Spiritual." *Callaloo* 13 (1990): 516–25.

Hopkins, Mary Francis, and Leon Perkins. "Second Person Point of View in Narrative." In *Critical Survey of Short Fiction,* edited by Frank N. Magill, 119–32. Englewood Cliffs, New Jersey: Salem Press, 1981.

Horvitz, Deborah. "Nameless Ghosts: Possession and Depossession in *Beloved.*" *Studies in American Fiction* 17 (1989): 157–67.

House, Elizabeth. "Toni Morrison's Ghost: The Beloved Who Is Not Beloved." *Studies in American Fiction* 18 (1990): 17–26.

Iser, Wolfgang. *The Act of Reading.* Baltimore: Johns Hopkins University Press, 1978.

Johnson, Barbara, and Marjorie Garber. "Secret Sharing: Reading Conrad Psychoanalytically." *College English* 49 (1987): 628–40.

Johnson, Barbara. *The Wake of Deconstruction.* Lewisburg, Pennsylvania: Bucknell Press, 1994.

Kacandes, Irene. "Are You in the Text? The 'Literary Performative' in Postmodernist Fiction." *Text and Performance Quarterly* 13 (1993): 139–53.

Kimball, Roger. "Moral Homicide: Illiberal Education in America." *New Criterion* 9, no. 8 (1991): 5–11.

———. *Tenured Radicals.* New York: Harper and Row, 1990.

Knapp, Steven, and Walter Benn Michaels. "Against Theory." *Critical Inquiry* 8, no. 4 (1982): 723–42.

———. "Against Theory 2: Hermeneutics and Deconstruction." *Critical Inquiry* 14, no. 1 (1987): 49–68.

Krause, Sidney J. "Hemingway's 'My Old Man.'" *Explicator* 20 (January 1962): Item 39.

Lardner, Ring. "Haircut." In *The Best Short Stories of Ring Lardner,* 29–33. New York: Scribner's, 1957.

Leath, Helen. "Washing the Dirty Linen in Private: An Analysis of Katherine Anne Porter's 'Magic.'" *Conference of College Teachers of English Studies* (September 1985): 50–53.

Leiter, Louis H. "Echo Structures: Conrad's 'The Secret Sharer.'" *Twentieth-Century Literature* 5, no. 4 (1960): 159–75.

Lewis, Robert. *Hemingway on Love.* Austin: University of Texas Press, 1965.

Lockridge, Ernest. "F. Scott Fitzgerald's *Trompe l'Oeil* and *The Great Gatsby*'s Buried Plot." *Journal of Narrative Technique* 17 (1987): 163–83.

Lodge, David. "Analysis and Interpretation of the Realist Text: A Pluralistic Approach to Ernest Hemingway's 'Cat in the Rain.'" *Poetics Today* 1 (1980): 5-19.

Loofburrow, John. *Thackeray and the Form of Fiction.* Princeton: Princeton University Press, 1964.

Mailloux, Steven. "Interpretation." In *Critical Terms for Literary Study,* edited by Thomas McLaughlin and Frank Lentricchia, 121–34. Chicago: University of Chicago Press, 1990.

Marcus, Jane. "Britannia Rules *The Waves.*" In *Decolonizing Tradition: New Views of the Twentieth-Century British Literary Canon,* edited by Karen R. Lawrence, 136–62. Urbana: University of Illinois Press, 1992.

McHale, Brian. *Postmodernist Fiction.* London: Methuen, 1987.

McMaster, Juliet. *Thackeray: The Major Novels.* Toronto: University of Toronto Press, 1971.

Miller, J. Hillis. "Narrative." In *Critical Terms for Literary Study,* edited by Thomas McLaughlin and Frank Lentricchia, 67–79. Chicago: University of Chicago Press, 1990.

Moore, Lorrie. *Self-Help.* New York: New American Library, 1985.

Morrison, Toni. *Beloved.* New York: Knopf, 1987.

———. *Playing in the Dark: Whiteness and the Literary Imagination.* Cambridge: Harvard University Press, 1992.

———. "Unspeakable Things Unspoken: The Afro-American Presence in American Literature." *Michigan Quarterly Review* 28 (1989): 1–34.

Morrissette, Bruce. "Narrative 'You' in Contemporary Literature." *Comparative Literature Studies* 2 (1965): 1–24.

Murphy, Michael. "'The Secret Sharer': Conrad's *Turn of the Winch.*" *Conradiana* 18, no. 3 (1986): 193–200.

Nabokov, Vladimir. *The Annotated "Lolita."* Edited by Alfred Appel. New York: McGraw-Hill, 1970.

Nagel, James. "Catherine Barkley and Retrospective Narration in *A Farewell to Arms*." In *Ernest Hemingway: Six Decades of Criticism,* edited by Linda Wagner-Martin, 171–93. East Lansing: Michigan State University Press, 1987.

Neuhaus, Ron. "Gatsby and the Failure of the Omniscient 'I.'" *University of Denver Quarterly* 12 (1977): 303–12.

Oldsey, Bernard. *Hemingway's Hidden Craft: The Writing of "A Farewell to Arms."* State College: Pennsylvania State University Press, 1979.

Olson, Elder. *On Value Judgments in the Arts and Other Essays.* Chicago: University of Chicago Press, 1976.

O'Sullivan, Gerry. Review of *Illiberal Education. Humanist* 52 (January/February 1992): 43–45.

Page, Philip. "Circularity in Toni Morrison's *Beloved*." *African American Review* 26 (autumn 1992): 31–39.

Phelan, James. "A Monologic Imagination." *Narrative* 2, no. 3 (1994): 270–71.

———. *Reading People, Reading Plots: Character, Progression, and the Interpretation of Narrative.* Chicago: University of Chicago Press, 1989.

———. *Worlds from Words: A Theory of Language in Fiction.* Chicago: University of Chicago Press, 1981.

Phelan, James, and Peter J. Rabinowitz, eds. *Understanding Narrative.* Columbus: Ohio State University Press, 1994.

Poe, Edgar Allen. "The Cask of Amontillado." In *The Collected Tales and Poems of Edgar Allen Poe,* 274–79. New York: Modern Library, 1992.

Porter, Katherine Anne. "Magic." *The Collected Stories of Katherine Anne Porter,* 42–44. Franklin Center, Pennsylvania: The Franklin Library, 1981.

Prince, Gerald. *A Dictionary of Narratology.* Lincoln: University of Nebraska Press, 1987.

———. "Introduction a l'étude du narrataire." *Poétique* 14 (1973): 178–96. Reprinted and translated as "Introduction to the Study of the Narratee." In *Reader Response Criticism: From Formalism to Post-Structuralism,* edited by Jane P. Tompkins, 7–25. Baltimore: Johns Hopkins University Press, 1980.

———. "The Narratee Revisited." *Style* 19 (1985): 299–303.

Rabinowitz, Peter J. *Before Reading.* Ithaca: Cornell University Press, 1987.

———. "'Betraying the Sender': The Rhetoric and Ethics of Fragile Texts." *Narrative* 2 (1994): 201–13.

———. "Truth in Fiction: A Reexamination of Audiences." *Critical Inquiry* 4 (1976): 121–41.

Rader, Ralph. "The Dramatic Monologue and Related Lyric Forms." *Critical Inquiry* 3 (1976): 131–51.

Ressler, Steve. *Joseph Conrad: Consciousness and Integrity*. New York: New York University Press, 1988.

Reynolds, Michael. *Hemingway's First War: The Making of "A Farewell to Arms."* Princeton: Princeton University Press, 1976.

Richardson, Brian. "The Politics and Poetics of Second Person Narration." *Genre* 24 (1991): 309–30.

Richter, Harvena. *Virginia Woolf: The Inward Voyage*. Princeton: Princeton University Press, 1970.

Rigney, Barbara. *The Voices of Toni Morrison*. Columbus: Ohio State University Press, 1991.

Rorty, Richard. *Philosophy and the Mirror of Nature*. Princeton: Princeton University Press, 1979.

Rosenblatt, Louise. *The Reader, the Text, the Poem*. Carbondale: Southern Illinois University Press, 1978.

Rovit, Earl. *Ernest Hemingway*. New York: Twayne, 1963.

Rushdy, Ashraf H. A. "Daughters Signifyin(g) History: The Example of Toni Morrison's *Beloved*." *American Literature* 64 (1992): 567–97.

Sale, Maggie. "Call and Response as Critical Method: African-American Oral Traditions and *Beloved*." *African American Review* 26 (autumn 1992): 41–50.

Scarry, Elaine. "Enemy and Father: Comic Equilibrium in No. 14 of *Vanity Fair*." *Journal of Narrative Technique* 10 (1980): 145–55.

Schapiro, Barbara. "The Bonds of Love and the Boundaries of Self in Toni Morrison's *Beloved*." *Contemporary Literature* 32 (1991): 194–210.

Schneider, Daniel. "Hemingway's *A Farewell to Arms:* The Novel as Pure Poetry." In *Ernest Hemingway: Five Decades of Criticism,* edited by Linda Wagner, 252–66. East Lansing: Michigan State University Press, 1974.

Scholes, Robert. *Protocols of Reading*. New Haven: Yale University Press, 1989.

———. "Responsible Extravagance: Reading after Post Structuralism." *Narrative* 1 (1993): 3–11.

———. *Textual Power*. New Haven: Yale University Press, 1985.

Sharp, Ronald. *Friendship and Literature*. Durham, North Carolina: Duke University Press, 1986.

Shaw, Harry. "Loose Narrators: Display, Engagement, and the Search for a Place in History in Realist Fiction." *Narrative* 3 (1995): 95–116.

Sinha, S. K. *Thackeray: A Study in Technique*. Salzburg Studies in English Literature 86. Salzburg: Institut für Anglistik und Amerikanistik, 1979.

Sipiora, Philip. "The Ethical Narration of 'My Old Man.'" In *Hemingway's Neglected Short Fiction,* edited by Susan Beegel, 43–60. Ann Arbor: UMI Research Press, 1989.

Sitter, Deborah Ayer. "The Making of a Man: Dialogic Meaning in *Beloved.*" *African American Review* 26 (autumn 1992): 17–29.

Smith, Barbara Herrnstein. "Narrative Versions, Narrative Theories." *Critical Inquiry* 7 (1980): 213–36.

Smith, Paul. *A Reader's Guide to the Short Stories of Ernest Hemingway.* Boston: G. K. Hall, 1989.

Steig, Michael. *Stories of Reading.* Baltimore: Johns Hopkins University Press, 1989.

Sterne, Laurence. *Tristram Shandy.* New York: Norton, 1980.

Thackeray, William Makepeace. *Vanity Fair: A Novel without a Hero.* 1847–48. Boston: Houghton Mifflin, 1963.

Tillotson, Geoffrey. *Thackeray the Novelist.* Cambridge: Cambridge University Press, 1954.

Troy, Mark. "' . . . of no particular significance except to myself': Narrative Posture in Conrad's 'The Secret Sharer.'" *Studia Neophilogica* 56 (1984): 35–50.

Tyson, Lois. *Psychological Politics of the American Dream: The Commodification of Subjectivity in Twentieth-Century American Literature.* Columbus: Ohio State University Press, 1994.

Waldhorn, Arthur. *A Reader's Guide to Ernest Hemingway.* New York: Farrar, Straus and Giroux, 1972.

Warhol, Robyn. *Gendered Interventions.* New Brunswick, N.J.: Rutgers University Press, 1989.

Wheatley, James. *Patterns in Thackeray's Fiction.* Middleton, Conn.: Wesleyan University Press, 1967.

Wilt, Judith. *Abortion, Choice, and Contemporary Fiction.* Chicago: University of Chicago Press, 1989.

Woolf, Virginia. *The Waves.* New York: Harcourt Brace, 1931.

Wright, Austin. *Recalcitrance, Faulkner, and the Professors.* Iowa City: University of Iowa Press, 1989.

Wyatt, Jean. "Giving Body to the Word: The Maternal Symbolic in Toni Morrison's *Beloved.*" *PMLA* 108 (1993): 474–88.

Ziff, Larzer. "The Social Basis of Hemingway's Style." In *Ernest Hemingway: Six Decades of Criticism,* edited by Linda Wagner-Martin, 147–54. East Lansing: Michigan State University Press, 1987.

Index

The Theory and Interpretation of Narrative Series

James Phelan and Peter J. Rabinowitz, Editors

Because the series editors believe that the most significant work in narrative studies today contributes both to our knowledge of specific narratives and to our understanding of narrative in general, studies in the series typically offer interpretations of individual narratives and address significant theoretical issues underlying those interpretations. The series does not privilege any one critical perspective but is open to work from any strong theoretical position.

Framing *Anna Karenina*
Tolstoy, the Woman Question, and the Victorian Novel
Amy Mandelker

Understanding Narrative
Edited by James Phelan and Peter J. Rabinowitz

Psychological Politics of the American Dream
The Commodification of Subjectivity in Twentieth-Century American Literature
Lois Tyson